African Adventurer's Guide To

NAMIBIA

African Adventurer's Guide To

NAMIBIA

Willie and Sandra Olivier

SOUTHERN
BOOK PUBLISHERS

ISBN 1 86812 752 4

Published by
Southern Book Publishers (Pty) Ltd
(A member of the New Holland Struik Publishing Group)
PO Box 5563, Rivonia 2128

While the authors and the publisher have endeavoured to verify all facts, they will not be held responsible for any inconvenience that may result from possible inaccuracies in this book.

The authors and publishers would welcome any information or comments which would assist in updating and improving future editions. Please contact: The Editor, *African Adventurer's Guide to Namibia*, Southern Book Publishers, P O Box 5563, Rivonia 2128, South Africa.

Cover photograph by Heinrich van den Berg (ABPL)
Cover design by Micha McKerr
Maps by Michael Thayer
Set in Optima 10/12
Designed and typeset by Micha McKerr
Reproduction by Positive Proof cc, Randburg
Printed and bound by Creda Communications, Eliot Avenue, Epping 11, 7460

ACKNOWLEDGEMENTS

Much of the information in this guide is based on our *Visitors' Guide to Namibia* (originally published in 1989), which was made possible by the enthusiastic co-operation, assistance and advice of many people – often on an informal basis – whom we would like to thank sincerely. We appreciate the assistance of all and, should anyone have been omitted inadvertently, we apologise. Our gratitude is due especially to the following: Ministry of Wildlife staff including Dr Hugh Berry (Etosha), Peter Bridgeford (Naukluft), Treigue Cooper (Waterberg), Dr Malan Lindeque (Etosha), Rudi Loutit (Kaokoveld) and Dr Rob Simmons (birding). In addition, we are also indebted to the following people who have since left the ministry: Chris Hines (birding), Brian Jones (northeastern Namibia), Dr Eugéne Joubert, Achim Lensin (Namib), Dr Hentie Schrader (freshwater fish) and Dr Tony Williams (birding).

Our gratitude also to the following specialists: Dr John Kinahan (archaeology), Dr Roy Miller (geology), the late Dr Mike Muller (flora), Marion and Gunther Schelke (Luderitzbücht Safaris) and Dr Mary Seely (Namib Desert). Our research was also made easier by the efficient staff of the Esdorff Reference Library and the National Monuments Council who allowed us to examine their records.

We are also grateful to the following people and establishments for accommodation made available on our travels: Damaraland Camp (Wilderness Safaris Namibia), Epako Lodge, Etendeka Mountain Camp, Dusty and Karin Rodgers of Impalila Island Lodge, Intu-Africa Lodge, Eric and Nancy Hessemans of Kulala Lodge, Lianshulu Lodge, Mount Etjo Safari Lodge, John and Jeanie Rabie of Namibgrens Rest Camp, Namib-Naukluft Lodge, Okonjima Lodge, Ongava Lodge, the late Louw Schoeman of Skeleton Coast Safaris, Swakopmund Hotel and Entertainment Centre (Stocks and Stocks) and Sossusvlei Karos Lodge. In addition, Marc and Elinor Dürr of Tok Tokkie Trails and Gideon and Sakki Davids of Sossusvlei On Foot hikes shared their knowledge of the Namib with us.

To Friedrich Neuhaus of Ondese Travel and Safaris, Babie Ahrens of Eden Travel and Dennis Rundle (formerly of Wilderness Safaris Namibia), thank you for updating us on the growing number of accommodation establishments in Namibia.

Finally our appreciation to all Southern Book Publishers, particularly Basil van Rooyen for initially having the faith in us to way back in 1988, Louise Grantham for taking the initiative to revamp the guide, commissioning editor Reneé Ferreira and copy-editor David Pearson.

CONTENTS

List of Maps

HOW TO USE THIS GUIDE

Namibia's excellent infrastructure makes exploring the country relatively easy compared to many other African countries. To take in as much as possible of this intriguing country, you will, however, have to cover long distances. *African Adventurer's Guide to Namibia* will help you make the best use of your time by showing you how to plan your trip around aspects and activities of particular interest to you.

The structure of the book

Chapters 1 to 5 provide a general introduction to the country and deal with the basics of travelling to and in Namibia. Chapter 2, 'Why visit Namibia?', gives a general résumé of Namibia's main tourist attractions, while detailed descriptions of game parks, national monuments, towns and places of interest in each region are given in chapters 6 to 12, or in the relevant route description. Once you have a broad idea of what you want to see and do on your visit to Namibia, the best times for visiting, and how to get around, you are ready to tackle the more detailed information in the second part of the book.

Chapters 6 to 12 cover the main tourist areas in Namibia. For practical purposes the country has been divided into six tourist regions – Windhoek and Central, Northern, Western and Northeastern Namibia, the Namib Desert (including the Skeleton Coast Park) and Southern Namibia. These tourist regions are shown on the map on pp 50-51. These regions were demarcated by the authors and are not official tourist or administrative regions.

Chapter 13, 'Where to stay in Namibia', provides information about Namibia's grading system for hotels, guest farms, lodges and rest camps as well as a comprehensive list of accommodation establishments. Chapter 14 includes a list of Namibian diplomatic missions abroad and diplomatic representatives accredited to Namibia, as well as useful contact details.

Planning your trip

Namibia is renowned for its game parks and resorts, places of historical significance and stark, beautiful landscapes. Faced with so many choices, travellers often find the wide range of tourist destinations and attractions overwhelming. The information in chapters 6 to 12 will help you plan a holiday to suit your specific interests. Each chapter starts with a brief introduction to the specific region, followed by detailed information on its top attractions and in-depth descriptions of the main tourist routes. The main tourist attractions are clearly cross-referenced to the route(s) by means of a route symbol in the margin. In addition, symbols alongside the text have been used to show at a glance the different activities, attractions and accommodation options available. For easy reference, a list of these symbols can be found on the front cover flap.

The 25 tourist routes cover Namibia's major tourist attractions and, in addition, describe many other places of interest along the different routes. Symbols in the margin show at a glance which activities and features may be of interest to the traveller. For practical reasons, routes sometimes extend into adjoining tourist regions. Each route description is preceded by the direct distance, time, road conditions, the availability of fuel and linking routes. Distances and times are estimates only and exclude detours and lengthy stops. For example, *Route 7: Okahandja to Etosha via Tsumeb* excludes detours to Mount Etjo, Okonjima and Lake Guinas. Distances measured during our travels frequently differed from those on road maps which, to add to our confusion, often differed not only from one map to the other, but also from those on distance markers along the road. Discrepancies are generally small, but distances should be treated as approximately only.

For Windhoek, Swakopmund, Walvis Bay and Lüderitz, walking tours are suggested that take in the towns' historical and cultural highlights. Names of accommodation establishments and restaurants are provided under the headings *Where to stay* and *Where to eat*. This, however, does not imply any recommendation.

Owing to the increasing number of accommodation establishments, only selected establishments have been included in the descriptions of top attractions and in the route descriptions. These establishments were selected on the basis of our own experience, or on the recommendation of tour operators. The *Namibia Accommodation Guide for Tourists*, which is updated annually, is available from the Ministry of Environment and Tourism, Private Bag 13346, Windhoek, Namibia. Copies can also be obtained from Namibia Tourism offices abroad (see p 299).

Authors' notes

Namibia has known human conflict for many centuries and battlefields, military graveyards, fortifications and monuments are included purely from a historical point of view and not to perpetuate colonial history.

Tree names in the text follow the South African *National List of Indigenous Trees*, while the scientific names of species not listed in the *National List of Indigenous Trees* follow their common names. Bird names follow *Roberts' Birds of Southern Africa* (1993, 6th edition).

Namibia's tourist industry is growing rapidly and while care has been taken to ensure that the information is up to date, information does change. This is especially the case with telephone numbers.

Introduction To Namibia

Geography

Namibia lies in southwestern Africa between latitudes 17° and 29° south. Covering 824 269 km², it is nearly four times the size of Great Britain. It is bounded in the west by the cold Atlantic Ocean, and in the east by South Africa and Botswana. Its northern boundary is shared by Angola and Zambia, while the northeastern tip lies at the junction of its boundaries with Zambia, Zimbabwe and Botswana. The Gariep (Orange) River forms a natural boundary with its southern neighbour, South Africa.

The country's topography is dominated by three distinct features. The west is characterised by a narrow **coastal plain**, extending from the coast inland for up to 120 km. This is Namibia's famed Namib Desert, one of the most fascinating deserts in the world.

At the eastern edge of the coastal plain lies an **eroded escarpment** which forms part of southern Africa's Great Escarpment. It stretches from the Kunene River southward to just north of the Huab River, where it disintegrates. South of the Ugab River is the Brandberg, with the 2 579 m high Königstein, the highest point in Namibia. The escarpment reappears in the Khomas Hochland and continues to the Gariep (Orange) River. Altitudes range from 1 500 m to 2 000 m above sea level.

To the east of the eroded escarpment lies a vast **interior plateau**, with elevations of 1 000 m to 1 500 m. The landscape of the interior plateau is dominated by extensive plains, except in the southeast and the northeast, where Kalahari dunes are conspicuous.

Namibia has few perennial rivers. In the north of the country the Kunene and Kavango rivers form natural boundaries with Angola, while the Kwando-Linyanti-Chobe system forms the southern boundary with Botswana. The Zambezi River, in turn, provides a natural boundary with Zambia. The only perennial river in the south of the country is the Gariep, or Orange, River.

Climate

With an average rainfall of 270 mm a year, which is extremely erratic, and a high potential evaporation, Namibia is the most arid country south of the Sahara. More than 70 per cent of this rain is recorded from December to March, and the rain, as well as the length of the rainy season, increases from the coast inland and from the south northward. This trend is reflected by the following average annual rainfall figures:

Swakopmund	8 mm
Keetmanshoop	146 mm
Windhoek	365 mm
Grootfontein	611 mm
Katima Mulilo	700 mm

Rain usually falls in the afternoons as thunderstorms, accompanied by lightning, which soon pass over.

May to September is usually considered the best time to visit the interior. Daytime temperatures are pleasant, but evenings and early mornings are cold, with frost occurring occasionally. Snowfalls are occasionally recorded in the south of the country, but are an unusual phenomenon in Windhoek, which had snow in 1994 and 1984.

The summer months are hot and temperatures of over 35 °C are not uncommon, especially in the far south, the southeast and from Rundu eastward. Fortunately the humidity is relatively low, except in the northeast of the country, where it can reach 88 per cent at 08:00 in February. Minimum and maximum temperatures in the central highlands are about two degrees lower than those of the adjacent interior plateau.

The following table gives a good idea of average maximum and minimum temperatures throughout the country:

	Jan	*April*	*July*	*Oct*
Swakopmund	20/16	19/13	17/9	16/11
Keetmanshoop	35/18	29/14	21/5	31/13
Windhoek	30/17	26/13	20/6	29/15
Grootfontein	30/18	27/13	24/4	32/16
Rundu	31/19	30/15	26/6	35/18

Temperatures along the coast are more moderate than those of the interior and in summer the coast offers welcome relief from the hot temperatures further inland. Fog occurs on average 117 days a year at Lüderitz, most often from February to May. Swakopmund has an average of 113 foggy days – fog being most prevalent from May to August. East winds, locally known as berg winds, can cause the occasional sandstorm as well as unusually high temperatures of up to 40 °C over the Namib and along the coast during these months.

History

Early inhabitants

One of the most exciting discoveries in the search for the origins of modern man was made when an American-French paleontology team discovered the fossilised jawbone of an apelike creature in the Otavi area in June 1991. The age of the fossil was estimated at between 12 and 15 million years, suggesting that the creature lived before the Miocene hominoids evolved into two branches; one leading to humans and the other to chimpanzees and gorillas. The first such discovery south of Kenya and Uganda, it was named *Otavipithecus namibiensis.*

There is also much evidence of Early and Middle Stone Age people having roamed the plains, deserts and mountains of Namibia. The Later Stone Age people left a wealth of rock paintings and engravings, the most significant being the painted slabs discovered in the Apollo 11 shelter in the Huns mountains in southern Namibia. Dated between 27 000 and 25 000 years old, the paintings provide the oldest evidence of artistic expression on the African continent. Other important sites are the rock engravings at Twyfelfontein (see p 139) and the rock paintings of the Brandberg (see p 130).

Prior to the migration of Bantu-speaking peoples into Namibia, the country was inhabited by San hunter-gatherers, also referred to as Bushmen, who lived in small bands throughout the country. Then, about 2 600 years ago, Khoikhoi pastoralists (the ancestors of the Nama people), with their fat-tailed sheep, migrated into Namibia from Botswana.

About the 9th century, Bantu-speaking people started arriving in Namibia, settling in the north of the country. The Herero, who reached the Kaokoland in the mid-1500s, lived there for about two centuries before settling in the central and eastern parts of the country. Other groups, notably the Oorlam Nama and the Basters, migrated into Namibia from the south during the 19th century.

The Portuguese navigator Diego Cão became the first European to set foot on Namibian soil when he landed at Cape Cross, some 120 km north of Swakopmund, in 1486. Nearly four centuries passed, however, before Britain annexed the Walvis Bay enclave in 1878. Germany also began showing increasing interest in the territory and five years later, the German flag was raised at Lüderitz. On 24 April 1884 the area surrounding

Lüderitz was declared a German protectorate and German rule was further extended by the signing of so-called "protection treaties" with several chiefs.

War years

The leader of the Witbooi Nama, Chief Hendrik Witbooi, however, refused to sign such a treaty and in 1893 Captain Curt von François attacked and destroyed Witbooi's stronghold at Hoornkrans near the Gamsberg. Numerous skirmishes followed, until Major Theodor Leutwein launched an attack on Witbooi in the Naukluft mountains in August 1894. Having failed to defeat the Witboois after nine days, Leutwein agreed to negotiate when Chief Hendrik Witbooi offered a conditional surrender.

In 1903 the Bondelswarts in the south of the country rose against colonial rule after an aborted attempt to apprehend their leader by force. Fearing the loss of their land, the Herero in central Namibia took up arms on 11 January 1904. Seizing the opportunity, several hundred Ndonga warriors attacked Fort Namutoni on 28 January 1904, razing it to the ground the following day. Following the defeat of the Hereros seven months later at Waterberg, General Lothar von Trotha issued his infamous extermination order, forcing thousands of Herero to flee eastward into the Omaheke sandveld and present-day Botswana.

War also spread to the south of the country in August 1904 when the German *Schutztruppe* clashed with Jakob Morenga. Early in October 1904, the Witboois went to war and were soon joined by other Nama chiefs in a struggle which lasted until 31 March 1907.

After the military defeat of Namibia's people, tribal lands were systematically expropriated by the German colonial administration. Following the outbreak of World War I in 1914, the South African government invaded the territory to protect the Cape sea route, should the Suez Canal be closed. German colonial rule came to an end when its forces surrendered to South Africa's Union Forces on 9 July 1915.

South Africa assumed responsibility for the territory, which was administered as a protectorate until the League of Nations conferred a Class C Mandate over the territory on South Africa on 17 December 1920. The German administrative structures were adopted with little change, and by 1921 the area of farmland awarded to white farmers had increased significantly. A limited form of self-government, for whites only, was given in 1925.

After World War II, the Trusteeship Council of the United Nations assumed the responsibilities of the League's Permanent Mandates Commission. South Africa, however, refused to recognise the United Nations as the successor to the League of Nations in 1946. A request by

South Africa to incorporate South West Africa as a fifth province was rejected and in 1948 South Africa ceased to submit annual reports to the UN. A lengthy dispute with the world body ensued, resulting in four advisory opinions by the International Court of Justice and numerous UN General Assembly resolutions.

Struggle for independence

Resistance to South Africa's illegal occupation of South West Africa mounted and in 1959 the South West Africa National Union (SWANU) was founded. In September that year the Owamboland People's Organisation (OPO), formed in Cape Town in 1958 to oppose the contract labour system, joined forces with SWANU. However, on 19 April 1960 the alliance split and the OPO was transformed into the South West Africa People's Organisation (SWAPO).

The National Party government in South Africa enforced its apartheid policies on the people of South West Africa. In 1962 the Odendaal Commission was appointed to devise a homeland system for the country's indigenous population groups. The Commission recommended the creation of 10 ethnic homelands which would ultimately govern themselves.

In July 1966, Swapo decided to use all means, including armed struggle, to achieve the liberation of Namibia. The first shots of the liberation war were fired when the South African Police attacked a People's Liberation Army of Namibia (PLAN) base at Ongulumbashe, 20 km west of Tsandi in the Omusati Region, on 26 August 1966. Two PLAN fighters were shot dead, another died of his wounds some time later, while nine were arrested.

South African cooperation with the Portuguese government in Angola made it impossible for Swapo to operate in the north of the country, forcing it to infiltrate northeastern Caprivi from bases in Zambia. Following Angola's independence on 11 November 1975, Swapo enjoyed the support of the MPLA government and relocated its bases to that country.

To counter Swapo, the South African government arranged a convention of internal political parties to deliberate on the future of South West Africa. On 18 August 1976 the Turnhalle Conference decided that an interim government should be formed and that the country should become independent before 31 March 1978.

On 4 May 1978 the South African Defence Force carried out a pre-emptive strike on Cassinga, a Swapo base in southern Angola. Statistics on the number of casualties vary considerably, and Swapo maintains that mostly innocent women and children were killed in the attack.

Despite the attack on Cassinga, diplomatic initiatives begun by the Western Contact Group in April 1978 continued, resulting in the adoption of Resolution 435 by the UN Security Council on 29 September 1978. The South African government subsequently expressed concern about several aspects of the Secretary-General's report on the implementation of the proposals and unilaterally decided to go ahead with elections. The elections, held from 4 to 8 December 1978, were won by the Democratic Turnhalle Alliance (DTA) which drew 81 per cent of the vote and in May 1979 the Constituent Assembly decided to establish a National Assembly. In January 1983 the National Assembly was abolished after the Chairman of the Minister's Council, Dirk Mudge, resigned in protest when a bill on public holidays was referred back to the National Assembly by the South African Administrator-General. Legislative and executive powers were then transferred to the Administrator-General.

In September 1983 several internal political parties announced that they would participate in a multi-party conference. The first meeting of the Multi-Party Conference (MPC) was held on 12 November 1983 and in May the following year representatives of the MPC and Swapo held talks on Namibian independence in Lusaka, Zambia. The talks were inconclusive and Swapo did not sign the Lusaka Declaration.

South Africa, meanwhile, continued its policy of diplomacy and military action in the hope of defeating Swapo militarily and isolating it from the masses in its power base in Owambo, northern Namibia. It also became increasingly involved in hot-pursuit cross-border operations and assisting Unita in its fight against the MPLA.

To counter South African assistance to Unita, Cuba and Russia took greater roles in the Angolan conflict and in October 1987 the SADF and Unita were involved in the biggest land battle fought in sub-Saharan Africa, at the Lomba River in southeastern Angola. This was followed by the battle of Cuito Cuanavale, where a military stalemate forced all sides in the conflict to consider a peaceful solution, rather than further escalation of the war.

Peace and independence

Agreement on a new initiative to pave the way to Namibia's independence was reached in March 1988 between South Africa's Minister of Foreign Affairs, Pik Botha, and the American Secretary of State for African Affairs, Dr Chester Crocker. Further diplomatic initiatives resulted in the New York Agreement, signed on 22 December 1988 by the governments of South Africa, Angola and Cuba. It provided for the implementation of UN Resolution 435 and the withdrawal of an estimated 50 000 Cuban troops from Angola.

The agreement was implemented on 1 April 1989 and was overseen by the Special Representative of the UN Secretary General, Marthi Athisaari.

Assisting him was the United Nations Transitional Assistance Group (UNTAG), a body comprised of a 4 426-strong military component, 1 500 people in a policing role and 437 civilians.

Namibians went to the polls to elect a Constituent Assembly, charged with drawing up a constitution for the country, in November 1989. In a 97 per cent poll, Swapo won 41 of the 72 seats, and the Democratic Turnhalle Alliance 21. The United Democratic Front won four seats, Action Christian National three, and three smaller parties one seat each.

The country's constitution was unanimously adopted on 9 February 1990 and Namibia became independent on 21 March 1990. Swapo leader Sam Nujoma became the first President, and Hage Geingob was appointed the country's first Prime Minister.

Population

Namibia is one of the most sparsely populated countries in Africa, with 1,6 million people and an average population density of just under two people per square kilometre. The highest population densities are in the north, with up to 26 people per square kilometre. In the arid south of the country, the population density is as low as one person per three square kilometres. About 32 per cent of the country's people live in rural areas.

Namibia's population is a mosaic of 11 cultural groups. The largest group, the **Oshiwambo**, live mainly in the four northern regions. The Kwanyama are the largest of the eight Oshiwambo cultural groups and also live north of the Namibian-Angolan border. They are primarily subsistence crop farmers, cultivating mainly *mahangu* (millet).

The second largest group is the **Kavango**, comprising five cultural groups, of the Kavango Region. The northeast of the country is home to the **Caprivian people**; the two main cultural groups are the Masubia and the Mafwe.

The **Herero-speaking** people comprise the Herero of north-central and eastern Namibia, the Mbanderu of eastern Namibia, and the Himba, who live in the arid northwest of the country. They are pastoralists and cattle still play an important part in their culture.

The **Basters** stem from intermarriage between the early farmers of the Cape Colony and Khoikhoi women. They migrated from the Cape in the 1800s and settled at the hot water spring at Rehoboth in 1870. Despite the pejorative meaning of the name Baster (half-caste), they are a proud and fiercely independent people and speak mainly Afrikaans. The Basters are skilled at crafts, especially building, and also practise smallstock farming on farms in what was formerly known as the Rehoboth Gebiet. (*Gebiet* is the Afrikaans term for area.)

Although sharing the language of the Nama of southern Namibia, **Damaras** are considered negroid and their origin is still shrouded in mystery. They live in the arid northwestern parts of Namibia, where they eke out an existence with smallstock farming.

The **Nama** people, descendants of the Khoikhoi, are found in the south of Namibia, with small groups of Topnaar Nama also occurring further north along the Kuiseb River and in the Sesfontein area. Small in stature and with a yellowish complexion, they have a language characterised by explosive click sounds. They are traditionally pastoralists.

The **San**, the most marginalised group in Namibia, live mainly in the area generally referred to as Bushmanland and western Caprivi. Those living outside these areas have to a large extent become assimilated with other cultures and many work as farm labourers.

Namibia's smallest population group, the **Tswanas**, number less than 7 000 people. Related to the Tswanas of neighbouring Botswana, they farm with livestock, mainly in the Epikuro and Aminius areas in the east of the country.

Namibia's white population is of **Afrikaans**, **English** and **German** extraction. They have settled in urban areas and on commercial farms. The **coloured people**, originally from the Western and Northern Cape in South Africa, live mainly in urban areas.

Language

English is the official language and travellers should generally have little difficulty communicating, except in some of the remote rural areas. Prior to independence in 1990, Afrikaans was the official language and it is still the *lingua franca*; the only exception is the Caprivi Region, where English is spoken. German is widely spoken in Windhoek, Swakopmund, Lüderitz and some smaller towns. Oshiwambo is the most widely spoken of Namibia's indigenous languages.

Economy

Namibia has a mixed economy allowing for several forms of ownership. Following independence, the government embarked on a policy to create an environment conducive to economic growth.

Namibia's *per capita* gross national product is the seventh highest in Africa and its economy is classified by the World Bank as lower-middle income. This description is misleading, though, as income is extremely unevenly distributed due to past inequalities, as a result of which 5 per cent of the population earn more than 70 per cent of the national income.

The primary industries (mining, agriculture and fishing) account for more than 25 per cent of GDP. However, these industries are very susceptible to external influences such as world commodity prices, drought and unfavourable oceanic conditions; hence their contribution to GDP can vary from year to year.

Namibia is one of the top seven **diamond** producing countries in the world. Diamonds are mined at Oranjemund, Auchas, 40 km northeast of Oranjemund on the banks of the Orange River, and at Elisabeth Bay south of Lüderitz. Significant deposits of diamonds occur offshore and marine diamonds accounted for about 35 per cent of NAMDEB's production of 1,36 million carats in 1997.

The country is also a major producer of **uranium**, which is mined at Rössing, 65 km inland from Swakopmund. It is the largest open-cast uranium mine in the world and when the mine reaches the end of its life span, the pit will cover over 5 km^2. Rössing's output represents about 6 per cent of world production.

Other important minerals and metals include copper, lead and zinc, while a variety of semi-precious stones (quartz, agate and tourmaline) and dimension stone (marble) are also mined.

Large **gas reserves** have been discovered 4,7 km under water, 150 km offshore of Oranjemund. Estimates are that the Kudu Gas Field has reserves in excess of three trillion cubic feet. The feasibility of developing the gas field is still being determined. Exploration for oil along the Namibian coast is still continuing.

Namibia's agricultural industry is characterised by a commercial sector of mainly white farmers and dry-land subsistence farming in the communal areas. Livestock is the mainstay of agriculture, with beef and mutton production accounting for about 75 per cent of gross agricultural income. **Commercial cattle farming** is practised mainly in the eastern and central parts, while **smallstock** is reared for meat and karakul pelts in the south of the country. South Africa is the major market for livestock and meat, but Namibia also has an annual quota of 13 000 tonnes of boneless meat to the European Community.

Agronomy contributes less than 3 per cent to total agricultural income. Cereals, mainly maize, are grown in the Otavi-Tsumeb-Grootfontein triangle, while fruit and vegetables are cultivated under irrigation along the Orange River, at Hardap Dam and Stampriet.

In the past few years, **game farming** has grown rapidly and numerous guest farms and lodges have been stocked with a wide variety of species. The country is also a popular destination with trophy hunters, especially from Europe. **Ostrich farming** is practised on a small scale, mainly in the south of the country.

Fisheries is another important economic sector. Following Namibia's independence, a 200-mile Exclusive Economic Zone was proclaimed along Namibia's coast and stringent conservation measures were implemented to ensure the recovery of the severely depleted fish resources. As a result, the contribution of fisheries to the GDP grew from 3,4 per cent in 1989 to 9,3 per cent in 1995, making it the third largest economic sector. However, from 1993 to 1995, the marine environment was adversely affected by unfavourable environmental conditions, resulting in the reduction of fish stocks. Since then stocks have, however, recovered.

Pelagic fishing of pilchard, anchovy and horse-mackerel is the most important sector of the industry, and harvesting white fish (such as hake) is another important activity. Lüderitz is the centre of Namibia's **rock lobster** industry.

Namibia's small population and reliance on imports from South Africa has resulted in an underdeveloped **manufacturing sector**. To reduce dependence on the primary sector, attract investment and create employment, the government has embarked on a programme of industrial development. Increasing emphasis is being placed on local processing of raw materials, with the Export Processing Zones Act offering lucrative incentives to investors to manufacture goods for export. Several companies have set up industries in the Walvis Bay Export Processing Zone since it became operational in 1995.

A feature of the Namibian economy is the prominent role played by the state, with government expenditure contributing more than 23 per cent to the country's GDP. The budget for the 1998-99 financial year made provision for expenditure of N$6 784 million. The largest recipient was basic education, which received 21 per cent of the budget, while 13,5 per cent was allocated to health and social services.

Government

Namibia is a democratic, non-secular and unitary state founded on the principles of democracy, the rule of law and justice for all. The country's constitution has been hailed as a model. Among its provisions are the entrenchment of certain fundamental freedoms, environmental protection and the requirement for a two-thirds majority to amend the constitution.

The constitution provides for a separation of the powers of the executive, legislature and judiciary. The executive consists of the President and the Cabinet. The President heads the executive and is elected by popular vote for a five-year term. The bicameral legislature consists of the 72-member National Assembly and the National Council. Members of the

National Assembly are elected for a five-year term on the basis of party lists and proportional representation. The National Council is comprised of 26 representatives; two from each of the country's 13 regions. They are elected for a six-year term by members of Regional Councils. The National Council reviews bills passed by the National Assembly and recommends legislation of regional concern. The judiciary, consisting of a Supreme Court, High Court and lower courts, is independent and subject only to the Constitution and the laws of the country.

Regional government is entrusted to 13 regional councils divided into constituencies. The candidate receiving the most votes in each constituency is elected to the regional council. The administration of government at local level is the responsibility of municipalities and village councils.

Following independence, the government adopted a policy of national reconciliation to unite former enemies. A policy of affirmative action to "ensure" the advancement of the formerly disadvantaged majority was also implemented.

Another area that received attention was that of land ownership, which was central to the liberation struggle. As a result of the South African government's homelands policy, 75 per cent of the population lived on 43 per cent of the land at the time of independence. The (Commercial) Land Reform Act was adopted in 1995 and came into force in October the following year. Central to the act is the principle of willing buyer, willing seller. Land acquistion has, however, been slow and there are increasing calls to amend legislation to enable the government to expropriate land.

As a result of the government's policies and its commitment to democracy, the country has enjoyed peace and stability since independence. Despite incentives to foreign ventures, the response has been slow, but an increasing number of companies are starting to invest in Namibia.

WHY VISIT NAMIBIA?

Namibia's wide variety of attractions and activities cater to the interests, needs and demands of each and every visitor. Combined with an excellent infrastructure and accommodation facilities, these have made the country one of the top 10 tourist destinations in Africa.

The Landscape

Among Namibia's many attractions are its starkly beautiful landscapes, which range from the awe-inspiring depths of the Fish River Canyon (see p 233) and the rock-strewn plains of the Kaokoveld to the vast dune seas and gravel plains of the Namib. Feared by mariners of old, the windswept plains and dunes of the famed Skeleton Coast (see p 198, Skeleton Coast Park) present yet another of the many faces of the Namib Desert.

Extinct volcanoes, weirdly shaped rock formations such as the Vingerklip (see route 11) and the Giant's Playground (see route 20), as well as dinosaur footprints (see route 9) add to the incredible diversity Namibia has to offer.

Contrasting sharply with these arid environments are the woodlands and wetlands of northeastern Namibia. Here you will find papyrus-fringed channels, backwaters carpeted with delicate water lilies, oxbow lakes and floodplains that attract red lechwe, sitatunga and puku – species restricted in Namibia to the northeast of the country.

Among Namibia's attractions are many unique plants and trees. Heading the list of unique species is the *Welwitschia mirabilis* (see routes 2, 16) which has defied botanical classification. Viewed from a distance, the shredded leaves of the welwitschia resemble a stranded octypus. Characteristic of the rocky outcrops of the Kaokoland is the bottle tree, while Namibia's rich diversity of lichens have attracted worldwide attention. In the extreme south of the country there are numerous succulents that are endemic to southern Namibia and the adjoining Richtersveld in South Africa.

Rock engravings and paintings testify to the habitation of the country thousands of years ago, while numerous places of more recent historic significance can also be visited. There is Twyfelfontein (see p 139 and route 11), one of Africa's most spectacular open-air art galleries and the Brandberg (see p 130 and route 13), where more than 40 000 paintings were delicately executed by Later Stone Age people.

With its German heritage, towns such as Swakopmund and Lüderitz have a distinctly colonial atmosphere, with many well-preserved German buildings. Even more fascinating are the diamond mining ghost towns of Kolmanskop (see p 236 and route 24) and Elisabeth Bay (see p 245) near Lüderitz.

Photography

All of Namibia's attractions combine to make it a popular destination with photographers and, in recent years, many award-winning photographs have been taken in the country.

Because of the harsh sunlight, films with an ASA rating of between 50 and 100 are recommended for landscape photography. Early morning and late afternoons are the most rewarding times for photography, but should you take photographs in bright sunlight a polarising filter is useful for reducing glare. Dust and fine sand are frequently a problem, especially in the Namib Desert, and you should store your camera and lenses in a dust-proof bag. Remember to bring a blower brush and lens-cleaning tissues and take care not to scratch the surface of your lenses when cleaning them. A coolbox is recommended for storing films.

Game Parks and Wildlife Viewing

Namibia's 19 state-owned conservation areas and resorts cover about 15 per cent of the country's land surface. Although game numbers are lower than those of other African countries, the **Etosha National Park** (see p 99) ranks as one of Africa's great game parks and route 7 or 8 is a must for wildlife enthusiasts. Other options for those keen on game viewing include the **Waterberg Plateau Park** (see p 108 and route 7) and **Khaudum Game Park** (see p 161 and route 15). Despite the relatively low game populations in the **Mudumu** and **Mamili national parks** (see route 14), their wilderness atmosphere is an attraction to those seeking a total escape into the wilds.

Outside of the state-owned conservation areas, the arid **northwest** of the country is home to **desert-dwelling elephants, black rhino** (see also chapter 8, Etosha National Park) and **giraffe**. These uniquely adapted animals have attracted international attention and have inspired artists such as David Shepherd, Paul Augustinus and Paul Bosman to capture them on canvas. For visitors keen on exchanging the highways for the byways routes 11 and 12 are compulsory when visiting Namibia. Be warned though, the animals are wild and you will only see them if luck is on your side! Also take care to respect them.

While it is inevitably the big species that attract the most attention, Namibia has a stunning variety of small creatures that are specially adapted to survive in the inhospitable **Namib Desert** (see chapter 11). Those who are prepared to set aside time to discover this wonderful world will be richly rewarded. Routes 2, 3, 4, 5, 16 and 18 are ideally suited to those with a passion for deserts.

Wildlife viewing need not, however, be restricted to state-owned conservation areas. In the past few years the number of fine **lodges** and **privately owned conservation areas** has increased considerably. Many of these areas offer excellent opportunities for wildlife viewing and are described under the relevant routes.

Culture

Namibia's people are yet another attraction and offer a variety of cultural experiences. As 67 per cent of the country's people live in rural areas, traditional homesteads and practices are still frequently seen once the highways are exchanged for the byways.

In the far northwest, the **Himba** people continue to pursue a largely traditional way of life, moving about constantly with their herds of cattle and goats. Highly recommended for those interested in learning more about these people is a safari with Kaokohimba Safaris. In addition to drives and walks through the Kaokoveld landscape, visits are also paid to Ovahimba villages. Contact **Kaokohimba Safaris**, P O Box 11580, Windhoek, tel and fax (061) 22-2378.

In Bushmanland and western Caprivi the last remnants of the **San** people are inextricably caught up between pursuing their traditional way of life and adapting to the demands of the 21st century.

Visitors with a keen interest in the culture of the San people will benefit by taking advantage of a specialised tour.

!Na!Hore Safaris, P O Box 5103, Windhoek, tel and fax (061) 22-0124, conduct trips to the ancestral lands of the Jung-kwa San of Bushmanland. Tours are guided by conservationist Alan Cilliers and San trackers. As relatively long distances are covered on foot through loose sand, participants must be fit.

A less demanding option is one of the **Muramba Bushman Trails**, conducted by San expert Reinhard Friedrich, who speaks the Heikum language fluently, and a San tracker. On the 2,5 km guided trail the uses of various plants are pointed out, while trailists will also learn more about the beliefs and culture of the Heikum. There are also two trails of 4,5 and 12 km which can be done with a guide or self-guided.

Overnight visitors can spend the night in a typical Heikum hut, equipped with two beds, a kettle and hotplate. Communal ablutions are provided. There is also a camp site with tables and benches, places to braai (barbecue) and water. From Tsumeb, take the C75 north to Tsintsabis for 64 km and turn right onto the D3016, which is followed for 6 km to the signposted turnoff. Advance reservations are essential. P O Box 689, Tsumeb, tel (06738) ask for 6222, fax (061) 25-9914.

Colourfully dressed Herero women draw attention in Windhoek and the north-central and eastern parts of the country. The annual **Red Flag Herero** and **Green Flag (Mbanderu) ceremonies** at Okahandja (see route 1) are among the most colourful cultural events in the country. Not as well known, but no less spectacular, is Omaruru's **White Flag Herero ceremony** (see route 9), while the **Witbooi Festival** in Gibeon (see route 20) provides a fascinating insight into the resistance of the Witbooi Nama against German colonialism.

If you happen to be in the country towards the end of April, **WIKA**, the Windhoek Karneval, should not be missed. The German-style carnival features a coronation ball, a colourful street procession, youth carnival, ladies evening, an international evening and a masked ball.

Angling

The Namibian coast has long been regarded as an anglers' paradise and every year thousands of hopeful fishermen crowd the shores. Camping facilities at popular angling spots in the National West Coast Tourist Recreation Area are provided at Mile 4, Mile 14, Jakkalsputz, Mile 72 and Mile 108 (see route 17). Camping facilities are available at Torra Bay and bungalows at Terrace Bay in the Skeleton Coast Park.

To protect the country's surf and rock angling species from overexploitation, the total number of kob, steenbras, blacktail or galjoen caught by an angler may not exceed 30, while a maximum of eight galjoen may be caught. For processed fish the limit is 30 kg, but a limit of 8 kg applies to galjoen.

Angling with polychaete (bristle) worm is prohibited. The daily limits on the collection of bait per person are as follows: barnacles, coelenterates, echinoderms, hermit crabs, prawns and molluscs (other than those listed) five of each, black mussels 50, limpets 15 and periwinkle 25. The limit on white mussel, with an inner diameter of at least 38 mm, is 25. A maximum of 2 kg red bait (without shell) that has been washed ashore may be collected. With a few exceptions, marine invertebrate animals may only be collected by hand.

Seven rock lobsters per person may be caught daily during the season, which stretches from 1 November to 30 April. The minimum size is 65 mm, measured in a straight line down the middle of the back. It is forbidden to be in possession of female rock lobsters carrying eggs or showing signs of the eggs having been stripped off, or any rock lobster (male or female) with a very soft shell.

Rock lobsters may be caught between sunrise and sunset and the methods of collection are restricted to diving from the shore (the only permissible artificial breathing apparatus is a snorkel) and the use of a ring net. Collection in the rock lobster reserve, which extends from Dias Point to Agate Beach at Lüderitz, is prohibited.

Regulations change from time to time, making it advisable to obtain the latest angling regulations from the Ministry of Fisheries and Marine Resources at:

- Swakopmund, Sea Fisheries Institute, Strand Street (South), tel (064) 40-5744, fax 40-4385
- Walvis Bay, 214 1st Street, tel (064) 20-5968, fax 20-5008
- Lüderitz, Old Hospital, Kreplin Street, Shark Island, tel (063) 20-2415, fax 20-3337

Favoured dams for freshwater angling include Daan Viljoen Game Park near Windhoek (see route 2), Von Bach Dam near Okahandja (see route 1), Hardap Dam near Mariental (see route 20), Naute Dam near Keetmanshoop (see route 25) and Ai-Ais on the Fish River (see route 20). Popular species include large- and smallmouth bass, carp, yellowfish, Mozambique tilapia and barbel. Licences can be obtained at the resort offices.

The Kavango, Kwando-Linyanti and Zambezi rivers (see chapter 10) in the north of the country are the habitat of several fine angling species. Especially sought after is the rapacious tigerfish, while threespot tilapia, bream, nembwe, pink happy and barbel also inhabit the rivers.

There are currently (December 1998) few regulations with regard to freshwater angling, but comprehensive legislation is being considered. For further information, contact the Ministry of Fisheries and Marine Resources in Windhoek, tel (061) 205-3911.

Backpacking, Trailing & Rock Climbing

Despite few perennial rivers and high summer temperatures, several areas in Namibia lend themselves to rock climbing, backpacking and trailing. Self-guided overnight trails in state-owned conservation areas include the

Fish River Canyon (see p 233), Naukluft (see p 190), Sweet Thorn (see route 2) and the Waterberg (see p 110) hikes. Guided wilderness trails are conducted in the Waterberg Plateau Park (see p 110) and along the Ugab River (see p 199), which forms the southern boundary of the Skeleton Coast Park. Several farmers have established hiking trails on their farms. Among these are the Dassie (see route 4), Namib Feral Horse (see route 24) and Oas hiking trails.

Other self-guided options include exploring Brukkaros (see route 20), an extinct volcano in the south of the country and the Brandberg (see route 13). Owing to the extremely rugged terrain and limited water, excursions into the Brandberg should, however, only be undertaken by experienced and fit climbers. It is also advisable to be accompanied by someone who knows the mountain. For those unfamiliar with it, a safe option is to take a guided trail with **Damaraland Trails and Tours**. Tour guide Joe Walter knows the Brandberg intimately and on his Rock Art Safari six days are spent examining the rock paintings of the Brandberg. P O Box 3073, Windhoek, tel (061) 23-4610, fax 23-9616. Alternatively, you can hire the services of the **Brandberg Mountain Guides**, indigenous guides living around the mountain. Contact NACOBTA, P O Box 86099, Windhoek, tel (061) 25-0558, fax 22-2647. The **Namibian Mountaineering Club** has an active programme. P O Box 2488, Windhoek, Namibia.

Those unable to undertake a hiking or guided wilderness trail can take to the hills on any of a number of short walks. Day walks have been laid out in the Naukluft (see p 188) and Namib (see p 186) sections of the Namib-Naukluft Park, Hardap (see route 20) and Daan Viljoen game parks (see route 2), Skeleton Coast Park (see p 198) and the Waterberg Plateau Park (see p 108).

One of the greatest challenges to rock climbers is the Spitzkoppe (see p 136), also known as the Matterhorn of Namibia. Rising some 700 m above the surrounding plains, its sheer granite walls can be ascended along a number of routes.

Canoeing and Rafting

Two of Namibia's boundary rivers, the Kunene and Orange rivers, are ideally suited to canoeing. The 120 km stretch of the **Kunene River** between Ruacana and Epupa falls is generally wide and slow-flowing, with few rapids. However, at Ondorusso and Enyandi the river increases its pace, creating a series of exciting rapids up to Grade Four. Unless you are an accomplished canoeist, it is inadvisable to explore the river without a guide. Guided trips are offered by two companies, **Whitewater Eco Tours** (WET), P O Box 30024, Windhoek, tel and fax (061) 22-7363, and **Felix**

Unite Namibian River Adventures, P O Box 3, Noordoewer, tel (063) 29-7161, fax 29-7250.

The **Orange River**, which forms Namibia's southern boundary with South Africa, is far more popular and accessible. Organised canoeing trips depart from a base camp a few kilometres downstream from Noordoewer. Rapids are generally Grade Two. Contact **Felix Unite Namibian River Adventures**, P O Box 3, Noordoewer, tel (063) 29-7161, fax 29-7250, or **River Tours and Safaris**, P O Box 474, Rivonia 2128, South Africa, tel (011) 803-9775, fax 803-9603, or **The River Rafters**, P O Box 314, Bergvliet 7864, South Africa, tel (021) 712-5094/5, fax 712-5241.

If you prefer something less adrenaline-charged, you can opt for a **sea-kayak tour** of Walvis Bay lagoon and the offshore coastal areas with Joe Meintjies. **Eco-Marine Kayak Tours**, tel and fax (064) 20-3144.

4x4 Driving

The rough tracks in Namibia's remote regions make the country an ideal destination for those keen to venture off the beaten track. Prime destinations include the Kaokoveld in the northwest (see route 12), Bushmanland and Khaudum Game Reserve in the east (see route 15 p 110) and the Mudumu and Mamili national parks (see route 15) in the far northeast of the country. An increasing number of 4x4 trails offer another option to those with a spirit of adventure. The first organised trail to be established in the country, the STF Trail links the Kalahari Desert in the east with the Namib Desert in the west.

The **Naukluft 4x4 Trail** (see p 191), the first route to be established in a state-owned conservation area, covers 72 km of mountainous terrain and the plateau of the Naukluft mountains. With several steep ascents, rough descents and narrow mountain passes, the trail presents a challenge to the driving skills of even experienced drivers.

A pleasant trail in the central part of the country is the **Isabis 4x4 Trail** (see route 4), which traverses the rugged terrain of the Gamsberg region for 70 km. The two-day route can be extended by exploring the tracks on the farm **Weener** (see p 91) nearby. Visitors can also tackle the steep, zigzag track to the top of the **Gamsberg**, but must be accompanied by a guide (see routes 3, 4).

The **Windhoek-Okahandja 4x4 Trail** enables travellers to explore the off-the-beaten track routes of the Windhoek Valley. Starting on the farm Okapuka, (see p 76) 30 km north of Windhoek, the trail covers 120 km of gravel tracks, mountain roads and sandy beds of rivers. A choice of three overnight stops is available. P O Box 5955, Windhoek, tel (061) 23-4607, fax 23-4690.

The **Uri Desert Run** is a guided, self-drive tour conducted in specially designed off-road vehicles (Uris) to tourist attractions in the south of Namibia from March to November. Tours are tailored to suit groups of three to 10 people and last from four to 14 days. In addition to well-known tourist attractions such as the Fish River Canyon (see p 233), Sossusvlei (see p 194) and Sesriem (see p 193), stops are also made at farms along the way. Accommodation varies from sleeping under the stars to rustic farm lodgings and *pensions*. Two people share a Uri, one being the driver. Trips start and end in Keetmanshoop. P O Box 83, Koës, tel and fax (063) ask for 2021 or 2003.

Horseback Trails

Horseback safaris offer yet another perspective of the magnificent scenery, flora and fauna of Namibia. Guided trails are conducted from Waldi and Lumpi Fristche's farm, Hilton, in the Khomas Hochland. Trails range from four days in the saddle exploring the Namib to the 13-day Damaraland and Skeleton Coast ride. One of the most popular tours is the 400 km trip from the Khomas Hochland to Swakopmund. Nine days are spent in the saddle on the journey, descending the escarpment and then traversing the Namib Desert. **Reit Safaris**, P O Box 20706, Windhoek, tel (062) 57-2102, fax (061) 23-8890.

Birdwatching

To date over 630 bird species, including vagrants, have been recorded in Namibia. Of special interest to birders are the endemic dune lark and the near endemics of north-central and northwestern Namibia. Among these are Hartlaub's francolin, Rüppell's korhaan, Monteiro's hornbill, Bradfield's swift, Gray's lark, Carp's black tit, Herero chat, rockrunner and white-tailed shrike (see also Waterberg Plateau Park, p 108 and route 7). Two species that reach the southern limit of their distribution along the Kunene River are the Cinderella waxbill and the rufous-tailed palm thrush.

Northeastern Namibia is home to about 130 species occurring nowhere else in the country. "Specials" include slaty egret, western banded snake eagle, rock pratincole, coppery-tailed coucal, Pel's fishing owl, Narina trogon, greater swamp warbler, pink-throated longclaw, swamp boubou and brown firefinch. The best area for birding in Namibia is undoubtedly the Mahango Game Park (see p 163), where more than 450 species have been recorded to date.

The Walvis Bay-Swakopmund coastal area offers excellent birding and during the summer months experienced birders can tick up to 90 species in a day. The Walvis Bay wetlands (see p 213) are among the most important coastal wetlands in Africa. Other good birding spots include the Bird Paradise on the eastern outskirts of Walvis Bay, the rocky shores between Walvis Bay and Swakopmund, Swakop River Mouth, Swakop sewerage works and the saltworks north of Swakopmund.

Over 250 species have been recorded in the central highlands, where birding is especially rewarding just before the summer rains. "Specials" such as Monteiro's hornbill, rockrunner and white-tailed shrike can be ticked in the Daan Viljoen Game Park (see p 87), while a variety of waterbirds are attracted to Avis Dam on the eastern outskirts of Windhoek on the rare occasions that the dam holds water.

In the Etosha National Park (see routes 7, 8) you are unlikely to tick more than 100 species during dry cycles, but during wet cycles the number of species can exceed 300. Fischer's Pan is the best wetland area in the park, while the Andoni Plains attract species such as crowned crane and pink-billed lark. The Namutoni area is one of the best places to see black-faced babbler, while at Halali the chances of spotting bare-cheeked babbler and violet wood hoopoe are good.

Some 150 species occur in the desert and semi-desert areas. Among the typical Namib species are Ludwig's bustard, Rüppell's korhaan, and Stark's and Gray's larks. Your best chances of sighting the Herero chat are at Spitzkoppe (see p 136) or on the road between Khorixas and Twyfelfontein. At Elim Dune near Sesriem there is a possibility of ticking dune lark, while Gray's lark favours the gravel plains of the coastal strip between Aus in southern Namibia and southwestern Angola.

November through to April are generally the most rewarding months for birdwatching, as a large number of Palaearctic and intra-African migrants can also be seen. Specialist birding safaris are conducted by **The Namibian Naturalist**. These high-quality tours are expertly guided by three professional biologists, Chris Hines, David Ward and Steve Braine. P O Box 784, Windhoek, tel (061) 23-6692, fax 23-6693.

The **Namibia Bird Club** organises regular meetings and outings. Contact them at P O Box 67, Windhoek, Namibia.

Sports

Namibians are a sport-loving nation with a keen interest in **soccer**. The participation of the national team, the Brave Warriors, in the African Cup of Nations and World Cup soccer, has done much to enhance interest in the sport. Also popular is **athletics**, no doubt as a result of the outstanding performances of Frank Fredericks, one of the world's top athletes in the 100 and 200 m.

In Windhoek and the larger towns, there are opportunities for playing **tennis, squash** and **golf**.

The **Windhoek Country Club**, on the southern outskirts of Windhoek, has a pleasant course. The **Rossmund** golf course, outside Swakopmund, is situated in the Swakop River valley amid the stark plains of the Namib Desert. The 18-hole course is said to be one of only five desert courses in the world and it is not unusual to see springbok grazing on the verdant fairways. **Tsumeb** and **Oranjemund** also have well-maintained courses. Among the country's more unusual courses is the one at **Henties Bay**, where golfers are confronted with white sandy fairways, and the 9-hole course at **Katima Mulilo** which is "mowed" at night by hippos.

In summer, public **swimming pools** are a popular refuge for those seeking to escape the heat. Windhoek has two public swimming pools, one near Maruea Park, and the other in the western suburbs. Elsewhere in the country there are public swimming pools at Keetmanshoop, Omaruru, Otjiwarongo and Grootfontein, as well as at the three rest camps in Etosha, Hobas, Hardap Dam and Waterberg. There is a heated pool at the Health & Racquet Club at Maruea Park in Windhoek and an Olympic-size heated pool at Swakopmund. Ai-Ais, Rehoboth and Gross Barmen have hot water outdoor pools. Along the coast the hydroslide and pool at Dolphin Park between Swakopmund and Walvis Bay are popular.

Few people brave the usually cold sea temperatures along the west coast. In addition, swimming can be dangerous due to crosscurrents and steep slopes in the sea bed. However, the **Mole basin** at Swakopmund offers safe swimming, as does the **Langstrand tidal pool** between Swakopmund and Walvis Bay. A number of **protected bays along the Lüderitz Peninsula** (see p 242) offer pleasant conditions for a dip.

Water sports

With a number of dams spread around the country, a variety of water sports are pursued at weekends on the Naute (see route 25), Hardap (see route 20) and Von Bach (see route 1) dams over weekends. **Powerboating, water-skiing, yachting** and **windsurfing** are especially popular. Fresh breezes along the coast create ideal conditions for **boardsailing, windsurfing** and **yachting**, and the Walvis Bay lagoon is much favoured by water-sport enthusiasts.

Air sports

Atmospheric conditions over Namibia are ideal and offer opportunities for air sports. Bitterwasser, north of Mariental, has an international reputation for **soaring (gliding)** and several records have been set here. Bitterwasser becomes a hive of activity from October to January, when an international array of gliding pilots gather here to make use of the excellent thermals and visibility. Bitterwasser, P O Box 13003, Windhoek, tel (06672) 3830, fax (061) 25-0621.

Skydiving (parachuting) takes place at Windhoek's Eros Airport at weekends, tel (061) 22-3548. The Etosha Skydiving Centre, based at Tsumeb, meets less frequently. Swakopmund has an active skydiving club and a jump at the coast offers skydivers spectacular views of the desert and the ocean. Desert boogies are arranged from time to time. For details, tel (064) 40-2841.

Commercial **ballooning** operations are conducted from Mövenpick Sossusvlei Lodge (see p 194), Kulala Lodge (see route 19) and Camp Mwisho (see route 19) by **Namib Sky Adventure Safari**, P O Box 5197, Windhoek, tel (063) 29-3233, fax 29-3241. Hot-air balloon flights are also conducted from Sossusvlei Wilderness Camp (see routes 18, 22).

Dune sports

The coastal dunes between Swakopmund and Walvis Bay lend themselves to a variety of dune sports. Popular activities include **duneboarding** and **parasailing** from the dunes at Langstrand Resort. Contact **Swakopmund Adventure Centre**, P O Box 1388, Swakopmund, tel (064) 40-2737.

Stargazing

With amazingly clear skies, minimal air pollution and hardly any glare from city lights, Namibia is considered one of the best stargazing locations in the world. In addition, its location offers excellent views of the central section of the Milky Way, as well as stars, planets and deep-sky objects in the southern and northern hemispheres.

The **Cuno Hoffmeister Memorial Observatory** on the Auas mountains, just south of Windhoek, provides ideal opportunities to study the Namibian night sky. The observatory was established through the initiative of one of Namibia's foremost amateur astronomers, Mrs Sonja Enke. Contact her on tel (061) 23-8982, fax 23-8850.

Several lodges have small telescopes and offer opportunities for stargazing, among them Mövenpick Sossusvlei Lodge, Sossusvlei Wilderness Camp and the Damaraland Wilderness Camp.

Caving

Although the country does not have many caves, it does offer some exciting caving experiences for specialist speleologists and the general public.

Following the discovery of **Dragon's Breath Cave** on a farm in the Grootfontein district in July 1986, Namibia has attracted the attention of speleologists worldwide. With a surface area of 2 ha, Dragon's Breath is the largest underground lake in the world and is roughly three times the size of the famous Amphitheatre of the Cango Caves in South Africa's Western Cape Province. The depth of the water ranges from 37 m to 89 m. Access is extremely difficult; the crack which provides access is in places only 30 cm wide and the last 30 m of the 55 m descent is free hanging. As a result the cave is not open to the general public. Members of speleological societies might, however, be successful if they approach the Southern African Speleological Association.

Also of interest is the **Ghaub Cave** in the Kombat area, but once again access and logistics are rather difficult and enquiries should best be made through the Southern African Speleological Association. The cave is about 500 m long and leads to two chambers; one about 6 m high while the main chamber is about 10 m high. Over the years the cave, unfortunately, suffered at the hands of vandals and few of the stalactites, limestone crystals and other formations remain.

Caves open to the general public are **Arnhem**, at 4,5 km the sixth longest in southern Africa (see p 72 and route 6) and the **Munsterland Caves** (see route 11).

Geology & Geomorphology

With its interesting rock formations and rocks dating back more than 2 000 million years ago, Namibia is a haven for the amateur geologist, geomorphologist and rock, gemstone and mineral collectors.

Among the country's most striking formations and landscapes are the awesome Fish River Canyon (see p 233) and the Giant's Playground (see route 20) in the south of the country. The Namib Desert (see chapter 11) with its sand dunes and gravel plains has attracted the attention of scientists and tourists from around the world. In western Namibia (see chapter 9), contorted layers of rock, cone-shaped peaks, table-top mountains and lava flows have created a treasure chest for hobby geologists. Best-known among the attractions of this region are the Spitzkoppe (see p 136) and the Vingerklip (see p 140).

Shopping

For visitors wishing to take reminders of their visit to Namibia home, there is a wide variety of local crafts. Especially popular are the **Herero dolls** which are sold at the entrance to the Gustav Voigts Centre in

Independence Avenue, Windhoek, while **Kavango woodcarvings** are another typical Namibian craft. Outside of Windhoek they can be bought at Okahandja, at stalls along the road between Mururani Gate and Rundu and in Rundu itself. In Windhoek there are a number of street markets and craft outlets that should not be missed (see chapter 6, p 65).

Jewellery with a distinctive Namibian design, inspired by the country's wide open spaces and varied cultures, is hand-crafted by a number of highly trained goldsmiths in Windhoek and Swakopmund. Local semi-precious stones like tourmaline, amethyst, topaz and aquamarine are incorporated into the designs.

Collectors of rocks, gems and minerals should not miss a visit to Sidney Pieters of The House of Gems at the lower end of Stübel Street and Rocks and Gems in Independence Avenue, Windhoek. There are also **gemstone shops** in Swakopmund and Tsumeb.

Unique to Namibia are the **Swakara garments** manufactured from locally produced karakul pelts. These pelts are renowned throughout the world for their high quality and among the garments are reversible coats, jackets and capes tailored to the latest international fashions. In addition to Swakara garments a variety of leather goods, including ostrich skin bags and purses, are also sold by outlets in Windhoek.

Also popular are **hand-woven karakul carpets, rugs and wall-hangings**. Dunes and typical Namibian landscapes feature prominently in many designs, while others feature farmlife, intricate abstract and geometric patterns and coastal scenery. There are a number of weaving centres to the east of Windhoek and route 6 is especially recommended for those keen on this type of art. Also worth visiting is Karakulia in Swakopmund (see p 200) and Der Webervogel in Karibib (see Route 1).

Famous far outside the borders of Namibia are the well-known **Swakopmunders**, shoes with kudu leather uppers, manufactured by the Swakopmund Tannery since the early 1960s. A wide range of belts, bags, and other leather goods, as well as treated game skins, are also on sale.

A useful brochure for those interested in arts and crafts is published by the Arts and Crafts Guild of Namibia, P O Box 20709, Windhoek, tel (061) 22-3831 or 25-2468 or 25-1422, fax 25-2125.

Hunting & Hunting Safaris

Namibia is highly rated for the opportunities it affords to hunters. To ensure the orderly utilisation of wildlife, all aspects of hunting are strictly controlled by law.

Game is classified in three categories: specially protected, protected and huntable. Springbok, kudu, gemsbok (oryx), buffalo, warthog and bushpig are huntable game and may be shot during the hunting season, usually between May and July.

A permit is required for huntable game and prospective hunters must obtain written permission from the farm owner, who decides what animals may be hunted and the price. The letter of permission must then be submitted to a Ministry of Environment and Tourism (MET) office, or police station, which will issue the necessary hunting permit.

Bag limits are three head of big game, or two head of big and four head of small game, or 12 head of small game per hunter per year. The permit must be carried by the hunter during the hunt (unless accompanied by the owner), between the hunt and return home, and as long as the meat is in his or her possession.

Trophy hunters may also hunt protected and specially protected game throughout the year, except during December and January, provided the necessary permit has been obtained from the MET. Trophy hunting permits are only issued to those who can produce proof that they will be hunting under the guidance of a registered professional hunter or hunting guide, a list of whom can be obtained from the Directorate of Wildlife Management, Windhoek, tel (061) 26-3131.

Trophy hunting concessions have been granted in several communal areas in the northeast of the country. The species which may be hunted and the quotas are determined annually by the MET. Details can be obtained from the Directorate of Wildlife Management, Windhoek, tel (061) 26-3131.

The hunting season for game birds is usually August and September, but may vary. Visitors to Namibia hunting on a trophy permit may shoot only two birds of each of the species listed on the permit. A permit is not required to shoot huntable birds during the season, but hunters must be in possession of the written permission of the landowner. At the time of writing (December 1998) 20 bird species were classified as huntable, but the list could change and it is advisable to consult the Directorate of Wildlife Management on current regulations.

Most hunting guides, master guides and professional hunters are members of the Namibia Professional Hunters' Association (NPHA), which represents the interests of the trophy hunting industry. Among its objectives is the marketing of Namibia as a hunting destination abroad. Tel (061) 23-4455.

PLANNING YOUR TRIP

Planning Your Itinerary

Namibia offers so many diverse attractions and adventure activities that the question of what to include and what to leave out inevitably comes up. This will no doubt result in long planning sessions and frequent changes in plans before your itinerary is finalised. The following hints and suggested itineraries will hopefully make planning your trip a lot easier.

To assist you with your planning, refer to the symbols in the page margins in chapters 6 to 12 to identify areas likely to be of interest to you. This will enable you to plan your trip around your specific interests without being side-tracked by attractions, or activities, that do not particularly appeal to you.

A common complaint is that visitors do not realise that 400 km of travelling on gravel roads takes a lot more out of you than the same distance on a motorway, *autobahn*, or dual carriage highway. Although the recommended maximum speed on gravel roads is 100 km per hour you will often not exceed 80 km per hour. Allowing for the occasional stop along the way, this will reduce your *average* speed to 60 km per hour. With this in mind and the vast distances between towns, do not make the mistake of trying to see too much in too little time. After all, it is not worthwhile driving a couple of hundred of kilometres to a destination and then having hardly any time to enjoy it before racing off to the next attraction!

On 4x4 tracks your progress will be even slower and in some areas of the Khaudum Game Park and the Kaokoveld your average speed can be as little as 10 km per hour. As a general rule, though, you should not expect to do more than 20 km per hour on average in 4x4 country.

Fuel is available at all towns and some farming settlements throughout Namibia, but could be a problem at remote settlements like Tsumkwe. Distances between towns are, however, often vast, making it advisable to plan your refilling stops accordingly. When venturing off the highways into Bushmanland, Khaudum and the Kaokoveld, ensure that you have sufficient spare fuel to get you to the next refuelling stop, bearing in mind that fuel consumption is much higher when driving in low range. Also bear in mind that many of the pumps at farms are only open until 17:00 or 18:00 and could be closed over weekends.

Owing to the vast distances between attractions, air charter is becoming increasingly popular in Namibia, especially for visitors with limited time. Although rather costly, visitors can see the country's most popular attractions in a much shorter time. If you consider this option, bear in mind that the costs are considerably lower when you book as a small group as all the seats can be taken up.

Suggested Itineraries

The following suggested itineraries can be combined into longer tours, or adapted to suit personal preferences. For example, visitors travelling to Namibia via Noordoewer border post can join the 12-day southern tour at Ai-Ais, while those travelling to Namibia via Victoria Falls and Chobe National Park can join the northeastern Namibia Lodge and Camping Safari at Katima Mulilo and follow the tour in reverse. Distances are approximate only and allowance should be made for detours.

8-Day Highlights of Namibia tour

DAY	DESTINATION	DISTANCE
1	Windhoek – Sesriem via Spreetshoogte	310 km
2	Sesriem – Sossusvlei – Sesriem	130 km
3	Sesriem – Swakopmund	350 km
4	Swakopmund, including Welwitschia Drive	160 km
5	Swakopmund – Cape Cross – Twyfelfontein – Vingerklip	650 km
6	Vingerklip – Etosha National Park (Okaukuejo)	220 km
7	Etosha National Park (Namutoni)	150 km
8	Etosha National Park – Windhoek	540 km

12-Day Southern Tour

DAY	DESTINATION	DISTANCE
1	Windhoek – Hardap Dam – Keetmanshoop	540 km
2	Keetmanshoop – Ai-Ais	260 km
3	Ai-Ais – Fish River Canyon/Hobas	100 km
4	Hobas – Lüderitz	420 km
5&6	Lüderitz	50 km
7	Lüderitz – Duwisib Castle – Maltahöhe	430 km
8	Maltahöhe – Sesriem	180 km

9	Sesriem – Sossusvlei – Sesriem	130 km
10	Sesriem – Naukluft	120 km
11	Naukluft (at leisure or 4x4 trail)	30 km
12	Naukluft – Windhoek	245/290 km

11-Day Northern Tour

DAY	DESTINATION	DISTANCE
1	Windhoek – Omaruru (Epako Lodge)	210 km
2	Omaruru – Brandberg – Khorixas	330 km
3	Khorixas – Petrified Forest – Twyfelfontein – Vingerklip	290 km
4	Vingerklip – Etosha National Park (Okaukuejo)	220 km
5	Etosha National Park (Okaukuejo)	100 km
6	Etosha National Park (Halali)	100 km
7	Etosha National Park (Namutoni)	120 km
8	Etosha National Park – Waterberg	380 km
9	Waterberg (at leisure)	–
10	Waterberg – Gross Barmen	230 km
11	Gross Barmen – Windhoek	100 km

14-Day Northwestern Namibia 4x4 Lodge and Camping Safari

DAY	DESTINATION	DISTANCE
1	Windhoek – Kamanjab (Kavita/Hobatere)	515/555 km
2	Kamanjab – Epupa	455/475 km
3	Epupa (at leisure)	–
4	Epupa – Marienfluss	250 km
5	Marienfluss	50 km
6	Marienfluss – Purros	240 km
7	Purros – Sesfontein	105 km
8	Sesfontein – Palmwag/Etendeka Mountain Camp	105 km
9	Palmwag/Etendeka Mountain Camp	50 km
10	Palmwag/Etendeka – The Damaraland Wilderness Camp	70 km
11	The Damaraland Wilderness Camp	–
12	The Damaraland Wilderness Camp – Twyfelfontein – Khorixas	185 km
13	Khorixas – Vingerklip – Brandberg	135 km
14	Brandberg – Windhoek	370 km

20-Day Northeastern Namibia 4x4 Lodge and Camping Safari

DAY	DESTINATION	DISTANCE
1	Windhoek – Waterberg Plateau Park	280 km
2	Waterberg Plateau Park (at leisure)	–
3	Waterberg Plateau Park – Tsumkwe	600 km
4	Tsumkwe area	50 km
5	Tsumkwe – Khaudum Game Park (Sikereti)	75 km
6	Khaudum Game Park (Sikereti)	50 km
7	Khaudum Game Park (Sikereti – Khaudum Camp)	140 km
8	Khaudum Game Park (Khaudum Camp)	90 km
9	Khaudum Game Park – Popa Falls	150 km
10	Popa Falls – Mahango Game Park – Popa Falls	80 km
11	Popa Falls – Caprivi Game Park (Nambwa camp site on Kwando)	230 km
12	Caprivi Game Park (Nambwa camp site on Kwando)	30 km
13	Caprivi Game Park – Mudumu National Park (Lianshulu Lodge)	85 km
14	Mudumu National Park (Lianshulu Lodge)	20 km
15	Mudumu National Park (Lianshulu Lodge) – Mamili National Park	70 km
16	Mamili National Park	40 km
17	Mamili National Park	40 km
18	Mamili National Park – Popa Falls	300 km
or	Mamili National Park – Katima Mulilo	160 km
19	Popa Falls – Grootfontein	450 km
or	Katima Mulilo – Chobe National Park/ Victoria Falls	125/210 km
20	Grootfontein – Windhoek	470 km

What to Pack

For summer light clothing – cotton shirts, shorts or skirts – is recommended. Long-sleeved shirts and cotton trousers are a good idea if your skin is sensitive to the sun, and also to keep mosquitoes at bay after sunset. Rain gear is handy for afternoon thunderstorms.

In winter the days are sunny and clear, while early mornings and nights can be bitterly cold. Light clothing is suitable for winter daywear, but for early mornings, evenings and nights warm trousers, jerseys, jacket, gloves and warm socks should be packed.

Miscellaneous items that should be included are a sunhat, sunscreen cream, insect repellent, anti-malaria tablets, sunglasses, binoculars, sturdy walking shoes and a bathing costume.

Entry & Customs Regulations

A list of Namibian diplomatic missions abroad and diplomatic representatives accredited to Namibia, together with their addresses, telephone and fax numbers, is provided in chapter 14.

Entry formalities

Visitors must be in possession of a valid passport, visa (see list of nationals of countries exempted from visas below), a return ticket and sufficient funds to support themselves for the duration of their stay. Temporary residence permits are issued on arrival for up to 90 days, but can be extended by applying well in advance to the Ministry of Home Affairs, Private Bag 13200, Windhoek, tel (061) 292-9111, fax 22-3817.

Passport holders of the following countries are exempted from visa requirements, provided that they do not intend remaining in Namibia for more than three months, are bona fide tourists or business travellers, have a return ticket and sufficient funds to support themselves during their stay.

- **Africa**: Angola, Botswana, Kenya, Lesotho, Malawi, Mozambique, South Africa, Tanzania, Zambia and Zimbabwe
- **Americas and Caribbean**: Canada and the United States of America
- **Australasia**: Australia, New Zealand
- **Far East**: Japan, Malaysia and Singapore
- **Europe**: Austria, Belgium, Denmark, France, Germany, Iceland, Ireland, Italy, Lichtenstein, Luxembourg, Netherlands, Norway, Portugal, Russia, Spain, Sweden, Switzerland and United Kingdom

Border posts

Hosea Kutako International, Eros and Mpacha airports, as well as the towns of Gobabis, Grootfontein, Karasburg, Katima Mulilo, Keetmanshoop, Lüderitz, Ondangwa, Oranjemund, Rosh Pinah, Rundu and Walvis Bay, are recognised immigration points.

Overland travellers may enter and exit Namibia at the following points:

Angola
Omahenene	08:00-18:00
Oshikango	08:00-18:00
Ruacana	08:00-18:00

Botswana
Buitepos	07:00-19:00
Mohembo	06:00-18:00
Ngoma	06:00-18:00
Impalila	08:00-17:00

South Africa
Ariamsvlei	24 hours
Hohlweg	06:00-22:00
Klein Menasse	06:00-22:00
Noordoewer	24 hours
Oranjemund	06:00-22:00 (special permission required from NAMDEB)
Velloorsdrift	06:00-22:00

Zambia
Wenela	06:00-18:00

The opening and closing times of Namibian border posts are not affected by the change to Namibian Winter Time, as South African Standard Time (SAST) is followed.

Customs

Visitors importing goods from Botswana, Lesotho, South Africa and Swaziland (Southern African Customs Union) are exempt from paying import duty. Duty-free allowances for visitors include personal effects, sporting and recreational equipment and the following consumables: 2 ℓ wine, 1 ℓ spirits, 400 cigarettes, 50 cigars, 250 g cigarette or pipe tobacco, 250 ml toilet water, 50 ml perfume; other new or used clothing and goods with a total value of less than N\$500. Visitors have the option of paying a flat-rate assessment of 20 per cent on goods valued up to N\$1 000, over and above the duty-free allowance. Should you decide not to make use of the flat-rate assessment, or if the value of the imports exceeds N\$1 000, customs duty is payable on each item.

Duty-free allowances are exempted from General Sales Tax (GST), but on all other imports GST of 10 per cent, and Additional Sales Duty (ASD) ranging from 5 to 25 per cent, are payable at the point of entry. The GST-ASD system is to be replaced with VAT (Value Added Tax) in October 1999.

Health

No vaccinations are required by visitors to Namibia. Although the country is virtually free of tropical diseases, visitors to the northern regions must be aware of malaria and bilharzia.

Tap water in towns is purified and you need have no hesitation in drinking it. Water obtained from boreholes is very often brackish and can taste unpleasant, but is by no means a health risk. However, in rural communal areas caution should be exercised.

Medical insurance is advisable. **Medrescue Namibia**, a member of Medical Rescue International, has branches in Windhoek, tel (061) 23-0505, and Walvis Bay, tel (064) 20-8222. Medical emergency services include medical evacuation, guaranteed hospital admission, dispatch of emergency medicines and repatriation of mortal remains. P O Box 31220, Windhoek. **Aeromed Namibia**, a member of Europassistance, also provides a medical emergency service. P O Box 80274, Windhoek, tel (061) 24-9777.

Private medical facilities in Windhoek (Medi Clinic, tel (061) 22-2687 and the Catholic Hospital, tel (061) 23-7237), Otjiwarongo (Medi Clinic, tel (067) 30-3734) and Swakopmund (Cottage Hospital, tel (064) 46-2321) are of a good standard and equipped to deal with most emergencies.

Private doctors in Windhoek are listed under Medical Practitioners in the Telecom Namibia directory.

AIDS

Namibia has a high incidence of HIV (AIDS), especially in the northeast of the country, making casual and unprotected sex unwise.

When travelling in remote areas it is advisable to carry a pack of sterile needles and syringes.

All blood is screened for AIDS and hepatitis B by the Blood Transfusion Service of Namibia. The blood is tested in accordance with internationally recognised methods and is subject to strict controls.

Malaria

As elsewhere in Africa, the risk of malaria has increased considerably in Namibia during the past few years. It is caused by a parasite transmitted through the bite of an infected female *Anopheles* mosquito. The *Plasmodium falciparum* parasite is not only becoming increasingly resistant to prophylaxis, but is also spreading further south. Although malaria occurs mainly in northern Namibia, cases have also been reported in the central areas and occasionally in the south. The area between Mariental and Otjiwarongo is a very low risk area, while Waterberg, Grootfontein,

Tsumeb and Etosha National Park lie within a low risk area where there is usually only a risk during summer. Malaria is endemic in the northern parts of the Kavango and Caprivi regions; the risk is especially high from October to May.

It is advisable to take prophylaxis in both malaria epidemic and endemic areas throughout the year. Consult your doctor at least a week before visiting a malarial area, and note that chloroquine prophylaxis is no longer effective against *Plasmodium falciparum* mosquitoes in many areas of southern Africa.

Symptoms of malaria are similar to those of flu and include fever, shivering, headaches, muscular aches, vomiting and diarrhoea. These symptoms usually show up within two weeks after being infected and it is important to seek medical advice immediately. If these symptoms are experienced on returning home, medical attention must be sought urgently and the doctor informed that you had visited a malarial area.

While reducing the risk, prophylaxis is no guarantee that malaria will not be contracted. Mosquitoes feed mainly at night and the following additional precautions must, therefore, be taken between dawn and dusk to reduce the risk:

- Wear long-sleeved shirts, socks and trousers.
- Apply an insect repellent to exposed skin.
- Spray your room with an insecticide to kill any mosquitoes that may have entered during the day.
- Burn mosquito coils in your room or tent.
- Sleep under a mosquito net.

Bilharzia

This disease is caused by a parasite which lives in water and attacks the intestines, bladder and other organs of its hosts. Bilharzia is usually associated with human habitation, so avoid drinking water (unless it has been thoroughly boiled), swimming or washing in rivers or streams downstream of inhabited areas. The Kavango and the Kwando-Linyanti-Chobe river systems in the northeast and the Kunene River in the north of the country carry bilharzia.

Symptoms take at least six weeks to appear, but after three to four weeks there could be general lethargy and weakness. Any sign of blood in the faeces should be reported to a doctor as soon as possible.

Sleeping sickness

Sleeping sickness is caused by a parasite transmitted by the bite of an infected tsetse fly. The fly is a little larger than the common house fly, grey, with scissor-like wings and difficult to swat because of its hard body. Only visitors to the Caprivi Region run a risk, although the incidence is low because of a successful eradication campaign.

Bites can be prevented by wearing long-sleeved shirts and trousers in dull colours, and applying insect repellent to the exposed skin. A sharp pain will indicate a bite, but this does not necessarily result in the disease being transmitted. If the bite becomes sore or inflamed, consult a doctor as soon as possible. Other symptoms include swelling of the lymph glands and severe headaches.

Currency & Banks

Namibia has its own currency, the Namibian dollar, which is divided into 100 cents. Notes are available in N$200, N$100, N$50, N$20 and N$10 denominations, while coins are available in N$5, N$1, 50c, 10c, 5c.

The Namibian dollar is on par with the South African rand, which is also legal tender in Namibia. The Namibian dollar is, however, not accepted in South Africa and other southern African countries. It is, therefore, important to convert Namibian dollars to foreign currency before leaving the country.

A Bank Windhoek *bureau de change* operates at Windhoek's Hosea Kutako International Airport. Namibia Bureau de Change (a Thomas Cook representative) is situated in the Jack Levinson Arcade in the city centre, as is the *bureau de change* of First National Bank of Namibia. Other banks in Windhoek also have *bureaux de change* or foreign exchange departments.

There is a wide network of commercial banks in Namibia – First National Bank of Namibia, Standard Bank Namibia, Bank Windhoek and Commercial Bank of Namibia.

Visa, Mastercard, Diners Club and American Express credit cards are widely accepted by hotels, shops, restaurants and Namibia Wildlife Resorts rest camps. Some *pensions*, guest farms and shops, however, prefer cash or traveller's cheques, while shops and filling stations in rural areas only deal in cash.

Automatic teller machines, linked to Saswitch (a South African electronic banking network), are available in Windhoek and all major towns.

Banking hours
Monday-Friday   09:00-15:30
Saturday   08:30-11:00
In some country towns banks still close for lunch between 13:00 and 14:00.

Public Holidays

The following public holidays are observed in Namibia:
New Year's Day – 1 January
Independence Day – 21 March
Good Friday – March-April
Easter Monday – March-April
Workers' Day – 1 May
Cassinga Day – 4 May
Ascension Day – 40 days after Easter
Africa Day – 25 May
Heroes' Day – 26 August
Human Rights Day – 10 December
Christmas Day – 25 December
Family Day – 26 December

Business Hours

Shops
Monday to Friday	08:00-17:00 or 17:30
Saturday	08:00-13:00

Offices
Monday to Friday	08:00-13:00 and 14:00-17:00
Saturday	Closed

Time

Namibia introduced differentiated standard times for summer and winter in 1994. Summer time is two hours ahead of Greenwich Mean Time (GMT +2) and commences at 02:00 on the first Sunday of September, ending at 02:00 on the first Sunday of April the following year. Winter time is one hour in advance of GMT (GMT +1) and commences at 02:00 on the first Sunday in April, ending at 02:00 on the first Sunday of September. Namibian Winter Time is hence one hour behind South African Standard Time. In the northeast of the country, however, many shops, businesses and offices continue to operate on Namibian Summer Time, as this region lies much further to the east than the rest of the country.

Electricity

Electricity of 220 volt AC is supplied and sockets are for round three-pin plugs, 15 amp types.

Posts & Telecommunications

The postal service in Namibia is operated by Nampost, a government-owned enterprise, with post offices throughout the country. Its services are generally efficient and reliable.

Telecommunication services in Namibia are provided by Telecom Namibia, an independent state-owned enterprise with more than 50 offices throughout the country.

Namibia has an excellent telecommunications system, with direct dialling to over 200 international destinations. The international country code for overseas calls to Namibia is 264, while area codes in the country are preceded by a 0. When calling from outside Namibia, the 0 of the area code must be omitted. All major towns are served by fully automated exchanges, and automation is rapidly being extended to rural areas. Some manual exchanges are, however, still in operation in rural areas.

Coin- and card-operated public phones are provided at post offices, police stations and public places. Cards are sold at TeleShops and Nampost offices and shops.

The cellular network is operated by Mobile Telecommunications Ltd (MTC). The network covers Windhoek and virtually all major towns and their immediate surroundings. MTC has roaming agreements with MTN and Vodacom in South Africa, as well as with networks in Belgium, Denmark, Germany, Mauritius, Netherlands, Spain, Sweden, Switzerland, Turkey and the United Kingdom.

HOW TO GET THERE

Getting to Namibia by air from Europe and southern African countries is easy, either by direct flights or making use of connecting flights. All the major road links with neighbouring countries are tarred and in excellent condition, making the country easily accessible by sedan car. Regular scheduled coach services operate between Windhoek, Johannesburg, Cape Town and Victoria Falls.

Air

Air Namibia, the country's national carrier, has several weekly international flights linking Windhoek with Frankfurt and London. The airline has a code-sharing agreement with the German airline LTU which flies once a week from Düsseldorf/Munich to Windhoek. Air Namibia also has a cooperation agreement with TAAG Angolan Airlines for a weekly flight from Windhoek to Luanda and Lisbon.

The airline has regular regional flights between Windhoek and Cape Town, Johannesburg, Harare, Luanda, Lusaka, Maun and Livingstone (Victoria Falls).

Beechcraft 1900s are operated on domestic routes, a Boeing 737 serves regional sectors and a Boeing 767-300 ER international routes.

South African Airways, British Airways operated by Comair, Lufthansa, LTU and **TAAG Angolan Airlines** all have regular flights to Windhoek.

The Hosea Kutako International Airport is some 45 km from the city centre, but a bus service is available for all incoming and departing passengers. The service operates between the bus terminus on the corner of Independence Avenue and Peter Müller Street in the centre of Windhoek and the airport. Eros Airport, 4 km from the city centre, handles charter and domestic scheduled flights.

Road

The most direct approach from Johannesburg in South Africa to Windhoek is via Botswana, along the Trans-Kalahari Highway, and Buitepos, a distance of about 1 400 km. Opened in December 1997, the fully tarred route has reduced the distance between Johannesburg and Windhoek by 400 km. Travellers using the highway as a transit route must exit Botswana before the border posts close. Only Botswanan currency (Pula) is accepted for fuel and other *en route* purchases.

The alternative route (also fully tarred), from Johannesburg via Upington to Windhoek through the Naroegas-Ariamsvlei border post, is a distance of about 1 970 km. The main approach route from Cape Town via the Vioolsdrif-Noordoewer border posts is also fully tarred; the distance to Windhoek is 1 493 km. Other entry points are: Noenieput-Hohlweg, Rietfontein-Klein Menasse, Onseepkans-Velloorsdrif. These approaches are all along gravel roads. Plans are afoot to reopen the Mata Mata border post on the western boundary of the Kalahari Gemsbok National Park in South Africa.

The Trans-Caprivi Highway between Rundu and Ngoma is fully tarred, except for a 56 km stretch between Katima Mulilo and Ngoma border post. Tarring of this section is scheduled to be completed by March 2000. From Ngoma in Botswana the road through Chobe National Park is tarred.

The gravel surfaced D3403 from Divundu to the Mohembo-Mamuno border post is negotiable by sedan car, but can be impassable to sedan cars after rains. The 32 km road is scheduled to be tarred. From Mamuno in Botswana the road to Shakawe and Maun is tarred.

There is only one border post between Namibia and Zambia, Wenela near Katima Mulilo. From here tourists can either travel through western Zambia, or take the ferry across the Zambezi River to Sesheke. The ferry to Sesheke, operated by the Zambian authorities, is scheduled to be replaced by a bridge forming part of the Trans-Caprivi Highway.

The main approach linking Namibia and Angola via Oshikango is in the process of being rehabilitated. Incidents of banditry are reported in Angola from time to time and given the uneasy political situation, casual travellers seldom use the road.

Bus

Intercape Mainliner operates luxury bus services from Johannesburg and Cape Town to Windhoek. Departures from Johannesburg via Upington are on Tuesdays, Thursdays, Fridays and Sundays, with arrival in Windhoek the following day after a 21-hour journey. A service from Johannesburg to Windhoek along the Trans-Kalahari Highway is also operated. Departures from Windhoek and Johannesburg are on Sundays, Tuesdays and Fridays. The journey takes just under 18 hours. Departures from Cape Town are on Sundays, Tuesdays, Thursdays and Fridays, with arrival in Windhoek the following day after 18 hours. The company operates a scheduled service between Windhoek and Victoria Falls on Fridays and Mondays, taking 18 hours. Victoria Falls departures are on Sundays and Wednesdays. Reservations can be made with Computicket in South Africa, tel (011) 445-8445, or Intercape offices in Johannesburg, tel (011) 333-5231, and Windhoek, tel (061) 22-7847.

Ekonolux operates a weekly service between Walvis Bay and Cape Town. The southbound service departs Walvis Bay on Fridays, arriving in Cape Town the next day. The northbound service leaves Cape Town on Sundays, arriving in Walvis Bay early Monday morning. Tel (064) 20-5935.

The **NamVic Shuttle** is a weekly service in an air-conditioned microbus between Victoria Falls-Windhoek and vice versa. The price is inclusive of tented accommodation at a rustic safari lodge on the Kwando River on the first day. For bookings in Windhoek, tel (061) 23-6880 or (061) 24-7668.

Rail

StarLine provides a train service from Keetmanshoop to Upington in South Africa on Wednesdays and Saturdays. There is, however, no connecting passenger train service from Upington. The return service departs Upington on Sundays and Thursdays. Daily overnight services between Windhoek-Keetmanshoop-Windhoek, except Saturdays, provide convenient connections both ways. StarLine Central Reservations, Windhoek, tel (061) 298-2032.

GETTING AROUND IN NAMIBIA

By Road

Namibia's road system is one of the best in Africa and all the country's major towns are connected by tarred roads, which cover about 5 150 km of the total network of approximately 40 000 km.

Motoring and traffic regulations

Motorists in Namibia, as in neighbouring countries (except Angola), drive on the left-hand side of the road. As a rule the speed limit on main roads is 120 km/h, while a limit of 60 km/h is in force in urban areas. The wearing of seat belts is compulsory for the driver and front-seat passenger.

Visitors, excluding residents of neighbouring states, must have a valid international driving licence if they intend driving in Namibia.

International road signs are used. Major routes are either tarred or have a well-maintained gravel surface and are indicated by a "B" followed by the route number in a five-sided road sign.

Secondary routes have gravel surfaces varying from good to fair. The route number is preceded by a "C" in a rectangular road sign. Main routes (MR) are indicated by a route number in a diamond-shaped or rectangular road sign.

District roads are indicated with a "D" followed by the route number in a small rectangular road sign. The condition of these roads varies from good to poor and the surface can become sandy and corrugated.

The route number for farm roads used to be preceded by a "P", but this is being replaced by an "F". These roads are best avoided in sedan cars.

Towns, accommodation establishments and tourist attractions are well signposted along all routes. Distances are generally indicated at 10 km intervals on major routes, but not on others.

The country's roads are notorious for accidents involving animals, especially kudu. This is usually only a problem between dusk and dawn, making it advisable to drive slowly, or avoid night driving altogether. Warthogs are also a menace, especially after good rains when the grass on the verges is long.

Motoring hints

Distances between towns are often quite considerable and secondary, district and farm roads usually carry very little traffic. You should, therefore, be as well prepared as possible to cope with an emergency when travelling off the main routes. One of the most important rules is: never set off on a journey without a full 10 ℓ container of water.

Ensure that your spare tyre is inflated and in a good condition. It is comforting to have two spares, as tyres are not always available at small rural towns. If this is not possible, carry an inner tube and gaiter and have the tyre repaired at the first opportunity. On extended four-wheel drive trips, two spare wheels, tyre levers, spare inner tubes and a puncture repair kit are essential.

Many foreign visitors, unaccustomed to driving on gravel roads, lose their lives on the country's roads each year. Keep the following in mind:

- Slow down – 80 km/h is a reasonable speed.
- Check the condition of tyres regularly, as rattles and bumps can mask a flat tyre until it is too late and the wheel rim is ruined.
- When travelling in the dust of a vehicle ahead, or one approaching, switch on headlights to ensure that you are visible.
- Do not overtake if vision is impaired by dust from a vehicle ahead of you – you might be surprised by a donkey cart or a speeding car.
- Constantly glance in your side- and rear-view mirrors. Some roads are seldom used and it is easy to forget that other drivers could also be on the road.
- Take an occasional break when travelling on long stretches of gravel road.
- To avoid skidding, decelerate gradually rather than braking suddenly.
- The surfaces of road verges are often deceptive, so do not take chances by stopping alongside the road unless you are satisfied that the surface is hard.
- Concentrate on the road – sandy patches, often in riverbeds, or disintegrated surfaces, could cause you to lose control over the vehicle.
- If a road has not been graded for some time, gravel accumulates in the middle of the road. Reduce speed when changing from one track to another.
- Bad corrugations can cause a vehicle to lose grip. Avoid braking suddenly or turning the steering wheel hard – decelerate and bring the vehicle slowly back into the track.

- Cattle grids are encountered frequently on minor roads. Slow down considerably when approaching them, as the road surface just before and after the crossing is often badly rutted.
- Many roads are crossed by barely noticeable river and stream courses which you would surmise never carry much water. Causeways are uncommon and after rain the road surface is often washed away – a dangerous situation if you are travelling at speed.

Tips for four-wheel driving

For the inexperienced, the most important advice is: don't venture into the unknown unless you are well acquainted with your vehicle and know how to use it! On the first few outings it is reassuring to be part of a two-vehicle expedition, accompanied by an experienced off-road driver. This will give you an opportunity to gain experience.

Although one usually learns by making mistakes, the following hints may prove useful:

In sand
- Remain in existing tracks – in deep sand the vehicle will simply follow the track.
- Do not allow the vehicle to get bogged down to its axles before taking action. Deflate tyres before entering thick sand (although this is not a good idea if you do not have a pump), lock the free-wheel hubs (if fitted) and engage four-wheel drive.
- Long sandy stretches are best negotiated in the early morning when the sand is still cool and more compact.
- In the past few years several vehicles have been reduced to smouldering heaps of metal on trips through long grass. This was the result of long grass accumulating under the protection plate and the driving shaft and then catching fire. Make regular checks under the vehicle and always carry a fire extinguisher.
- Grass seeds blocking the flow of air to the radiator can cause overheating. Fit a fine mesh grille in front of the radiator and remove grass seeds regularly.

Rocky terrain
- Low profile tyres should preferably not be used in rocky terrain as the side walls are easily punctured.
- Tyre pressure is best left at normal, or slightly under normal.
- Try to judge the ground clearance of the vehicle – if unsure get a passenger to check whether an obstacle can be cleared.
- Steep ascents and descents should be tackled in low range.

Environmental considerations

The increasing popularity of four-wheel drive vehicles has opened up many areas and the large number of people is beginning to destroy the unspoilt character of these places. Unfortunately, some drivers seem to think they are free to go where they choose – without considering the sensitivity of the area. For those able to explore remote areas the basic rule is: follow existing tracks. To casual tourists much of the Namibian landscape may appear barren, but uniquely adapted plant and animal life exist there. One thoughtless driver could not only scar the landscape for decades, but also cause irreversible damage to sensitive ecosystems.

Having a four-wheel drive vehicle does not entitle you to drive wherever you desire. Permits are required from the relevant authorities and should you enter an area illegally, you are liable to a heavy fine.

When camping, do not bury refuse – it is inevitably exposed by the elements and broken bottles and cans with jagged edges are dangerous to humans and animals. Refuse that cannot be burnt must be taken with you until it can be properly disposed of.

Trees are scarce in most areas, so take your own supply of wood. Do not make fires under a tree or on tree roots, and never break off seemingly dead branches. Fireplaces dotted around in a small area are unsightly, so rather use existing fireplaces. Let the fire burn to ash, ensuring that it is completely burnt out, and remove all rocks – the wind will soon scatter the ashes, leaving little evidence of a fireplace.

Human waste should be buried and paper should preferably be burnt (don't set the veld on fire though!), or buried deep enough so that it is not easily uncovered.

Choose camp sites with care. Never camp near a waterhole, as you could scare animals away from water which is vital to their survival.

When animals are encountered outside game reserves (e.g. in the Kaokoveld), never approach too closely and ensure that they can move freely. Some of the river valleys in the Kaokoveld are very narrow and animals trapped by pursuing vehicles are not only potentially dangerous to humans, but could injure themselves in an attempt to escape.

All rock paintings and archaeological sites are protected by law and nothing should be tampered with in any way or removed.

Maps

Members of the Automobile Association can visit the AA of Namibia office in Windhoek at Carl List House, corner of Independence Avenue and Peter Müller Street, tel (061) 22-4201, for general information, maps and road reports. Membership cards must be produced.

The most useful road map is the one issued free of charge by the Ministry of Transport and Communications. It is available at tourist information offices.

For those venturing off the beaten track, topographical maps are advisable. These are available from the Office of the Surveyor-General, Ministry of Lands, Resettlement and Rehabilitation, Private Bag 13182, Windhoek, Namibia, tel (061) 24-5056. The office is situated on the corner of Robert Mugabe Avenue and Lazarette Street.

Vehicle hire

Sedan cars and four-wheel drive vehicles can be hired in Windhoek and other major towns. Enquiries should be made regarding drop-off charges if the vehicle is not returned to the depot from where it was collected.

As vehicle rental companies have proliferated in Namibia during the past few years it is advisable to deal with members of CARAN – the Car Rental Association of Namibia. They are required to adhere to high standards regarding the condition of the vehicle, back-up services in case of a breakdown and emergency medical services.

The following are members of CARAN:

Asco Car Hire, P O Box 40214, Windhoek, tel (061) 23-3064, fax 23-2245 – sedans, microbuses, 4x4 vehicles, fully equipped 4x4 vehicles, camping equipment

Avis-Rent-A-Car, P O Box 2057, Windhoek, tel (061) 23-3166, fax 22-3072 – offices near Eros Airport in Windhoek, Windhoek International Airport, Walvis Bay Airport, Swakopmund

Budget-Rent-A-Car, P O Box 1754, Windhoek, tel (061) 22-8720, fax 22-7665 – offices in Windhoek City Centre, Windhoek International Airport and Walvis Bay

Bush-Veld Car Hire, P O Box 80240, Windhoek, tel (061) 25-1710, fax 23-0844

Camping Car Hire, P O Box 5526, Windhoek, tel (061) 23-7756, fax 23-7757 – sedans, microbuses, 4x4 vehicles, camping equipment

Caprivi Car Hire, P O Box 1837, Windhoek, tel (061) 23-2871, fax 23-2374 – sedans, microbuses, 4x4 vehicles, camping equipment

Classic Car Hire, P O Box 40222, Windhoek, tel (061) 24-6708, fax 24-6709 – sedans, 4x4 vehicles, camping equipment

Continental Self Drive, P O Box 11115, Windhoek, tel and fax (061) 24-8280

East End Landrover Hire, P O Box 11438, Windhoek, tel (061) 23-3869, fax 22-8855

Enyandi Car Hire, P O Box 264, Otjiwarongo, tel (067) 30-3898, fax 30-3892 – sedans, minibuses, 4x4 vehicles

Imperial Car Rental, P O Box 1387, Windhoek, tel (061) 22-7103, fax 22-2721

Into Namibia Car Rental, P O Box 31551, Windhoek, tel (061) 25-3591, fax 25-3593 – sedans, 4x4 vehicles equipped for camping

Leopard Tours Car & Camper Hire, P O Box 22731, Windhoek, tel (061) 23-6113, fax 23-6113

Odyssey Car Hire, P O Box 20938, Windhoek, tel (061) 22-3269, fax 22-8911 – sedans and 4x4 vehicles

Pegasus Car & Camper Hire, P O Box 21104, Windhoek, tel 25-1451, fax 25-4165 – sedans, minibuses, mini campers

RK 4x4 Hire, P O Box 31076, Windhoek, tel and fax (061) 22-3994

Savanna Car Rental, P O Box 5180, Windhoek, tel (061) 22-7778, fax 22-3292

Windhoek Car Hire, P O Box 1038, Windhoek, tel (061) 23-7935, fax 25-8972

Bus transport

Namibia has a poorly developed public transport system in urban areas. Windhoek's municipal bus service caters exclusively for workers commuting to the city centre and suburban areas.

Intercape Mainliner operates luxury coach services on several routes. From Windhoek to Walvis Bay, stops are made at Okahandja, Karibib, Usakos and Swakopmund. Windhoek departures are on Mondays, Wednesdays, Fridays and Saturdays and Walvis Bay departures are on Mondays, Wednesdays, Fridays and Sundays.

On the Windhoek-Cape Town route stops are made at Rehoboth, Mariental, Keetmanshoop, Grünau and Noordoewer. On the Windhoek-Johannesburg route stops are made at Rehoboth, Mariental, Keetmanshoop, Grünau, Karasburg and Ariamsvlei. The company also has a service from Windhoek to Oshikango on the Namibian-Angolan border on Fridays and Tuesdays. The Oshikango-Windhoek service operates on Thursdays and Sundays. Reservations can be made with Mainliner at tel (061) 22-7847.

Ekonolux buses stop at all towns between Walvis Bay and southern Namibia en route to Cape Town. They depart from Walvis Bay on Fridays at 07:30. Tel (064) 20-5935.

Major towns are linked to those in rural areas by TransNamib's **StarLine** road transport passenger service. The service is aimed at those with no other means of transport and fares are cheap, providing an alternative to hitchhiking for budget travellers. StarLine Central Reservations (061) 298-2032, fax 298-2383.

Taxis

Most taxis in Windhoek and other towns in Namibia ply their trade to workers travelling to the city centre and suburban areas and few cater for tourists. In Windhoek, radio taxis operate from the airport bus terminus on the corner of Peter Müller Street and Independence Avenue.

Hitchhiking

Hitchhiking is safe, but you should be prepared for long waits along some of the country's back roads. Also note that hitchhikers are not permitted in Etosha National Park.

Notices of lifts sought and offered are broadcast on the national service of the Namibia Broadcasting Corporation on weekdays between 12:30 and 13:00. Tel (061) 23-6381. Information on lifts can also be obtained on notice boards in the Windhoek Information and Publicity (WIP) office in the Post Street Mall, the reservations office of Namibia Wildlife Resorts and at backpackers' accommodation establishments.

By Rail

StarLine passenger train services are operated by TransNamib to and from Windhoek-Swakopmund-Walvis Bay, Windhoek-Tsumeb, Windhoek-Gobabis and Windhoek-Keetmanshoop-Ariamsvlei. There is also a service between Walvis Bay-Swakopmund and Tsumeb.

StarLine passenger trains are fitted with recliner seats and floor heating. They also offer video entertainment and vending machines with hot and cold beverages and light snacks. Seats must be booked in advance at any of the major stations. Fares are reasonable and there is a choice of economy or business class. StarLine Central Reservations, tel (061) 298-2032, fax 298-2383.

The luxurious **Desert Express** between Windhoek and Swakopmund offers the ultimate in rail travel. Each of the 24 sleeper compartments has its own *en suite* facilities, air-conditioning, underfloor heating, internal telephone and several music channels. Sitter class is available in the Starview coach – a coach with a glass-panelled roof. There is also a lounge, a restaurant and a bistro on board. On the westbound journey, operated daily except Thursdays, excursions are undertaken to Okapuka Ranch (see p 76) and the Moon Landscape near Swakopmund. On the eastbound journey, operated daily except Fridays, excursions are undertaken to Spitzkoppe (see p 136) and Okapuka Ranch. Desert Express, Private Bag 13204, Windhoek, tel (061) 298-2600, fax 298-2601.

Shongololo Express provides a 13-day train journey through Namibia, combined with excursions by microbus to attractions such as Sesriem (see p 193), Sossusvlei (see p 194), Lüderitz, the Fish River Canyon and Etosha National Park (see p 99). Stops are also made at Okahandja, Swakopmund and Otjiwarongo. Two passengers each are accommodated in specially adapted cabins. Amenities include a lounge, dining room, bar and a laundry service. Trips are conducted from Windhoek to Tsumeb (northbound) and in the opposite direction. P O Box 25303, Windhoek, tel (061) 25-0378, fax 25-5013.

By Air

Because of the vast distances covered in Namibia, air travel has become increasingly popular. Visitors can make use of scheduled flights or charter aircraft.

Scheduled flights

The country's national carrier, **Air Namibia**, has several scheduled flights a week from Windhoek to Katima Mulilo, Keetmanshoop, Lüderitz, Mokuti (adjoining Etosha), Ondangwa, Oranjemund and Swakopmund and back.

Aircraft charter

Visitors with itineraries which do not suit scheduled air routes can consider chartering an aircraft. The following companies can be contacted:

Atlantic Aviation, P O Box 465, Swakopmund, tel (064) 40-4749, fax 40-5832

Bush Pilots Namibia, P O Box 9224, Windhoek, tel and fax (061) 24-8316

Cedaro Aviation, P O Box 80378, Windhoek, tel (061) 23-5662, fax 22-1093

Comav, P O Box 80300, Windhoek, tel (061) 22-7512, fax 24-9864

Pleasure Flights & Safaris, P O Box 537, Swakopmund, tel and fax (064) 40-4500

WestAir Wings Charters, P O Box 407, Windhoek, tel (061) 22-1091, fax 23-2778

Aircraft maintenance

If you travel to Namibia in your own aircraft, the following addresses could be useful:

Westair Aviation, Eros Airport, P O Box 407, Windhoek, Namibia, tel (061) 23-7230, fax 23-2402 – full service for all types of aircraft and helicopters, e.g. routine maintenance and mandatory periodic inspections (MPIs)

Thompsons Radio (Pty) Ltd, Ausspannplatz, Windhoek, Namibia, tel (061) 23-7533, fax 23-7536 – radio repairs

Tours & Safaris

A wide range of coach tours, off-the-beaten track safaris and self-drive tours are conducted throughout the year, taking advantage of the good roads and excellent accommodation facilities.

Local tour operators are listed under Lüderitz (see p 244), Swakopmund (see p 209) and Walvis Bay (see p 217).

Scheduled coach and fly-in tours, overland safaris

A list of some countrywide operators, with an indication of the type of tours they specialise in, is given below.

Afro Venture Safaris, P O Box 2339, Randburg 2125, South Africa, tel (011) 807-3720, fax 807-3480 – camping and accommodated land and fly-in safaris

Botswana/Okavango Fly-in Safaris, P O Box 9004, Windhoek, tel (061) 22-5289, fax 23-7609 – fly-in safaris in Namibia and to the Okavango Delta, Zimbabwe and Zambia

Karibu Safaris, P O Box 35196, Northway 4056, Durban, South Africa, tel (031) 83-9774, fax 83-1957 – 13-day tour featuring the highlights of Namibia, starting and ending in Windhoek, and a 13-day tour starting in Victoria Falls, ending in Windhoek

Oryx Tours, P O Box 2058, Windhoek, tel (061) 21-7454, fax 26-3417 – scheduled, self-drive, group and special interest tours, fly-in safaris

Skeleton Coast Safaris, P O Box 2195, Windhoek, tel (061) 22-4248, fax 22-5713 – fly-in safaris to the Namib Desert and coastal regions, Kunene River and Etosha National Park

Southern Cross Safaris, P O Box 941, Windhoek, tel and fax (061) 25-1553 – camping safaris to the Namib Desert, Kaokoveld, Caprivi and Botswana

SWA Safaris, P O Box 20373, Windhoek, tel (061) 22-1193, fax 22-5387 – scheduled tours to major tourist attractions in Namibia

Springbok Atlas, P O Box 11165, Windhoek, tel (061) 21-5943, fax 21-5932 – scheduled coach tours to major tourist attractions in Namibia

Trans Namibia Tours, P O Box 20028, Windhoek, tel (061) 22-1549, fax 23-0960 – scheduled modular tours that can be combined, study and special interest tours, self-drive and fly-in tours

Wilderness Safaris Namibia, P O Box 6850, Windhoek, tel (061) 22-5178, fax 23-9455 – cross-country and fly-in safaris of Namibia, Botswana, Malawi, Zambia and Zimbabwe.

Specialist Safaris

Kidogo Safaris, P O Box 30566, Windhoek, tel and fax (061) 24-3827, specialises in reptile tours.

For details on other specialist safari operators, refer to the appropriate subheading in chapter 2.

Travel consultancies

There are several travel consultancies in Windhoek; among them the following provide a high degree of personalised service to incoming tourists:

Eden Travel, P O Box 6900, Windhoek, tel and fax (061) 23-4342

Namib Travel Shop, P O Box 6850, Windhoek, tel (061) 22-6174, fax 23-9455

Ondese Travel & Safaris, P O Box 6196, Windhoek, tel (061) 22-0876, fax 23-9700

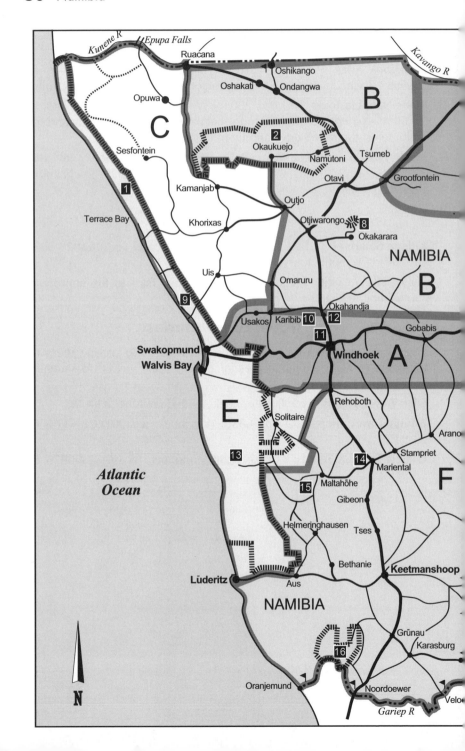

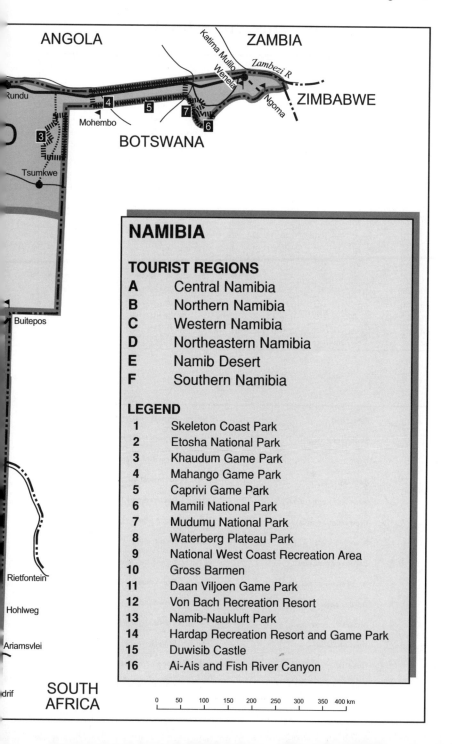

ANGOLA

ZAMBIA

Katima Mulilo

Wenela

Zambezi R

ZIMBABWE

Ngoma

Rundu

4

5

7

Mohembo

6

BOTSWANA

3

Tsumkwe

Buitepos

NAMIBIA

TOURIST REGIONS
A   Central Namibia
B   Northern Namibia
C   Western Namibia
D   Northeastern Namibia
E   Namib Desert
F   Southern Namibia

LEGEND
1   Skeleton Coast Park
2   Etosha National Park
3   Khaudum Game Park
4   Mahango Game Park
5   Caprivi Game Park
6   Mamili National Park
7   Mudumu National Park
8   Waterberg Plateau Park
9   National West Coast Recreation Area
10   Gross Barmen
11   Daan Viljoen Game Park
12   Von Bach Recreation Resort
13   Namib-Naukluft Park
14   Hardap Recreation Resort and Game Park
15   Duwisib Castle
16   Ai-Ais and Fish River Canyon

Rietfontein

Hohlweg

Ariamsvlei

drif

SOUTH
AFRICA

0   50   100   150   200   250   300   350   400 km

Distance Chart (km)

Aranos																					
569	Aus																				
493	134	Bethanie																			
218	898	822	Gobabis																		
850	1 145	1 069	657	Grootfontein																	
566	346	343	895	1 142	Karasburg																
581	876	800	388	403	873	Karibib															
358	211	157	687	934	208	665	Keetmanshoop														
692	125	259	1 021	1 268	471	999	334	Lüderitz													
248	249	257	498	824	540	555	332	374	Maltahöhe												
137	432	356	466	713	429	444	221	555	111	Mariental											
469	764	688	276	381	761	112	553	889	443	332	Okahandja										
642	937	861	449	342	934	61	726	1 060	616	505	173	Omaruru									
761	1 174	980	568	87	1 053	404	845	1 179	735	624	292	253	Otavi								
643	938	862	450	207	935	197	727	1 061	617	506	174	135	118	Otjiwarongo							
716	1 011	935	523	280	1 008	269	800	1 134	690	579	247	208	191	73	Outjo						
311	606	530	292	539	603	270	395	729	285	174	158	331	450	332	405	Rehoboth					
1 133	1 553	1 477	1 065	494	1 550	686	1 345	1 676	1 232	1 121	789	750	497	615	688	947	Ruacana				
756	1 051	975	563	598	1 048	175	840	731	482	619	287	236	489	371	444	445	684	Swakopmund			
824	1 119	1 043	631	60	1 116	377	907	1242	798	687	355	316	63	181	228	513	434	552	Tsumeb		
784	700	708	594	690	1 079	206	814	938	451	650	318	267	521	403	476	476	715	31	673	Walvis Bay	
395	693	618	205	452	690	181	482	816	372	261	71	242	363	245	318	87	860	356	426	389	Windhoek

Map Legend

Main road		Airport or landing strip	
Secondary road		Tourist transport	
4 x 4 track		Places of interest	
Railway line		Historical building	
International boundary		Rest camp or lodge	
Conservation area		Camp site	
River		Picnic site	
Large town or city		Swimming area	
Small town or settlement		♪18 Golf course	
Border post		Viewpoint	
Information centre		Thermal spring	
Post office		Waterhole	
Hospital		Landmark tree	
Parking area		Game-viewing hide	

WINDHOEK

Windhoek, capital of Namibia, is situated in the country's central Khomas Region. It lies in a valley bounded in the east by the Eros and Otjihavera mountains, the Auas mountains to the south and the rolling hills of the Khomas Hochland to the west.

The artesian springs in the area have attracted animals and people for thousands of years, inducing the Khoikhoi to name them Aigams (fire water), while the Herero referred to the springs as Otjomuise. In about 1840, Windhoek became the headquarters of the Nama-Oorlam Khoikhoi group under Jonker Afrikaner in central Namibia. The name Wind Hoock (Windy Corner) dates back to 1844, when it was used in a letter written by Jonker Afrikaner. This was seemingly a corruption of the name Winterhoek – a mountain range in the western Cape in South Africa, from where Jonker Afrikaner came.

German colonial administration was established in 1890 when Major Curt von François established a military post in Windhoek. Today, turn-of-the-century German colonial buildings stand alongside modern high-rise office blocks. Bustling pavement cafés give Windhoek a distinctly cosmopolitan atmosphere. Yet, it has an unmistakable African feeling about it. A rich diversity of cultures mingle on the streets, and Herero women wearing colourful Victorian dresses are still a common sight.

Windhoek is a friendly, clean city with an excellent infrastructure, offering visitors a wide choice of restaurants, sport and recreation facilities, and accommodation ranging from top-class hotels to congenial pensions (guesthouses).

Information

The **Windhoek Information and Publicity** (WIP) office is near the Independence Avenue end of the Post Street Mall. As you walk down Post Street Mall from Independence Avenue, keep an eye out for a signpost to the office, which is unfortunately

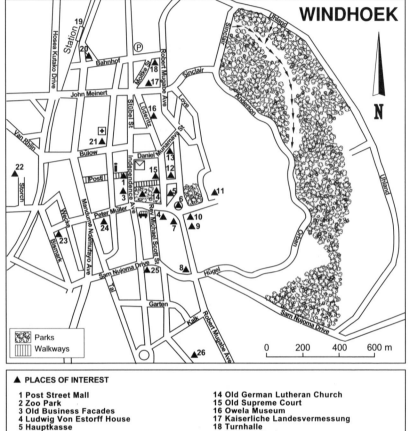

▲ PLACES OF INTEREST

1 Post Street Mall
2 Zoo Park
3 Old Business Facades
4 Ludwig Von Estorff House
5 Hauptkasse
6 Christuskirche
7 Kaiserliche Realschule
8 Officers' House
9 Alte Feste
10 Reiter Denkmal
11 Tintenpalast
12 Dernburg House
13 State House

14 Old German Lutheran Church
15 Old Supreme Court
16 Owela Museum
17 Kaiserliche Landesvermessung
18 Turnhalle
19 Railway Station
20 Owambo Campaign Memorial
21 Roman Catholic Church
22 Elisabeth House
23 Madchenheim
24 Orban School
25 Curt Von Francois Statue
26 Ten-Man House

stuck away in a corner of the mall. Information on Windhoek and surroundings. Tel (061) 290-2092, fax 290-2393. Open Monday to Friday 07:30 to 16:30; Saturday 08:00 to 13:00.

The **Namibia Tourism** office, Ground Floor, Continental Building, 272 Independence Avenue, provides information about tourist attractions and accommodation throughout Namibia. Tel (061) 284-2111, fax 284-2364. Open Monday to Friday 08:00 to 13:00 and 14:00 to 17:00.

The **Namibia Wildlife Resorts** office, corner of Molkte and John Meinert streets, handles reservations for NWR only. Tel (061) 23-6975 or 23-3845, fax 22-4900. Open Monday to Friday 08:00 to 17:00; reservations and cashier Monday to Friday 08:00 to 15:00.

What To Do In Windhoek

A walking tour

There is no better way to discover Windhoek than setting off on a self-guided two to three hour walking tour. Starting at the clock tower at the eastern end of the Post Street Mall, numbers on the map correspond with those in the text.

A favourite meeting place in Windhoek, the **clock tower** at the upper end of **Post Street Mall** (1) is a replica of the one which once graced the Deutsche-Afrika Bank, built in 1908. The Mall is a good place to hunt for curios from Namibia's Kavango Region, Zimbabwe and from as far afield as Kenya.

At the **Meteorite Fountain**, one of the largest collections of meteorites in the world, 32 from the Gibeon Shower (see p 254), can be seen.

The meteorites consist of 90-95 per cent iron, 8 per cent nickel (the Hoba meteorite near Grootfontein, by comparison, contains 16 per cent nickel), up to 0,5 per cent cobalt and as much as 0,04 per cent phosphorus. They also contain carbon, sulphur, chrome, copper and various trace elements.

The bubbly surface, melting seams and cavities have led scientists to believe that the meteorites' appearance is primarily due to atmospheric transformation at low temperatures, following the breakup of the parent body. Because of their dense and pure metallic structure, the arid climate of the Gibeon area and their relatively young age, only minor corrosion took place after the meteorites struck the earth.

Thirty-seven of these meteorites, with a mass of 12,6 tons, were brought to Windhoek between 1911 and 1913 by Dr P Range, the state geologist of the German Imperial Government. They were given to the *Landesmuseum* in Windhoek as a temporary measure, for safekeeping, and after World War I transferred to Zoo Park. In 1975 they were moved to the Alte Feste Museum, where they remained until the completion of the Post Street Mall in 1990.

Four of the meteorites were made available to museums and institutions in South Africa and abroad, leaving 33 of the 37 in Windhoek. The average mass of the meteorites is 348,5 kg, and the heaviest is 555,7 kg.

Zoo Park (2), with its shady trees, cool stream and pond, was once a zoo, hence the name. An interesting feature that should not be missed is the 1,5 m high **wonderstone column**, depicting an elephant hunt by Stone Age people. The column marks the site where the remains of at least two elephants and a variety of Stone Age tools were uncovered in 1962. It has been estimated that the elephants were slaughtered here some 5 000 years ago. The bones and artefacts were preserved *in situ* until 1990, when they were transferred to the State Museum, as the bones had partially disintegrated.

Looking south, an obelisk-shaped memorial, crowned by a golden eagle – the **Kriegerdenkmal (Soldiers' Memorial)** – attracts attention. This memorial was unveiled on 5 April 1897 in honour of *Schutztruppe* who died during the 1893-94 war against the renowned Nama chief, Hendrik Witbooi.

The **Old Business Facades** (3) in Independence Avenue are best viewed from the National Monuments Council plaque under the palm trees in the park. The three eye-catching buildings were designed by Willi Sander. **Erkrath Building** on the right was built in 1910 with business premises downstairs and a residence upstairs – a common feature of buildings of this period. **Gathemann House**, in the centre, dates back to 1913 and also had a residence above the ground floor business premises. Built for Heinrich Gathemann, then mayor of Klein Windhoek, it features an unusually steep roof – a European technique to prevent snow from accumulating! In 1920 Gathemann converted the **Hotel Kronprinz** into business premises. The name of the hotel and the year it was built can still be seen on the single-storey building on the left of the row of historical buildings.

Leaving Zoo Park through the gate at the southern end, you find yourself opposite the **street market** in **Peter Müller Street**, where a variety of handicrafts are on sale.

Ludwig von Estorff House (4) was built in 1891 as a canteen for military artisans. The shady veranda was added during alterations between 1898 and 1902. Ludwig von Estorff, a commander of the *Schutztruppe*, lived here from 1902 to 1910. The building subsequently served as a residence for senior officers, a hostel and a trade school. It now houses the National Library of Namibia.

Dating back to 1898-99, the **Hauptkasse** (5) formed part of the core of old Windhoek and originally housed the finance department of the German colonial government. It was also used as officers' quarters and a school hostel and now houses the Directorate of Agricultural Research and Training of the Ministry of Agriculture, Water and Rural Development.

Gottlieb Redecker was the architect of Windhoek's most prominent landmark, the imposing **Christuskirche** (6). It was built for the Evangelical Lutheran Church (ELC) as a symbol of gratitude for peace after the conclusion of various wars against the indigenous people. The design was based on that of a basilica with neo-Gothic and Art-Nouveau styles, and local sandstone was used as building material. The cornerstone was laid in 1907 and the church was consecrated on 16 October 1910.

The stained glass altar windows were donated by Kaiser Wilhelm II (who also donated the altar windows for the *Felsenkirche* at Lüderitz), and his wife, Augusta, donated the altar Bible. The brass bells were cast by the firm Schilling in Apolda, as were those of the ELC in Swakopmund. Guided tours are conducted on Wednesdays at 16:00 and 16:30 and on Saturdays at 11:00 and 11:30. Tel (061) 23-6002.

Built in 1907-8, the **Kaiserliche Realschule** (7) opened its three classrooms to 74 pupils in January 1909. It was enlarged in 1912-13 by building additional classrooms off the central hall, and the turret was modified to improve ventilation. The first German secondary school in Windhoek, it also served as both English and German primary schools in the course of time. It now houses offices of the Ministry of Basic Education and Culture.

The imposing **Officers' House** (8), on the corner of Sam Nujoma Drive and Robert Mugabe Avenue, was designed by Gottlieb Redecker and built in 1906-7 as a residence for senior government officials. The decorative brickwork around the windows, arches and doorway is characteristic of Putz architecture, fashionable in Germany at the time. The relatively steep roof with eaves was, however, not in keeping with the typical style in Germany. The building was restored in 1987 and today houses the Offices of the Ombudsman.

In 1890 Captain Curt von François decided to establish the headquarters of the *Schutztruppe* in Windhoek. The foundation stone of the **Alte Feste** (9) was laid on 18 October 1890 and the fort was completed two years later. In 1901 the western flank was demolished and rebuilt, and several changes made to the remainder of the building. It is the oldest building in Windhoek.

The historical section of the **State Museum** is housed in the historic fort. Namibia's independence process is depicted with photographs and memorabilia and the country's national symbols are on permanent display. There are also exhibits of indigenous pottery, antique household implements and furniture. Also of interest is a narrow-gauge locomotive and coaches. Open Monday to Friday 09:00-18:00; Saturday and Sunday 10:00-13:00, 15:00-18:00. Closed on public holidays.

The **Reiter Denkmal** (10), or **Equestrian Memorial**, honours those killed in the Nama and Herero wars of 1903-7. The larger than life-size monument of a mounted soldier was designed by Adolf Kurle and cast in Berlin. It was unveiled on 27 January 1912, the birthday of Kaiser Wilhelm II.

Situated on a hill behind the *Christuskirche*, the imposing **Tintenpalast** (11), or **Ink Palace**, housed the administrative offices of the German colonial administration. Its name appropriately referred to the large volume of writing that took place here.

When plans for the building were announced by Governor Von Schuckmann in 1910, the townsfolk unsuccessfully opposed the site of the new building, as they wanted it in the centre of town. The plans were drawn up by Gottlieb Redecker, who kept the design as simple and functional as possible to keep costs down. The building was completed in 1913 and the first meeting of the *Landesrat*, or local authority, was held here on 11 May 1914. In July the following year, the authority was disbanded, following the surrender of the German forces to South African Union forces.

The National Assembly of the Transitional Government of National Unity met here from 1985 to February 1989, when it was dissolved to pave the way for United Nations-supervised elections held in November 1989. It has been the seat of Namibia's National Assembly since independence.

Dernburg House (12) was built for high-ranking government officials and accommodated the German Secretary of State, Dr Dernburg, when he visited the country in July 1908. After he left, the house was used as offices for the governor.

As you walk down Park Street, **State House** (13), is to the right. It was built on the site of the former German Colonial Governor's residence which was demolished in 1958 to make way for a residence for the South African Administrator, and between 1977 and 1990, the Administrator-General. On independence it became the President's official residence. The only reminder of the original building is the retaining wall of the garden in Lüderitz Street.

One of Windhoek's earliest buildings, the **Old German Lutheran Church** (14) dates back to 1896. It was built by Tunschel and Wilke Company for the German Evangelical Lutheran Church and served as a place of worship until the *Christuskirche* was completed. It is still owned by the church and is now used as a nursery school.

The **Obergericht** or **Old Supreme Court** (15), facing the nursery school, was built in 1898-99 by the government builder, Carl Ludwig, as his home. However, his stately style was not to the liking of the governor and his contract was not renewed after its three-year period expired. Ludwig never occupied the home, which was used as a supreme court and still later as magistrate's courts.

Other places to see

Numerous other interesting buildings and places of interest worthwhile visiting are not included in this walk as it would become too tiring, especially on a hot day.

A visit to the **Owela Museum** (16), where the natural history section of the National Museum is housed, will give you some valuable background on the country's people and fauna. Open Monday to Friday 09:00-18:00; Saturday and Sunday 15:00-18:00. Closed on public holidays.

The **Kaiserliche Landesvermessung** (17) was built in 1902 to house the German administration's survey office. It consisted of a large drawing office, a fireproof archive where maps were stored and rooms for survey equipment. It was restored in 1988 after standing empty for a number of years and now houses the reservations office of Namibia Wildlife Resorts. Diagonally across from it, on the corner of Independence Avenue and John Meinert Street, is the **Kudu Monument**. The life-size monument was donated to Windhoek by a prominent Namibian businessman as a reminder of the thousands of kudus that died during the rinderpest epidemic of 1896.

Plans for the **Turnhalle** (18), the practice hall of the Windhoek Gymnasium Club, were drawn up by the architect Otto Busch and a single-storey building was completed in 1903. It was converted to a double-storey building in 1912-13.

The first session of the Constitutional Conference on Independence for Namibia took place here on 1 September 1975 and became known as the Turnhalle Conference. Following Namibia's independence, it became the seat of the second house of Parliament, the National Council.

The middle and southern wings of Windhoek's **Railway Station** (19) date back to 1912-13. At that time it became necessary to replace a 10-year-old prefabricated building, which became inadequate as a result of increased traffic after the railway line to Keetmanshoop was completed. Although there is uncertainty about the architect, the attractive building is a combination of several architectural styles and the only complaint at the time was that it lacked a restaurant. In 1919-20 the building was extended northward and 10 years later South African Railways extended the northern wing further. The extension is hardly noticeable however, as the original building style was cleverly retained.

A narrow-gauge locomotive, imported from Germany and assembled in Swakopmund in 1899, is the focal point of the station parking area. When coupled back-to-back with another locomotive, these steam engines were referred to as a *Zwilling* (*zwei* means two in German). Used singly, they were referred to as *Illing*. Over 100 were in use in the country by 1906 and saw service until World War I.

The **Transport Museum** on the upper level of the station building depicts the development of railways in Namibia from the German colonial administration until the end of the South African Railways era. Interesting exhibits include communications equipment and old railway furniture. Open Monday to Friday 09:00 to 12:00 and 14:00 to 15:30. Closed weekends and public holidays. Tel (061) 298-2079.

The **Owambo Campaign Memorial** (20), diagonally across from the station, is yet another reminder of the country's turbulent history. The stone obelisk was erected in 1916 following a combined South African and British attack against the Kwanyama king, Mandume, who had resisted the expansion of German colonialism. Oral tradition has it that Mandume committed suicide when his forces ran out of ammunition, but

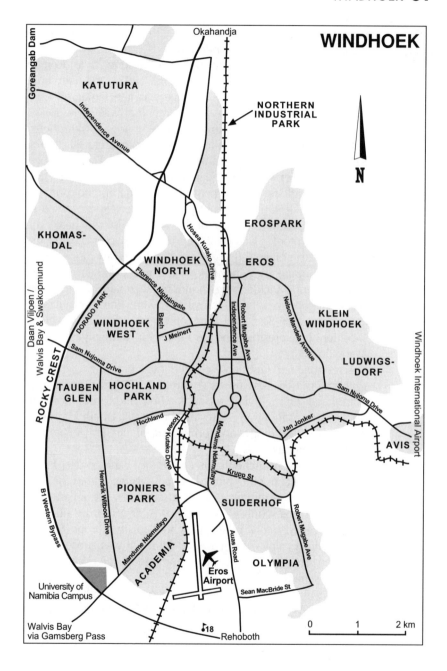

some historians suggest that he was gunned down when he led a charge against the combined force.

The cornerstone of the neo-Romanesque style **Roman Catholic Church** (21) was laid in March 1903. Originally built as a church with one spire, its nave was later enlarged eastward and the church altered to a cathedral with twin spires. The stained glass altar windows were made in Windhoek, while the lead glass windows were manufactured in the *Königliche Hofkunstalt* in München.

The weather vane on the pitched roof of **Elisabeth Haus** (22) leaves little to the imagination about the original purpose of the building. During the 73 years Elisabeth Haus served as a maternity home, 12 669 births were registered here. The inauguration took place on 24 April 1908, two years after the Deutsche Kolonialgesellschaft decided to collect money for a maternity home in Windhoek. The name honours Countess Elisabeth von Mecklenburg, honorary secretary of what later became known as the Frauverein vom Roten Kreutz für Deutsche Über See, and wife of Count Johan Albrecht zu Mecklenburg, president of the Deutsche Kolonialgesellschaft at the time.

Designed by Gottlieb Redecker, the building comprised four maternity wards, a sisters' ward, operating theatre, a large communal dining-living room, kitchen and store room. In 1914-15 the Sander annex to the south of Elisabeth Haus was added. The building now forms part of the Polytechnic of Namibia campus.

The stately **Mädchenheim** (23) dates back to 1914, but never served its original purpose of a boarding school for girls. The building was initially used as a secondary school after the Kaiserliche Realschule was vacated. After 1919 the building was converted into a boarding school for the Orban School, situated lower down Peter Müller Street. It was subsequently enlarged on several occasions and today serves as a pre-primary school.

By 1911 the growing number of pupils in Windhoek necessitated a new secondary school and a design competition was held. Of the 14 designs submitted, the one by Willi Sander was selected as the winning entry and on 20 April 1912 the **Orban School** (24) was officially opened. The modern block to the north was added in 1987 and the complex has since served as the conservatorium of the College of the Arts.

The **Curt von François Statue** (25) in front of the Windhoek municipal buildings was unveiled on 19 October 1965 when Windhoek was proclaimed a city. The work of Hennie Potgieter, it depicts the officer who established the headquarters of the German colonial administration in Windhoek in 1890.

Adolf Matheis drew up the plans of **Ten-Man House** (26), which provided accommodation to 10 single officials. Completed in 1906, the fort-like appearance of the H-shaped building is softened by wide verandas and relief work on the towers with their decorative turrets. Each of the four corners contained one-bedroomed flats with bathrooms, while one-bedroom flats without bathrooms were in the centre of the H.

Lending an air of romance to Windhoek are three castles – **Schwerinsburg, Sanderburg** and **Heinitzburg** – complete with turrets and watchtower rooms. Perched on the ridge separating the Windhoek and Klein Windhoek valleys, the castles were designed by the renowned architect, Willi Sander, and were built in the first two decades of the 1900s. The castles are not open to the public, except Heinitzburg, which has been turned into a stylish *pension*.

A variety of indigenous birds and reptiles can be viewed at **Wildlife Impressions**, 5 km east of the city centre along Sam Nujoma Drive. Among the poisonous snakes to be seen are mamba, Cape and Egyptian cobras and puffadder, as well as lizards and crocodiles. The complex also incorporates a wildlife museum, restaurant (open evenings) and curio shop. Open daily 09:00 to 18:00. Tel (061) 26-4538.

No visit to Namibia is complete without enjoying its high-quality beer, brewed in accordance with the Reinheitsgebot, or purity laws, issued by the Duke of Bavaria in 1516. **Guided tours of Namibia Breweries**, in Dortmund Street in Windhoek's Northern Industrial Area, are conducted on weekdays. The tours include a visit to the Namibia Breweries Museum, the brewing and bottling plants and beer tasting. Tours lasting about an hour and a half are conducted free of charge from 09:00 to 15:00 in groups numbering up to 25. Reservations must preferably be made a week in advance, but tours booked at shorter notice will be considered, should a tour guide and a suitable time be available. Tel (061) 26-2915.

The **Old Location Cemetery** in Hochland Road dates back to 1924, when it was set aside for black people living in the Old Location – Windhoek's black township before the forced removal of the people to Katutura. Of interest is the monument at the mass grave of the 13 people shot dead by the South African Police when a large crowd of people resisted the forced removals in 1959. More than 60 people were injured in the shooting.

Katutura, on the northwestern outskirts of Windhoek, was established in 1959 when Windhoek's black residents were forcefully removed from the Old Location (an area today known as Hochland Park) under South Africa's apartheid laws. The name, appropriately, means "the place where we do not wish to go". Today it is a sprawling residential area ranging from modest dwellings dating back to the 1970s and luxury houses to large informal settlements on the fringes. It is quite safe to drive through Katutura, but keep an eye out for taxis – their drivers are a law unto themselves.

The outdoors

Allow about an hour for the **Hofmeyer Walk**, an interesting route along the ridge separating Windhoek from the Klein Windhoek Valley. Vegetation typical of the area can be seen along the trail, which is especially attractive during autumn when the red flowers of the mountain aloe (*Aloe littoralis*), the emblem of the Windhoek city council, add a splash of colour to the surroundings. Birding can be rewarding and it is advisable to wear comfortable walking shoes.

Situated on the eastern outskirts of Windhoek, off Sam Nujoma Drive, **Avis Dam** is a favourite with Windhoek residents walking their dogs. The land surrounding the dam is leased to Greenspace and the Friends of Avis and is managed as a nature reserve. When the dam has water a large variety of birds is attracted to the area, providing excellent opportunities for birding close to the city centre.

Art, culture and entertainment

Occasional performances of formal drama, ballet and musicals are staged by the **National Theatre of Namibia**, 18 Robert Mugabe Avenue, tel (061) 23-7966. Housed in an old brewery, the **Warehouse Theatre**, 48 Tal Street, tel (061) 22-5059, is characterised by its lively, informal atmosphere. Live music, cabarets and plays are performed regularly. Classical music, ballet and modern dancing are performed from time to time by the **College of the Arts** in Peter Müller Street. Tel (061) 22-5841.

The **National Art Gallery of Namibia**, on the corner of John Meinert Street and Robert Mugabe Avenue, houses an extensive permanent collection of works by Namibian artists, among them John Muafangejo, Johannes Blatt, and Adolph Jentsch. Temporary exhibitions are held regularly. Tel (061) 24-0930.

Exhibitions are held from time to time at **Atelier Kendzia**, 14 Volans Street, tel (061) 22-5991 and the **Omba Gallery** in the Old Brewery Building.

An annual event on Windhoek's calendar is **WIKA**, an abbreviation for Windhoek Karneval. A local version of the great German festivals, the carnival features nine days of music, lots of beer, entertainment and humour. In addition to a colourful float procession, there are international and ladies nights, a masked ball and a children's carnival. It usually takes place from the end of April to early May.

Shopping

Shopping products in Windhoek range from hand-crafted jewellery and leather goods to karakul garments and traditional arts and crafts. When buying handicrafts at street markets, bear in mind that only cash is accepted. Although bargaining is acceptable, it is not practised to the same extent as in other African countries.

In addition to the street markets in Post Street Mall and Peter Müller Street, the **Namibia Crafts Centre**, 40 Tal Street, tel (061) 24-2222, is well worth a visit. A wide selection of traditional Namibian crafts – wood carvings, pottery, basketry, embroidery, carpets – is sold, and regular exhibits of handicrafts are held in the **Omba Gallery**. Light snacks and beverages are served at the **Craft Café**. The centre is open from Monday to Friday 09:00-17:30 (September to April) and 09:00-17:00 (May to August); Saturday 09:30-13:30; Sunday 10:00-14:00.

Tameka (a Herero word for "to create") in the Gustav Voigts Centre, Independence Avenue, markets a range of crafts produced by rural communities. Crafts include patchwork, embroidered textiles and decorative handicrafts.

Also well worth a visit is **Penduka**, on the western outskirts of the city, a non-profit development project working with women's groups producing needlework in underdeveloped areas. In addition to bed and table linen with unusual designs, a variety of other crafts are sold at the craft shop. Other attractions include a traditional village representing eight cultural groups of Namibia, hiking trails ranging from three hours to a day, a tearoom and traditional music. Open Monday to Saturday from 08:00 to 17:00. From Windhoek city centre, head for the Western Bypass (B2) which skirts the city, continue toward Okahandja and take the Brakwater turnoff into Monte Christo Road. Follow Monte Christo Road until you reach Otjomuise Road and turn left, followed by a right turn into Eveline Street. Turn right into Green Mountain Dam Road and follow the Penduka signs.

Where To Eat In Windhoek

Windhoek has a large variety of eating places, ranging from steak ranches to restaurants renowned for their outstanding cuisine.

Brazilian Coffee Shop, Frans Indongo Arcade, tel (061) 25-9722. Light snacks and a variety of coffees.

Café Restaurant Schneider, Jack Levinson Arcade, off Independence Avenue, tel (061) 22-6304. Popular meeting place in Windhoek with a continental atmosphere, breakfasts, good value-for-money lunches, light meals and cakes. Closed evenings.

Café Kaiserkrone, Kaiserkrone Centre, Post Street Mall, tel (061) 23-0141. Situated in a courtyard shaded by palm trees and large umbrellas. Specialises in Italian dishes.

Central Café, Jack Levinson Arcade, off Independence Avenue, tel (061) 22-2659. One of Windhoek's landmarks, with a lively atmosphere. Breakfast, light meals, lunches (veal specialities) and cakes. Closed evenings.

Chez Wou Chinese Restaurant, Windhoek Country Club Resort and Casino, tel (061) 205-5911. Variety of Chinese dishes.

Dros Restaurant, Post Street Mall, tel (061) 24-2740. Centrally situated for after work get togethers. Serves pizzas, steaks, chicken and fish.

Dunes Restaurant and Terrace, Kalahari Sands Hotel, Independence Avenue, tel (061) 22-2300. Buffet with carvery, hot plate stir-fry and salad bar, or à la carte menu with international cuisine. The terrace of the restaurant, a wooden deck shaded by awnings, overlooks Independence Avenue.

Fürstenhof Hotel, Hotel Fürstenhof,. 4 Romberg Street, tel 23-7380. Windhoek's most sophisticated restaurant. French and German cuisine, game dishes.

Gathemann Restaurant, Independence Avenue, tel (061) 22-3853. Continental cuisine with a balcony view of Independence Avenue and Zoo Park.

Gerts Klause, Sanlam Centre, Independence Avenue, tel (061) 23-5706. Continental dishes with eisbein and kassler specialities.

Golden Gate Coffee Roastery, Shop 13 Maerua Park, tel (061) 24-5326. Breakfast, light meals, cake and 17 different coffees.

Gourmet's Inn, 195 Jan Jonker Street, tel (061) 23-2360. International, game (ostrich, gemsbok and crocodile) and fish dishes.

Grand Canyon Spur, United House, Independence Avenue, tel (061) 23-1003. Popular family steakhouse offering steaks, burgers.

Homestead Restaurant, 53 Feld Street, tel (061) 22-1958. À la carte international dishes enjoyed in a homely atmosphere.

In's Wiener, Ground Floor, Wernhil Park, tel (061) 23-1082. Breakfast, light snacks, light lunches. Closed evenings.

Joe's Beer House, 440 Independence Avenue, tel (061) 23-2457. One of Windhoek's landmarks offers informal open-air dining in a large courtyard or under thatch. A wide selection of dishes, including the Sausage Tree specialities, and a variety of beers.

Kokerboom Restaurant, Windhoek Country Club Resort, tel (061) 205-5911. Elegant restaurant with a speciality buffet and international à la carte menu.

La Cave Restaurant, Carl List Building, Peter Müller Street, tel (061) 22-4173. À la carte international dishes.

Le Bistro, Corner Post Street Mall and Independence Avenue, tel (061) 22-8742. Bustling pavement bistro. Specialities include the Big Pan.

Luigi & the Fish, 90 Sam Nujoma Drive, Klein Windhoek, tel (061) 25-6398. Specialises in fish but also serves a range of steaks.

Marco Polo, Kaiserkrone Centre, Post Street Mall, tel (061) 23-0141. Pizzas and Italian dishes (evenings only).

Mike's Kitchen, First Floor, Wernhil Park, tel (061) 22-6596. Family steakhouse serving steaks, burgers, fish, vegetarian.

Mykonos Taverna, 324 Sam Nujoma Drive, Klein Windhoek, tel (061) 26-4459. Typical Greek menu and international dishes.

O'Hagans Irish Pub and Grill, Centaurus Street, Maerua Park, tel (061) 23-4677. Pub-style restaurant with à la carte menu; large selection of international and local beers.

Okambihi Restaurant, Kelvin Street, Southern Industrial Area, tel (061) 26-3204. Steaks and vegetarian platter.

O'Portuga Restaurant, Nelson Mandela Drive, tel (061) 27-2900. Authentic Portuguese cuisine in a relaxed setting.

Planet Italy, Stübel Street, tel (061) 25-5440. Usual Italian fare.

Saddles Steak Ranch, Maerua Park, Windhoek, tel (061) 23-3292. Usual steakhouse fare; steaks, burgers, spareribs, pizza.

Safari Hotel, Aviation Road, tel (061) 23-8560. Steakhouse and à la carte restaurant.

Sardinia Pizzeria-Eis Café, 39 Independence Avenue, tel (061) 22-5600. Homely Italian atmosphere for good food at good prices. Specialises in pastas, pizzas, veal and a variety of homemade ice creams.

The Cauldron, Gustav Voigts Centre, Independence Avenue, tel (061) 23-1040. Excellent value-for-money breakfasts and traditional lunch dishes.

Thüringerhof, Independence Avenue, tel (061) 22-6031.

Yang Tze Chinese Restaurant, Ae Gams Mall, Sam Nujoma Drive, tel (061) 23-4779. Chinese dishes.

Zum Wirt, Independence Avenue, tel (061) 23-4503. German home-style cooking at reasonable prices, lively beer garden.

Where To Stay In Windhoek

Hotels

Hotel Heinitzburg Garni, Heinitzburg Street. Built in 1914, the romantic castle overlooking the Windhoek Valley is the focal point of this hotel, which offers elegant accommodation. The tariff includes breakfast, while gourmet meals are served by prior arrangement. Facilities include a swimming pool.

Hotel Fürstenhof, Bulow Street. Extensively renovated in 1997, within walking distance of city centre, renowned for its excellent cuisine.

Kalahari Sands Hotel, Independence Avenue. Situated in the heart of Windhoek, this four-star hotel is popular with business people. Restaurant, pool, gymnasium and casino.

Safari Court and Safari Hotel, Aviation Road. Four star, 4 km from city centre, restaurant, swimming pool, shuttle to city.

Windhoek Country Club and Casino, Western Bypass. Tranquil setting on the outskirts of Windhoek adjacent to Windhoek Country Club. Restaurants, swimming pool, casino, conference facilities. Shuttle to city.

Guesthouses

Hotel Pension Christoph, cnr Robert Mugabe Avenue and Heinitzburg Street. Offers spacious bedrooms arranged around a courtyard with a swimming pool and an excellent buffet breakfast.

Hotel Pension Moni, 7 Rieks van der Walt Street. German hospitality, tranquil surroundings, swimming pool, tariff includes breakfast.

Hotel Pension Steiner, 11 Wecke Street. Comfortable accommodation near the centre of town, garden restaurant and swimming pool.

Hotel Pension Uhland, 147 Uhland Street. Comfortable accommodation, 10 minutes walk from city centre. Amenities include a lounge and swimming pool.

Pension Kleines Heim, 10 Volans Street. Built in 1911, the main building captures something of the old world charm of yesteryear. Spacious rooms, courtyard garden, swimming pool, restaurant.

Villa Verdi, 4 Verdi Street. Stylish accommodation, each room decorated in style of one of Namibia's cultural groups, secluded gardens, swimming pool, 5 minutes walk from city centre. Highly recommended.

Self-catering

Arebusch Travel Lodge, Golf Street. On southern outskirts of Windhoek, two- and five-bed chalets with air-con, television, telephone, rooms with separate bathroom, caravan park, camping area, shop, laundromat, swimming pool.

Jan Jonker Holiday Apartments, 183 Jan Jonker Road. Fully furnished holiday apartments for one to four persons.

Situated 22 km east of Windhoek on the way to Hosea Kutako International Airport, the **Trans Kalahari Caravan Park** offers partly grassed caravan and camping sites with electricity, braai places and communal ablutions. Other facilities include a service station, workshop, shop, information office and 4x4 and camper hire services.

Budget accommodation

Chameleon Backpackers, 22 Wagner Street. Spacious dormitories, double rooms, communal kitchen and entertainment area, swimming pool. Ten minutes from city centre.

Cardboard Box, 15 Johann Albrecht Street. Very popular with backpackers, conveniently close to city, double rooms, dormitories, common room with kitchen, television, bar.

Puccini, Puccini Street. Close to city, double rooms and dormitories, swimming pool, sauna, entertainment area.

Lodges and accommodation close to Windhoek

Auas Game Lodge, 45 km southeast of Windhoek. Accommodation at this 10 000 ha private nature reserve in luxury rooms with *en suite* facilities, poolside restaurant, swimming pool, guided game drives. Take the B1 south toward Rehoboth for 21 km and turn onto the D1463, which is followed for 22 km.

Heija Lodge, midway between Windhoek and Hosea Kutako International Airport (Otjihase Mine turnoff). Rooms (some equipped for self-catering), restaurant, swimming pool, game drives and horse riding.

Landhaus Aris, 21 km south of Aris on the B1 to Rehoboth. Stylish furnished rooms, swimming pool, sauna and gym. Excellent restaurant serving Mediterranean-style dishes.

Okapuka Ranch, 30 km north of Windhoek. A 12 000 ha game ranch offering excellent game viewing. Game drives, lion feed and braai offered for day visitors. P O Box 5955, Windhoek, tel (061) 23-4607, fax 23-4690.

Sundown Lodge, 25 km north of Windhoek in a country setting. Comfortable rooms on a bed and breakfast, full board or self-catering basis. Offers swimming pool, pool bar, games and sundown walks. Well priced. From Windhoek follow the B1 toward Okahandja for 25 km and then turn onto the D1474.

CENTRAL NAMIBIA

Central Namibia is an upland region dominated by the rolling hills, deeply incised river valleys and mountains of the Khomas Hochland. Tucked in the folds of this undulating highlands is Windhoek (see chapter 6), the capital and economic centre of the country. To the east and northeast of the capital are the Neudam highlands. Still further east, the uplands give way to the extensive plains of the interior plateau. Cattle and sheep farming is the main agricultural activity in the central parts, while the east is ideally suited to cattle. Copper is mined at Otjihase, east of Windhoek.

Arnhem Cave

6

Arnhem has the longest cave system in Namibia, the combined length of the passages measuring 4 501 m. The cave system was formed when seepage water dissolved layers of limestone and dolomite alternating with impermeable layers of quartz and shales. With the passing of time, the thin layers of quartz and shales collapsed to form the passages.

The temperature in the cave averages 24 °C, and the relative humidity ranges from 67 to 93 per cent. Although Arnhem Cave does not have many stalactites or stalagmites (it is too dry), a visit is nevertheless worthwhile. From the twin entrances, divided by a rock pillar, visitors enter the Twilight Zone, an enormous cavern measuring 122 m in length and 45 m in width, before continuing into the bowels of the earth. The excursion is, however, not suitable for people suffering from claustrophobia. Visitors must bring torches and are advised to wear old clothes, as the cave is dusty. Prior reservations are essential, tel (062) 57-3585.

Accommodation and amenities at Arnhem comprise self-catering chalets, a camp site, swimming pool and braai places. Meals can be provided on request. P O Box 11354, Windhoek, tel (061) 57-3585.

Bulls' Party & Phillip's Cave

Ameib Ranch, on the southern edge of the Erongos (see p 83) is best known for its rock paintings and its fascinating rock formations. Phillip's Cave, one of the best-known sites in the Erongos, is accessible only on foot and 45-60 minutes should be allowed each way for the walk from the car park. The walk is most enjoyable early in the morning or in the late afternoon, but should not be attempted by the unfit.

On entering **Phillip's Cave** your attention will be drawn by a painting of a large white elephant with an antelope superimposed in red paint. Also depicted are giraffe, zebra, ostrich and several human figures in various postures. These paintings were described in detail in the Abbé Breuil's book, *Phillip Cave*. However, his theories about the Mediterranean origin of the paintings have been rejected by archaeologists.

Best known among the fascinating rock formations is the **Bulls' Party**, a collection of round granite boulders resembling, with some imagination, a number of bulls engaged in conversation. A nearby outcrop has appropriately been named the **Elephant Head**, while an enormous 16 m high boulder which seems as if it has just come to rest is unlikely to escape attention. Endless hours can be spent exploring the area, but the heat becomes unbearable among the granite boulders at midday. A stream which rises among the jumble of rocks at the Bulls' Party trickles over the boulders for a short way before disappearing into the sand. Shady lunch spots can be found among the towering boulders.

A variety of wild animals is kept in enclosures at the ranch, but many visitors have objected to the small size of the enclosures and the conditions the animals are kept in.

Ameib offers fully inclusive accommodation in a guesthouse. There is a swimming pool and among the activities offered are game viewing, farm drives and horse riding. There is also a camp site with communal ablutions, tents and two fully furnished wooden bungalows.

Gross Barmen

Gross Barmen, southwest of Okahandja, is a popular stopover with visitors travelling to the Etosha National Park. Built on the banks of a tributary of the Swakop River, its main attraction is

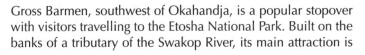

its thermal spring, which supplies water to an outdoor swimming pool and the glass-enclosed thermal hall. The "eye" of the spring can be seen between the outdoor pool and the restaurant complex. At its source the water temperature is about 65 °C, compared with temperatures of about 41 °C for the thermal hall pool and 29 °C for the outdoor pool. The water is rich in minerals such as sodium sulphate, sodium, sulphate, chloride, silicate, potash and fluoride.

The surrounding hillsides and a dam at the centre of the resort offer good opportunities for birding. A path has been cleared through the dense reedbeds fringing the dam and wooden benches provide excellent vantage points. Although there are no formal trails, visitors can ramble among the rocky outcrops or take a stroll along the riverbed.

Originally known as Otjikango, a Herero word meaning "a spring flowing weakly through rocky ground", the resort is on the site of the first Rhenish mission station for the Herero in Namibia. The mission station was founded in October 1844 by Carl Hugo Hahn and Heinrich Kleinschmidt, after the spring they had visited at Okahandja a few months earlier had dried up. Five days after their arrival at Okahandja, Jonker Afrikaner arrived unexpectedly and, on learning of their plight, encouraged them to settle at Otjikango. The station was named Neu-Barmen after the headquarters of the Rhenish Missionary Society at Barmen in Germany, but was later renamed Gross Barmen.

The mission station had to be abandoned on several occasions as it was in the line of attack between the warring Hereros and Namas. In 1890 it was closed when it became a branch of the Okahandja mission station. Sadly, all that remains are the ruins of the church and the mission house, marked by a solitary palm tree west of the dam.

The resort is open throughout the year. Visitors with reserved accommodation have unrestricted access, provided entrance and accommodation fees are paid during office hours. Day visitors are welcome, but must make prior reservations with the resort office, tel (062) 50-1091, and must leave the resort before 18:00.

Accommodation at **Gross Barmen Resort** ranges from two- and five-bed bungalows to two-bed rooms. There are also camping sites with field kitchens and communal ablutions. Amenities include a well-stocked shop, restaurant, kiosk, filling station, tennis court and a children's playpark. Picnic sites are available for day visitors.

Khomas Hochland

The Khomas Hochland lies between 1 750 and 2 000 m above sea level and forms part of the interior plateau of central Namibia. Extending westward from the Windhoek Valley to the Great Escarpment, it is bounded in the north by the Swakop River, with the Kuiseb River marking its southern boundary. It is a deeply dissected landscape crisscrossed by seasonal river valleys, sharp ridges and rolling hills. The similarity in altitude of many hill tops suggests the existence of an earlier erosion surface in its geological past. These levels are close to a surface formed during Karoo times, some 180 to 300 million years ago, which has been eroded over the last 100 million years.

The highland is comprised of mica schist of the Kuiseb Formation, which is Late Precambrian in age. Some 650 to 750 million years ago, sediments accumulated on the floor of a sea and were later metamorphosed during a mountain building phase to form schists. The schists were, in turn, folded and tilted some 500 to 600 million years ago. During several major erosion periods in the geological past, this mountain chain was reduced to the present landscape.

One of the best ways of seeing the Khomas Hochland is to follow route 2 from Windhoek to Swakopmund via the Bosua Pass. To the south, the Khomas Hochland borders on the Gamsberg region, which is often mistakenly assumed to form part of the Khomas Hochland.

ROUTE 1
WINDHOEK TO SWAKOPMUND

DISTANCE: 360 km **TIME**: Approximately 4 hours
ROAD CONDITIONS: Fully tarred **FUEL**: Available at all towns **LINKING ROUTES**: Route 9

From Windhoek (see p 53) the B1 stretches northward for 70 km to Okahandja along a valley formed millions of years ago when fracturing caused the floor to subside. To the west the valley is bounded by the Khomas Hochland, while the Eros and Otjihavero mountains form the eastern boundary of the valley.

The turnoff to **Okapuka Ranch** is signposted about 30 km north of Windhoek. Covering 12 000 ha of tree and shrub savanna, Okapuka is home to a variety of game, including kudu, gemsbok, springbok, blue wildebeest, eland, giraffe, crocodile and a host of smaller species.

One of the highlights of a visit to Okapuka is watching the lions feed from the safety of the Lion Bar, where meals can be enjoyed. Activities include game viewing and scenic drives into the mountains.

Day visitors can join a game drive, followed by watching the lions feed and a braai. A minimum of four people is required and prior reservations are essential.

Nestling against the slopes of the Otjihavero mountains, the main lodge has a spectacular view over the Windhoek Valley and the Khomas Hochland further west. It comprises a reception area, lounge and bar with a fireplace and restaurant, as well as a swimming pool. There is also a floodlit tennis court.

For 4x4 enthusiasts with time on hand, the **Windhoek-Okahandja 4x4 Trail** offers an alternative to travelling along the B1 (see p 18).

The turnoff to the **Von Bach Recreation Resort and Game Park** is signposted about 1,8 km south of Okahandja, from where it is about 2 km to the turnoff to the resort.

The focal point of the resort is the Sartorius Von Bach Dam, the main storage dam supplying water to Windhoek. Built to meet the future water requirements of the central areas of the country, it was completed in 1971 as part of the Eastern National Water Carrier System. The 270 m long dam wall in the upper reaches of the Swakop River impounds 48 560 000 m^3 of water and when full the dam covers a surface area of up to 50 km^2.

The **game park** covers 4 285 ha of extremely hilly terrain; the highest point is about 300 m above the dam wall in the southwestern corner. The southeastern section makes up two-thirds of the park when the dam is full and the northwestern part the remainder.

Only a few kudu, chacma baboon and smaller mammals occurred naturally in the area when the park was proclaimed in 1972 and Hartmann's mountain zebra, eland and ostriches were subsequently reintroduced. Opportunities for game viewing are limited though, as there are no tourist roads other than the one to the camping area on the southeastern banks of the dam.

The vegetation is thornbush savanna with ringwood tree, blue thorn, black thorn and red bushwillow among the dominant species. Good specimens of camel and sweet thorns can be seen below the dam wall.

A variety of water sports – water-skiing, windsurfing, yachting and boating – are enjoyed here. The dam is also popular with anglers and has been stocked with largemouth bass, blue kurper and smallmouth yellowfish, while carp and barbel also occur. Angling permits can be purchased at the entrance gate.

Accommodation at the **Von Bach Recreation Resort** comprises basic two-bed huts, served by communal ablutions. No bedding, crockery and cutlery are provided. Camp sites with communal ablutions are available on the shores of the dam.

Day visitors must make reservations with the resort office prior to their visit, tel (062) 50-1475. Picnic sites are available. There is no shop, restaurant or filling station. The resort is open throughout the year from sunrise to sunset.

Okahandja, at the junction of the routes to the north (see route 7) and the coast, is reached 70 km north of Windhoek. It is a pleasant little town with an abundance of trees, lending support to its claim of being the "Garden Town of Namibia".

The road leading into the town is lined with **Kavango crafts** fashioned by woodcarvers from the Kavango Region. On display are household implements, masks and furniture carved from teak wood. The demand for curios has, however, resulted in mass production and it will be worth your while to have a good look around before making a purchase. There are also large numbers of stalls on the northern outskirts of the town.

Much of Okahandja's early history is closely related to that of the Herero people. In 1843 Carl Hugo Hahn and Heinrich Kleinschmidt, two missionaries of the Rheinische Missionsgesellschaft, visited the area to establish a mission station for the Herero. A suitable site was located near a spring and named "Schmelen's Verwachting", after Heinrich Schmelen of the London Missionary Society, who had visited the area 16 years earlier. The first missionary, Friedrich Kolbe, settled here in 1849. As a result of the reign of terror of the Nama leader,

Jonker Afrikaner, he abandoned the mission station after three months and it was only reopened when peace returned to the area.

A small outcrop alongside the B1, about 600 m west of the turnoff to Gross Barmen, marks the site of **Moordkoppie**. A large number of followers of Herero Chief Kahitjenne were murdered here by a Nama force commanded by Jonker Afrikaner on 23 August 1850.

Several monuments and places of interest can be seen in Church Street, which runs parallel to Main Street. At the southern end of Church Street is the **Rhenish Mission Church**, built between 1871 and 1876 by the missionaries P H Diehl and J Irle. The graves of several German soldiers, missionaries and Herero leaders, including those of Trougoth and Willem Maharero, can be seen in the church cemetery.

Opposite the church are the **graves of Jonker Afrikaner**, captain of the Afrikaner tribe until his death in 1861, and of the Herero chiefs **Hosea Kutako** and **Clemens Kapuuo**. Chief Kutako is considered by many to be the father of black nationalism in Namibia and made the first direct petition to the United Nations against South African rule in the former South West Africa in 1946. As a demonstration of his commitment to unity, Kutako chose to be buried near a former enemy of the Herero people, Jonker Afrikaner, and not, as is customary, in the cemetery of his ancestors. Chief Clemens Kapuuo, the first president of the Democratic Turnhalle Alliance, was assassinated in Windhoek's Katutura township in 1978.

About 600 m further north along Church Street a signpost points the way to the **communal graves** of **Tjamuaha, Maharero** and **Samuel Maharero**. On the weekend before or after 26 August each year the Red Flag Hereros pay homage to their forefathers and the stately procession from the complex to the graves of Afrikaner, Kutako and Kapuuo has become a well-known event.

Okahandja is also of historical significance to the Mbanderu, Herero-speaking people united under the **Green Flag**. Their leader, Chief Kahimemua Nguvava, was executed by firing squad at Okahandja in June 1896 after a failed rebellion against German rule. His grave is situated in Skool Street, west of the railway line. It is the focal point of the annual Green Flag procession held in June when the Mbanderu pay homage to their slain leader.

Worthwhile visiting is **Ombo Ostrich Farm** on the western outskirts of the town. Take the B1 north toward Otjiwarongo for about 2 km and turn left onto the D2110. Just after turning left you pass the **Okakango Wildlife Garden**. Situated in peaceful surroundings, the Okakango Restaurant offers substantial breakfasts at very reasonable prices. Lunches (schnitzel, steak and daily specials), coffee and cake, as well as sundowners, are served. Open daily 07:00 to 18:00. Tel (062) 50-3280.

Continuing along a gravel road, **Ombo Ostrich Farm** is reached about 1 km on. A variety of displays relating to these interesting birds can be viewed in a museum which features a glass-fronted incubator room – some visitors are fortunate enough to see a chicken hatch! A fascinating insight into various aspects of the ostrich can be gained on a 45-minute guided tour. Starting at the museum, the tour includes a visit to the ostrich pens, where wild and domesticated ostriches can be viewed. Visitors are given an opportunity to feed the ostriches and to sit on one. Also to be seen are a pair of dwarf ostriches, emus from Australia and crocodiles.

A comprehensive range of souvenirs, such as ostrich eggs, jewellery and semi-precious stones, is sold by a well-stocked shop. Especially popular with children is an artificial cave where your own selection of semi-precious stones can be made. Light meals are served and the menu includes, when available, ostrich dishes and scrambled egg. Open throughout the year 08:00 to 17:00.

The MR87 to **Gross Barmen** (see p 73) is signposted about 1,6 km beyond the turnoff to Okahandja on the B2 bypassing Okahandja. From the turnoff it is 25 km along a tar road.

From Okahandja the B2 strikes west to reach Wilhelmstal after 59 km. The D1967 turning off here leads to Otjimbingwe, a historic settlement which was once the "capital" of the country. The 130 km detour is, however, only worthwhile if you have a keen interest in history.

Situated at the confluence of the Swakop and Omusema rivers, Otjimbingwe is a Herero name, translated as "place of refreshment" – a reference to the spring in the Omusema River. In 1849 the Rhenish missionary, Johannes Raath, established a mission station here and the **Rhenish Church** is the oldest place of worship for the Herero. It was built in 1867, and the tower was added in 1899. Although the Herero Chief, Zeraua, was not a Christian, he offered to have 10 000 bricks made for the church, which served as a refuge for women and children during attacks by the Nama on Otjimbingwe on more than one occasion.

Following the discovery of copper deposits in the area, the Walvisch Bay Mining Company (WBMC) established its headquarters at Otjimbingwe in 1854. In the same year a **trading store** opened its doors, selling arms, ammunition and liquor on credit, or bartering with the Herero and the Nama. When the copper boom came to an end in 1860, the explorer Charles John Andersson bought the WBMC assets in Otjimbingwe. The store was later purchased by Eduard Hälbich and still serves its original purpose.

By the 1860s increasing numbers of unscrupulous traders were active in the area, interfering with the missionary work at Otjimbingwe. To counteract the situation, the Missionshandelsgesellschaft was founded in Germany in 1871 to promote trade. Otjimbingwe served as the local headquarters, with branches established at Okahandja and Rehoboth. In 1872 an 8 m high **powder magazine** was erected to protect the society's trading ventures against frequent attacks by the Nama. Following the start of the second Nama-Herero war, the society suffered financially and in 1882 the tower passed into the hands of the Hälbich firm. No less than 30 unsuccessful attacks were made against the tower in the time before peace was established.

Otjimbingwe's strategic position, midway between Windhoek and Walvis Bay on the old ox-wagon route, prompted Reichs-Kommisar Heinrich Göring to establish the administrative seat of Deutsch-Südwestafrika here in 1885. The first post office was opened at Otjimbingwe in July 1888, a week after the country became a member of the Universal Postal Union on 1 July 1888.

An old **wind motor**, erected in 1896 by the firm Hälbich to generate power for the adjoining wagon factory, can be seen opposite the trading store. Power was derived from a windmill wheel with a diameter of 9 m, which turned a driving shaft attached to a gear on the ground. From here a belt ran to a long horizontal driving shaft inside the building, where several belts turned a variety of machines. The 8 hp motor generated power for, among others, a band saw, turntable and iron drill, and also supplied water from a nearby spring to the settlement.

Toward the end of 1890 the Germans transferred their headquarters to Windhoek. The settlement suffered another setback when the railway line between Windhoek and Swakopmund was completed in the early 1900s, following a more northerly route. Today, it seems hard to believe that Otjimbingwe was once the country's administrative centre.

Continuing west along the B2, the turnoff onto the C33 to Omaruru and Otjiwarongo (see route 7) is reached 2 km out of **Karibib**. Tourists often travel through this small town without stopping, but if you are interested in historic buildings, you would do well to stop here for a while.

Karibib is renowned for the high-quality marble quarried in the area since 1904. Considered the hardest in the world, Karibib marble has been used for the wall panels in the Prime Minister's Office in Windhoek (the former Legislative Assembly for Whites), the floors of the extensions to the Parliament buildings in Cape Town and at Frankfurt Airport.

The marble is quarried and transported to the Marmorwerke works in 20 tonne blocks, where it is cut into varying sizes by the largest granite saw in Africa, and then made into smaller blocks, washed and polished. Floor and bathroom tiles are particularly in demand, and a variety of ornaments and tombstones are also manufactured.

In July 1985, gold was discovered on the farm Navachab, 10 km southwest of Karibib. Production at the opencast mine started in November 1989 and in 1990 1 453 kg of gold was produced. The ore is low grade, about 2-3 grams a tonne, and about 750 000 tonnes of rock is treated annually. *The mine is not open to the public.*

On entering Karibib, the first building of interest is the **bakery and baker's quarters**. It dates back to 1913 and was one of six hotels during the town's heyday. In the 1950s the hotel's main building was converted into a bakery, a purpose it still serves today. It is an ideal stop for a snack (the freshly baked pies, pastries and bread are delicious) before continuing to the coast.

When the railway line between Swakopmund and Windhoek reached Karibib on 1 July 1900, there was a need for overnight accommodation in the town, as passenger trains initially only ran during the day. **The Rosemann Building** dates back to 1900, when it was built as a hotel and business premises for the firm Rosemann and Kronewitter. Although it has since been altered on numerous occasions, the facade has remained virtually unchanged and was declared a national monument in 1979.

Opposite the Rosemann Building is the **station**, which was completed in April 1901. In addition to the railway offices and waiting rooms, the building also housed a post office and a restaurant. Springbok, gemsbok and kudu dishes are served in the **Springbok Restaurant** in the western flank of the building. Tel (064) 55-0094.

Continuing down the street, the historic **Hälbich property**, comprising of four buildings, is passed on the left. The firm E Hälbich & Co moved to Karibib in 1900 after it was established at Otjimbingwe 27 years earlier.

The adjacent **Haus Woll** is easily mistaken for a church. The building dates back to the beginning of the 1900s, when a trader, George Woll, used part of it as a shop and the remainder as living quarters. The granite and Karibib marble building reflects the typical architectural style of the German colonial period.

With its wide range of minerals, gemstones, leatherware, stone and wood carvings, the **Henckert Tourist Centre** is a paradise for souvenir hunters. The centre incorporates a weavery, **Der Webervogel**, where rugs and wall-hangings are woven by hand from natural, undyed karakul sheep wool.

Etusis Lodge, a well-known guest farm in the area, lies southwest of Karibib amid 12 000 ha of savanna plains, interrupted in the west by the Otjipatera mountains. From Karibib, follow the C32 southward for 36 km to the signposted turnoff.

The lodge provides guests with an opportunity to view a diversity of animals, birds and plants in their natural habitat. Game to be seen include Hartmann's mountain zebra, kudu, gemsbok, springbok, klipspringer, common duiker and Damara dik-dik, as well as a variety of small mammals. There are several viewpoints overlooking waterholes and it is possible to overnight near one of the waterholes by special arrangement. Activities include 4x4 game-viewing trips, walks and horseback excursions. The mountainous area is ideal for hiking.

The main complex, comprising a reception area, restaurant and bar, overlooks a large dam where animals quench their thirst. Accommodation is in stone-built bungalows with thatched roofs, or in comfortable safari tents. There is also a small swimming pool.

Travelling from Karibib to Usakos, the landscape north of the B2 is dominated by the 2 319 m high **Erongo mountains**. They have a roughly circular diameter of about 35 km, and were formed by volcanic activity some 140 million years ago. Fractures which developed during a period of volcanism caused the centre of the volcano to subside. At the same time vast quantities of granite intruded into the Damara Sequence rocks and the overlying Karoo Sequence and lavas. Subsequent erosion exposed the granitic core, and fracturing below the surface and weathering fashioned impressive boulders. These boulders are characteristic of the Erongos and contribute much to the fascinating scenery.

From the earliest times people have been attracted to these mountains, as is evident from the wealth of rock paintings and engravings, with pottery and other relics providing evidence of more recent habitation.

About 2 km before Usakos, the C33 to Omaruru and Otjiwarongo (see route 7) branches off to the north. **Usakos**, on the southern bank of the Khan River, is 30 km west of Karibib. Tourists usually pass through without realising the important role Usakos played in the history of the country's railways.

The town developed around the railway workshops built here in the early 1900s to serve locomotives on the narrow-gauge Otavi Line. By 1907 Usakos had two hotels and a population of 300, and in time the workshops were rivalled only by those at De Aar in South Africa. In 1960 the steam locomotives were replaced by diesel engines and a modern workshop was opened in Windhoek, resulting in the depopulation of Usakos.

Reminders of the heyday of the railway era are the prominent **water tower** and the **locomotive** in front of the railway station. Locomotive No 40 was one of three Henschel heavy-duty units built in 1912 by the firm Henschel and Son in Casel, Germany. They were used on the narrow-gauge (600 mm) Otavi Line, between Kranzberg, about 20 km west of Karibib, and Tsumeb and Grootfontein. In 1960 the line was replaced with a 1,067 m track. The locomotives were originally manufactured with a steam dome and a sand dome. However, for practical purposes the sand dome was removed and sand boxes were fitted onto the locomotive's running boards. Locomotive No 41 can be seen in front of the Otjiwarongo station (see route 7).

An enterprising resident of Usakos has turned the station building into a guesthouse, offering accommodation to budget travellers. There is also a restaurant and it is planned to establish a small railway museum.

The turnoff to **Ameib Ranch**, renowned for Phillip's Cave and the Bulls' Party, (see p 73) is signposted in Usakos. To reach Ameib, follow the D1935 for roughly 13 km before turning right onto the D1937, continuing for about 16 km.

From Usakos, the B2 ascends steadily out of the Khan River Valley, reaching the turnoff to the Spitzkoppe after about 23 km (see route 13). Continuing further west, the landscape becomes increasingly arid. Dominating the scenery is the **Spitzkoppe** (see p 136 and route 13), one of Namibia's most prominent landmarks.

A road sign on the B2, 65 km west of Usakos, indicates the turnoff to Trekkopje station. Turn right and continue along the gravel road that crosses the railway line after less than 1 km. Turn right and follow the road to the fenced **military cemetery**, marked by a large tree.

Following the occupation of Swakopmund by South African forces in January 1915, the retreating Germans destroyed the Otavi Line between Swakopmund and Usakos, as well as the State Line as far as Welwitsch, 62 km east of Swakopmund. During the rebuilding of the Otavi Line between Swakopmund and Usakos to the 1,067 m standard gauge, the camp of the South African Engineering Corps was attacked by the Germans at Trekkopje. In the battle, fought on 26 April 1915, armoured vehicles were used for the first time by the South African forces, and although outnumbered, they defeated the Germans with the assistance of armoured cars with revolving machine-gun turrets.

About 19 km beyond Trekkopje station is the turnoff to **Rössing Mine** and Arandis, the town serving the mine. The mine is not open to casual visitors, but tours are conducted from Swakopmund (see p 209).

Uranium was discovered in the area in 1920 by a prospector, Captain Peter Louw, whose company later obtained a concession over an area of 1 000 km². Various attempts to interest mining companies failed, until a subsidiary of the multinational mining company Rio Tinto Zinc took an option on the concession in the mid-1960s. After four years of geophysical and geological surveys, Rössing Uranium was established in 1970.

Production of uranium oxide began in 1976, but full production was only reached two years later. The deposit covered an area of about 3 km in length and 1 km in width, making it the largest of its kind in the world. It is a low-grade deposit in tough, abrasive granite known as alaskite.

At full capacity about 100 000 tonnes of rock are recovered each week from the open pit, which is mined in 15 m deep benches and has an average slope of 45°.

Once the rock has been blasted it is loaded onto 150 tonne trucks and transported to two crushers with a capacity of 40 000 tonnes a day. After two more crushing stages, the rock particles undergo a series of processes, involving grinding, leaching, the separation of sand and slime and the thickening of the slime.

This is followed by several recovery stages until a yellow paste, ammonium diuranate, is recovered on rotating drum filters. In the final stage the yellow paste, also known as yellow cake, is dried and roasted at a temperature of more than 600 °C to form uranium oxide. This is then loaded into steel drums and exported overseas for further processing.

Another reminder of the South West Africa Campaign during World War I can be seen by taking a turnoff 47 km east of Swakopmund on the B2. Follow the track for about 1 km to the railway line, from where it is a short distance on foot to the platform overlooking the **regimental insignia** of the 2nd Durban Light Infantry.

Some of the South African soldiers assigned to patrol the railway line and prevent sabotage by the Germans occupied themselves by packing their names, initials or regimental badges in stone. A number of these insignia were laid out along the railway line – the best known being the 27 m by 12 m badge of the 2nd Durban Light Infantry. White quartz chips and dark brown rocks were used to show detail which is still visible today. To the right is the incomplete thistle of the Transvaal Scottish Regiment, whose Gaelic motto, *Alba nam duadh*, is just barely discernible.

Continuing along the B2, the scenery is dominated by the spectacularly eroded Swakop River Valley with its Moon Landscape, with Rössing Mountain a prominent landmark to the north. The coastal town of Swakopmund (see p 200) is 175 km west of Usakos.

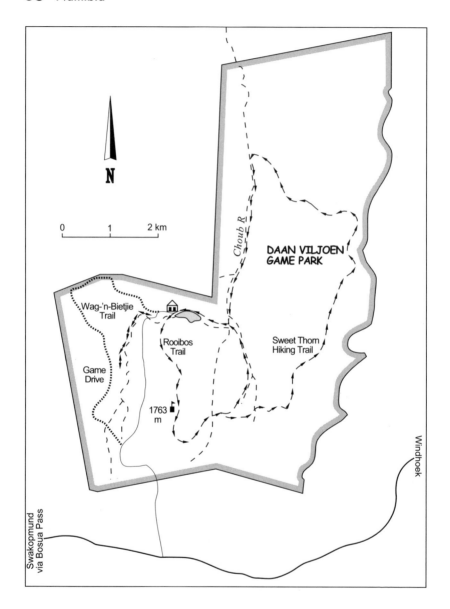

Great Escarpment Passes

From Windhoek, the adventurous traveller has a choice of five gravel-surface routes via the Khomas Hochland, the Gamsberg and the Escarpment to the Namib Desert and the coastal towns of Swakopmund and Walvis Bay. *It is advisable to enquire about road conditions after heavy rains from either the Department of Transport, or the Automobile Association of Namibia.* (See chapter 14 for contact details.)

ROUTE 2
WINDHOEK TO SWAKOPMUND VIA BOSUA PASS

DISTANCE: 340 km **TIME**: 6 to 7 hours
ROAD CONDITIONS: 21 km tar; rest usually good gravel, but can be corrugated **FUEL**: Windhoek, Swakopmund
LINKING ROUTES: Route 16

The direct route from Windhoek (see p 53) to Swakopmund (see p 200) through the Namib Desert is along the **Bosua Pass**, the most northerly of the passes. On account of its steep gradient (1:5) caravans are not permitted and the pass is best travelled from east to west.

In Windhoek, turn into Sam Nujoma Drive, either from Independence Avenue, or from Mandume Ndemufayo Avenue, and continue along the C28 for 14 km to the signposted turnoff to the **Daan Viljoen Game Park**. The entrance gate is reached 1,5 km on, with the park office 4 km further.

Situated among the undulating hills of the Khomas Hochland (see p 75), the park was proclaimed in 1966 after a former Administrator, Mr D T du P Viljoen, donated 2 700 ha of land for its establishment. It is the habitat of mammals typical of the Khomas Hochland, such as eland, Hartmann's mountain zebra, red hartebeest, blue wildebeest, kudu and springbok. Smaller species include klipspringer, steenbok, chacma baboon and rock dassie.

Among the more than 250 bird species recorded to date are several Namibian "specials", such as Monteiro's hornbill, rock-runner and white-tailed shrike. Commonly seen species include grey, red-billed and yellow-billed hornbills, short-toed rock thrush, crimson-breasted shrike and pale-winged starling.

Experienced birders could tick between 60 and 90 species a day, while those unfamiliar with birdwatching will find the guide, *Birds of Daan Viljoen Game Park*, a great help. It contains a short description of 58 species likely to be seen, plus colour photographs or illustrations, a description of habitat types and a checklist. The guide is sold at the park office.

The vegetation is a highland savanna with open hills characterised by scattered mountain thorn, Namibian resin tree and red bushwillow, also known as koedoebos. Other species include candle thorn, wild camphor bush and the sumach bean (*Elephantorrhiza suffruticosa*), locally known as looiwortelbos. Dense stands of camel thorn, sweet thorn, karree and buffalo thorn occur in the valleys.

Visitors can view the game park either by way of a 6 km circular drive or on foot. The 3 km **Wag-'n-Bietjie Trail** is ideal for families and those seeking an easy ramble. It starts near the park office, from where it follows the Augeigas River upstream for 1,5 km to the Stengel and Koch und Schultheiss dams, returning the same way. The 9 km **Rooibos Trail** follows a more strenuous, circular route, with magnificent views of the Windhoek Valley. It starts near the swimming pool and ends at the restaurant.

The **Sweet Thorn Hiking Trail**, a two-day overnight trail, winds for 32 km across undulating hills and through valleys. Along the route, hikers are rewarded with magnificent views and excellent opportunities to view a variety of game. Accommodation at the end of the first day's hike is in a basic shelter.

The dam at the rest camp has been stocked with barbel, kurper and black bass and angling permits are obtainable at the park office. However, during prolonged droughts the dam can dry up.

Picnic sites overlooking the dam are provided for day visitors. Day visitors must book through the park office, tel (061) 22-6806, fax 22-2393, and must leave the camp before 18:00.

The park is open throughout the year and overnight visitors with reserved accommodation may enter until midnight.

The **Daan Viljoen rest camp** on the banks of the Augeigas Dam comprises bungalows and camp sites. The bungalows and camp sites are served by field kitchens and communal ablutions. Breakfast is included in the tariff. There is a restaurant, kiosk and swimming pool, but no shop or filling station.

From Daan Viljoen Game Park, continue westward along the C28, ignoring the signpost 7 km further on to the **Matchless**

Mine. Commercial exploitation of the Matchless Mine dates back to 1856, when the Walvisch Bay Mining Company began exploiting copper deposits in central Namibia. The first manager of the mine was the renowned traveller, explorer and trader, Charles John Andersson, who supervised the mining operations from 1856 to 1858. The company abandoned its mining operations in 1860. In 1902 a subsidiary of the Deutsche Kolonialgesellschaft sank a trial shaft. No mining took place, however, and the mine was abandoned shortly afterward. In the late-1960s Tsumeb Corporation Limited conducted an extensive drilling survey and copper and sulphur were mined from 1970 to 1983. The mine closed in 1983 due to a decrease in world copper prices.

The tar road ends at the turnoff to the mine and 19 km on you pass the derelict, ghostly looking **Liebig House** on the farm Neu Heusis. The house dates back to around 1912, when it was built for the director of the Deutsche Farmgesellschaft. The farm was acquired in 1908 as headquarters for the company, which had also purchased other farms in the area for the purpose of cattle breeding.

Stop here, and take a stroll through the unusual double-storey building where, with little imagination, you can picture the once lavish lifestyle of the occupants. A fountain in the large room downstairs was once the focal point of the entertainment area, where a row of beautifully patterned tiles decorated some of the walls. Upstairs one can appreciate the expansive views the occupants enjoyed when they woke up.

Fourteen kilometres further west, at Karanab, you pass the ruins of the **Von François Fort**, named after Captain Curt Von François, who established the German colonial administration in Windhoek. The military post was built to protect the route between Swakopmund and Windhoek, but later served as a *Trockenpost* (drying-out post) for troops guilty of alcohol abuse.

Constructed of flat stones from the area, the fort blends in so well with its surroundings that it is easily overlooked. The mortar has withstood years of weathering, revealing how the walls were skilfully stacked. Looking through the "windows", you have a view of the Heusis River Valley and the surrounding hills, underlining the strategic importance of the post.

Further west, the road descends steeply along the **Bosua Pass** with its 1:5 gradient. It then meanders along valleys and through spectacular granite outcrops before reaching the eastern boundary of the Namib-Naukluft Park. From the boundary the road traverses the Namib section (see p 186) of the park. As you continue westward you will notice the strange-looking welwitschias alongside the road, where springbok and gemsbok are sometimes also seen. At the turnoff to the Welwitschia Plains route 16 joins in. The coastal town of Swakopmund (see p 200) is reached about 126 km after entering the park.

ROUTE 3
WINDHOEK TO WALVIS BAY VIA GAMSBERG PASS

DISTANCE: 355 km **TIME**: 7 hours **ROAD CONDITIONS**: 21 km tar; remainder gravel, usually good but can be corrugated **FUEL**: Windhoek, Walvis Bay **LINKING ROUTES**: Route 18

Although marginally longer than over the Us Pass (the most direct route to Walvis Bay), the route via the Gamsberg Pass is far more spectacular.

From Windhoek city centre travel south along Mandume Ndemufayo Avenue to the four-way intersection with the Western Bypass. Continuing along the C26, the tar road ends 5 km on and you then ascend along the Kupferberg Pass to the Khomas Hochland. About 36 km out of Windhoek the C26 turns left (signposted Walvis Bay via Gamsberg Pass).

Remain on the C26, and as you travel further, the scenery is increasingly dominated by Namibia's third highest mountain – the 2 347 m high **Gamsberg**. A large table-top mountain, it is said to derive its name from the Khoekhoen name *gan*, meaning "shut" or "closed" – a reference to the fact that one's view is obscured by the mountain.

Rising some 500 m above the interior plateau, the mountain consists of 1 000 million year-old granite, with a conspicuous horizontal capping of weather-resistant sandstone. The 25 m thick capping was formed about 200 million years ago when the area was covered by sediments, washed into a sea that covered most of southern Africa. Gamsberg has been protected from the ravages of subsequent erosion by its capping of sandstone.

Ignore the turnoff to Nauchas, 71 km beyond the previous turnoff, which lies at the junction of the roads to Spreetshoogte Pass (see route 4) and Remhoogte Pass. Continuing along the C26, **Weissenfels Guest Farm** is passed a further 8,7 km on. It is renowned for its hospitality and offers guests dramatic scenery, game viewing, horse riding and mountain biking.

For those with a spirit of adventure, the Gamsberg region offers a number of activities. Not to be missed is a **4x4 trip to the summit of the Gamsberg**. Guided trips lasting from five to eight hours are conducted in open 4x4 vehicles for groups of up to 10 people. Visitors can also use their own vehicles, but must be accompanied by a guide. Tel (062) 57-2108.

Another option is **mountain biking down Gamsberg Pass**. Transport is provided from Weissenfels Guest Farm to the summit of the pass, where bikers are provided with mountain bikes, crash helmets and gloves. After a short break at the bottom of the pass, transport is provided back to Weissenfels. The minimum group size for this activity is six people. Contact Joachim Cranz, tel (061) 22-8839 (office hours only).

There are other accommodation options in the area. On the farm **Gamsberg**, self-catering accommodation is available in an old restored farmhouse. Beds are provided, but guests must provide their own bedding. Contact Uschi Baur, tel (062) 57-2109. Farm **Weener**, at the foot of Gamsberg, has camp sites with braai facilities, a shower and toilet. Contact Rosalie van Heerden, tel (062) 57-2108.

It is worth stopping at the summit of the pass, 14 km beyond Weissenfels, from where you have magnificent views over the rolling hills and deep valleys of the escarpment. The pass snakes down the escarpment steeply and then meanders along valleys to join the C14 (signposted Walvis Bay) about 175 km out of Windhoek. Turn right here; the remaining 170-odd km to Walvis Bay (see route 18) winds along the Kuiseb Pass and then traverses the flat gravel plains of the Namib. This section is described from Swakopmund in route 18. Alternatively, you can turn left and continue with route 18 from Swakopmund to Sesriem and Sossusvlei.

ROUTE 4
WINDHOEK TO SOLITAIRE VIA SPREETSHOOGTE

DISTANCE: 230 km **TIME**: 4 hours **ROAD CONDITIONS**: 12 km tar; remainder gravel, usually good, but can be corrugated **FUEL**: Windhoek, Solitaire **LINKING ROUTES**: Route 18

Spreetshoogte Pass is popular with travellers heading from Windhoek to Sesriem (see p 193) and Sossusvlei (see p 194). From Windhoek, follow the directions for route 3 for the first 107 km and then turn left onto the D1265 (signposted Nauchas). After 15 km you will reach the turnoff to the **Isabis 4x4 Trail**.

Less than two hours' drive from Windhoek, this four-wheel drive trail features dramatic scenery of the Gaub basin of the Gamsberg region, peace and several challenging sections.

Among its other attractions are a deep, perennial pool in the Gaub River and a delightful camp site nestling against a cliff. Amenities include a fireplace, a flush toilet with views to three sides and a shower built in a crack of the cliff face. A shoulder-high reed screen provides privacy, but allows you to enjoy uninterrupted views of the surrounding countryside. A massive rock slab serves as a natural table, with smaller slabs arranged around the fireplace providing perfect seats.

Birding can be rewarding, especially after the summer rains, when a variety of birds are attracted to the pools in the rivers traversing the area. During the dry winter months the pools are a source of water for Hartmann's mountain zebras.

The trail network covers about 70 km of rough tracks on the farm Isabis and the adjoining farm Hornkrantz. Highlights include spectacular views into the Gaub Canyon and a scenic drive through the Rooiberg, a conglomeration of granite outcrops. Driving skills are tested by some sections of the trail, but none of them is dangerous, provided you are cautious.

Only one group, limited to a maximum of four vehicles, is allowed on the trail at a time. Reservations: Joachim Cranz, P O Box 9770, Windhoek, tel and fax (061) 22-8839 (office hours only).

The route then continues to the farm Nauchas, where you turn right onto the D1275. Nestling among spectacular granite outcrops, **Namibgrens rest camp** is reached 6 km beyond the turnoff.

Renowned for the Namibian hospitality of hosts Jeannie and John Rabie, Namibgrens offers guests peace and tranquillity and an opportunity to discover the scenic beauty of the area on foot, or by vehicle. Farm tours are offered to viewpoints along the escarpment edge, from where guests can enjoy distant vistas of the Namib Desert and the flat-topped Gamsberg to the north.

Those wanting to explore their surroundings even closer can set off on the **Dassie Hiking Trails**, a trail network covering 43 km. Options range from a day walk to a three-day circular trail. The route meanders around and over massive granite outcrops to hidden valleys and awe-inspiring viewpoints. Basic sleeping facilities are provided at a remote overnight hut high up in the mountains.

Guests staying at the rest camp are accommodated in comfortable rooms in an old farmhouse with lots of atmosphere. A communal kitchen is available for self-catering guests, although the excellent meals prepared by Jeannie Rabie are not to be missed. For those preferring even less sophisticated accommodation, a camp site with communal ablutions is available. Also worthwhile is a visit to the farm stall, where you can buy home-made delicacies such as prickly pear syrup, canned fruit, pickles and jams.

From Namibgrens continue for 9 km along the D1275 to the summit of **Spreetshoogte Pass**. The views from here are among the most spectacular in Namibia and it is a compulsory stop for photographers. A picnic spot, shaded for part of the day by a lone shepherd tree, is reached a short way below the summit.

With a gradient of 1:4 to 1:6, Spreetshoogte is Namibia's steepest pass and drops several hundred metres in less than 5 km. It is best travelled from east to west and is not suitable for caravans.

About 38 km from the summit, the D1275 joins the C14 to Solitaire. Turn left and continue for 9 km to Solitaire, where you can join route 18 to Sesriem and Sossusvlei. Alternatively, you can turn right and continue to Walvis Bay and Swakopmund.

Remhoogte Pass offers an alternative descent of the escarpment when travelling from Windhoek to Solitaire and Sesriem.

From Windhoek, follow the directions for route 4 to Nauchas farm. At Nauchas, ignore the turnoff to the right, continuing straight ahead on the D1261. The turnoff to **Swartfontein Guest Farm** is signposted 4 km south of Nauchas. Double rooms with *en suite* facilities are available in an old farmhouse. Activities include sunrise and sunset drives to the Spreetshoogte Pass and game drives. The road winds across the Remhoogte mountains and then descends into the valley carved by the Noab River, before joining the C14 about 73 km beyond Nauchas.

On joining the C14, you can either turn left, continuing to Büllsport and Naukluft, or you can take the D1273 short cut, which links up with Main Road 36 to Sesriem and Sossusvlei (see route 18).

 Situated on the plains to the northwest of the Naukluft mountains, **Ababis Guest Farm**, near the junction of the D1261 with the C14, offers guests a family atmosphere. Activities include farm trips, tours to Naukluft, Sesriem, Sossusvlei and flights over the dunes.

 # ROUTE 5
WINDHOEK TO NAUKLUFT AND SESRIEM VIA BÜLLSPORT

DISTANCE: 445 km **TIME**: 5 hours **ROAD CONDITIONS**: 90 km tar; remainder gravel, usually good, but can be corrugated **FUEL**: Windhoek, Rietoog, Büllsport, Sesriem **LINKING ROUTES**: Route 19

This route provides the most direct access from Windhoek (see p 53) to the Naukluft section of the Namib-Naukluft Park (see p 186). From Naukluft you can continue to Sesriem and Sossusvlei.

From Windhoek, take the B1 south to Rehoboth (see route 20) and turn right onto Main Road 47, which is followed past Klein Aub to the settlement of Rietoog. Just outside Rietoog, turn right onto the D1206 and follow it for 28 km to Büllsport.

 Büllsport Guest Farm, at the junction of the D1206 with the C14, is an ideal base for visits to the Naukluft mountains.

In addition to farm trips, tours are also offered to Duwisib Castle, Sesriem, Sossusvlei and the Zaris mountains. The farm has its own walking trails and four-wheel drive routes. Also of interest is an enormous rock arch, the Naukluft Bogenfels or Stone Window. Amenities include a swimming pool, farm shop and filling station.

From **Büllsport** take the C14 toward Maltahöhe for about 1 km to the turnoff onto the D854. Turn right here and continue for 10 km to the signposted turnoff to the Naukluft section (see p 188) of the Namib-Naukluft Park. The park office and camp site are reached 12 km beyond the turnoff.

Continuing further along the D854, the D850 turnoff to **Zebra River Lodge** is reached 32 km on. Travel for 19 km on the D850 to the signposted turnoff to the lodge, which is another 5 km on. Nestling in the scenic Tsaris mountains, the lodge is situated on a 13 000 ha farm among rugged mountain scenery.

The mountains, plateaus and plains are dissected by three spectacular canyons with springs. The farm is a paradise for nature lovers and outdoor enthusiasts. Among the activities are guided and unguided hikes, swimming in natural pools and farm tours in a 4x4 vehicle. Trips to Naukluft and Sossusvlei can also be arranged.

The lodge has earned a reputation for personalised service and excellent cuisine. Accommodation is in double rooms, or in a self-catering cottage, 3,5 km from the lodge.

Continuing along the D854, Main Road 36 is reached 34 km past the D850 turnoff. Turn right here and a few kilometres on you will pass the turnoff to the **Sossusvlei Wilderness Camp** on the farm Witwater. Guests are transferred from the covered parking area to the camp a further 6 km away.

Nestling among granite outcrops, the camp offers guests a unique desert experience, with expansive views over the gravel plains extending westward. Each of the nine chalets has been individually designed to fit in with its setting. Boulders were incorporated into the walls and a combination of brick, timber and thatch gives the chalets an earthy feel. To enable guests to enjoy unimpeded views from their chalets, the bedrooms and lounge have large foldaway sliding doors. Each chalet also has a deck with a private plunge pool. A walkway of timber and rock leads to the central lodge area, comprising a large deck, dining room, lounge, bar and curio shop.

Activities include guided trips to Sossusvlei, inclusive of a guided walk and a three-course breakfast. At the lodge guests can go on walks to explore the granite outcrops, and take guided and sundowner drives. After sunset, guests can view the night sky through a telescope from the stargazing circle. One of the main attractions, however, is a hot-air balloon flight, which offers a bird's-eye view of the desert. Of geological interest on the farm is the Hebron Fault, which occurred a few million years ago when calcified gravel deposits were displaced by earth movements.

From the turnoff to the camp, continue for 22 km along Main Road 36 and then turn left onto the D826 to Sesriem (see p 193) which is reached 12 km on.

ROUTE 6
WINDHOEK TO GOBABIS, THE TRANS-KALAHARI HIGHWAY AND BUITEPOS

DISTANCE: 315 km **TIME**: 3 hours **ROAD CONDITIONS**: Tar, except detours off B6 **FUEL**: Windhoek, Dordabis, Witvlei, Gobabis, Buitepos

The B6 from Windhoek (see p 53) to Gobabis initially takes you through rolling highlands, which eventually give way to scenic camel thorn savanna further east – ideal countryside for cattle farming.

About 15 km east of the city, the turnoff to **Heija Lodge** is signposted. The farm has been stocked with a variety of antelope and activities include game drives and horse riding. Amenities include a thatched restaurant overlooking a large dam. Accommodation is in rooms (some self-catering).

A road sign, 13 km further on along the B6, indicates the turnoff to **Dordabis**, 63 km along the C23. The settlement can justifiably be called the centre of Namibia's karakul weaving industry and those interested in finding out more about the industry will find a detour worthwhile.

The farm **Ibenstein** is 3 km south of Dordabis along the C15. Here karakul carpets and wall-hangings are woven by hand under the supervision of Berenike and Frank Gebhardt.

Open Monday to Friday 08:00 to 12:30 and 14:00 to 18:00 (September to April) and 06:30 to 11:30 and 13:00 to 17:00 (May to August). Weekends by prior arrangement. Tel (062) 56-0047.

To reach the farm **Kiripotib**, continue on the C15 to the turnoff onto the D1448, which is followed to the signposted turnoff. Visitors are welcome here, too, but should make prior arrangements by calling the owner, tel (062) 57-3319.

Continuing eastward of the Dordabis turnoff along the B6, **Hosea Kutako International Airport**, formerly Windhoek International Airport, is reached about 42 km out of the capital (see p 78 for a brief historical outline of Hosea Kutako). The airport was commissioned on 1 October 1965 after it was realised that the airport close to the city centre (Eros) would be unable to meet the requirements of jet aircraft. With mountains and hills surrounding Windhoek, the farm Ondekaremba was considered the most suitable site.

About 4 km east of the airport, you reach the turnoff onto Main Road 51, which is followed for 61 km to the junction with the D1472. Turn left and continue for 500 m to Farm Pepperkorrel, where the well-known **Dorka Teppiche** is located. Karakul carpets and wall-hangings have been woven here for over a decade, under the watchful eye of Volker Berner, a qualified textile designer who trained in Germany. His wife Dorte is renowned for her stone sculptures, which have been bought by several galleries, including the National Gallery in Cape Town, as well as for private collections. Tel (062) 57-3581.

To reach **Arnhem Cave** (see p 72) turn onto Main Road 51, signposted about 4 km beyond the Hosea Kutako International Airport. After 66 km turn left onto the D1506 and travel for 11 km to a T-junction where you turn right onto the D1808. The turnoff to the caves is signposted 4 km along this road.

Beyond the turnoff onto Main Road 51, the B6 heads east, passing through the farming settlement of Witvlei to **Gobabis**, 205 km east of Windhoek. The town is the centre of one of the country's most important cattle ranching areas; evidence of this is the statue of a bull as one enters Gobabis.

It is popularly accepted that the name Gobabis means "place of the elephants", but it has also been suggested that it is a Khoekhoen name meaning "place of arguing or discussing". The town developed around a mission station established in 1856 by the Rhenish missionary Eggers. In 1865 he was driven out of the mission station when he tried to establish peace between the Khauas Khoikhoi and the Damara. Missionary work was resumed only in 1876, but the missionaries were later forced to abandon their work when hostilities broke out between the Khauas Khoikhoi and the Herero. A military unit under the command of Lieutenant Lampe occupied Gobabis in March 1895 and in May the following year a rebellion by the Herero and the Khauas Khoikhoi was put down. Shortly afterward work on a fort commenced and the building was completed in 1897. Unfortunately, it was later demolished. The **Lazarette**, or old hospital, is the only building in the town dating back to this era.

Harnas Lion, Leopard and Cheetah Farm is reached by turning off the B6 onto the C22, about 3 km east of Gobabis. Continue along the C22 to Drimiopsis and then take the D1667 to the signposted turnoff to Harnas. Tel (062) 56-8020.

The farm has served as a sanctuary for orphaned and neglected wild animals since 1982, when Nick and Mariet van der Merwe took in the first animal. The number of animals in need of care has grown steadily and the farm is now home to more than 200 animals. In addition to tame lions, guests can also view leopard, cheetah, hyaena, wild dog, a variety of antelope, warthog, caracal and baboon in enclosures. Plans are afoot to enlarge the camps to provide a more natural habitat for the animals.

In addition to viewing the animals, there are also opportunities to watch them being fed. Other activities include game-viewing drives, walks, horse riding and donkey cart rides for children.

Accommodation is available in wooden bungalows, sleeping three. There is also a camp site with braai facilities, a swimming pool and children's playground.

The Trans-Kalahari Highway strikes 115 km eastward from Gobabis to Buitepos, the Namibian border post with Botswana. The road passes through scenic surroundings characterised by camel thorn trees, interspersed by stands of silver cluster-leaf, as it descends gradually to Buitepos. Travellers continuing to South Africa are advised to fill up here, or at Charles Hill, 10 km further on, as the next fuel stop is 387 km away, 5 km before reaching Kang.

From Buitepos it is about 1 100 km to Johannesburg.

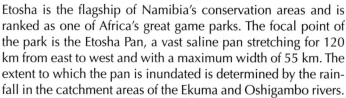

8

NORTHERN NAMIBIA

North of Okahandja the landscape alternates between plains, hills and low mountains, while the highland savanna gives way to thornbush savanna, mopane savanna in the west and mountain savanna in the Otavi-Tsumeb-Grootfontein triangle. The savannas are ideally suited to cattle ranching, while the Otavi-Tsumeb-Grootfontein triangle is an important maize-producing area. The four northern regions, formerly known as Owamboland, are home to about 45 per cent of Namibia's population.

Etosha National Park

Etosha is the flagship of Namibia's conservation areas and is ranked as one of Africa's great game parks. The focal point of the park is the Etosha Pan, a vast saline pan stretching for 120 km from east to west and with a maximum width of 55 km. The extent to which the pan is inundated is determined by the rainfall in the catchment areas of the Ekuma and Oshigambo rivers.

The animals are typical of the southern savanna plains of Africa and the most abundant large mammal is the springbok. Other commonly seen species are Burchell's zebra, gemsbok, kudu, blue wildebeest, giraffe and elephant. Red hartebeest and eland are seen less frequently.

Etosha is a sanctuary for the largest population of black rhino in the world. They occur mainly in the west, although there is always a good chance of spotting them at the Okaukuejo waterhole and in the Halali area. A small group of white rhino were reintroduced into the park in 1995; the species became locally extinct during the early 1900s.

An interesting antelope to keep an eye out for is the black-faced impala, a species endemic to northwestern Namibia and southwestern Angola. It is a subspecies of the impala, from which it can easily be distinguished by its purplish-black facial blaze, and dull brown body, also with a purplish-black sheen. About half the population lives in the Namutoni area, while smaller numbers occur around Halali and Ombika.

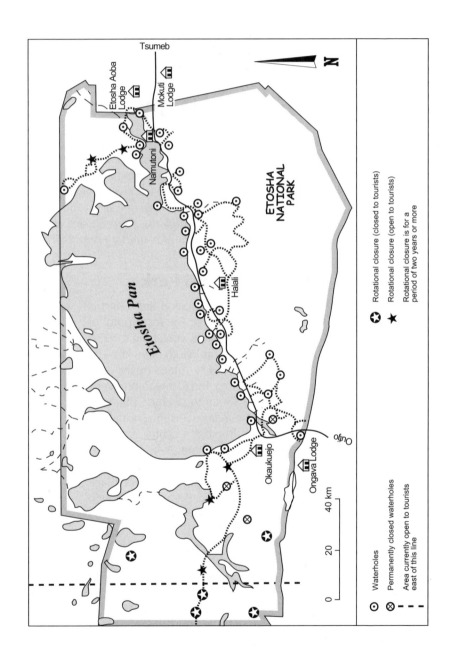

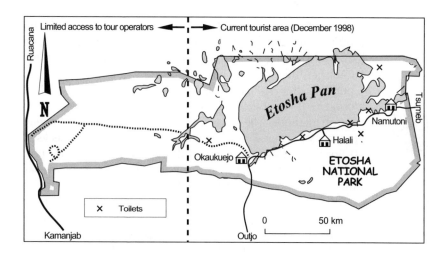

A small antelope that attracts considerable attention is the Damara dik-dik, which favours dense woodland and can usually be seen in the Bloubokdraai area south of Namutoni. It occurs in central and northern Namibia, as well as southern Angola, and reappears in East Africa after a 2 000 km break in its distribution.

Research on the drinking times of Etosha's animals has shown that blue wildebeest and springbok are daylight drinkers, while red hartebeest, kudu and eland are morning drinkers. Zebra, gemsbok and warthog drink predominantly in the afternoon, with black rhino, elephant, lion and jackal favouring the hours between 18:00 and midnight. About two-thirds of hyaenas were observed drinking between midnight and 06:00. Giraffe had no clear preferences.

The best time for game viewing is the dry season from May to October, when the animals congregate around the waterholes. Following the first summer rains, however, large herds of blue wildebeest, Burchell's zebra and springbok gather on the plains north and west of Okaukuejo. They remain there until about April, when diminishing ground water and grazing force them to migrate to the waterholes near Okaukuejo, before they move east onto the Gemsbokvlakte plains. The cycle is completed when the animals return to the plains north and west of Okaukuejo a few days after the first heavy rains of the following rainy season.

Etosha's elephant population fluctuates between 1 000 and 2 000 animals, as large numbers migrate to Kavango and the Kaokoveld during the wet season. As the surface water there diminishes, they migrate back to the park.

During the 1970s the park's lion population stood at around 500, necessitating either culling or practising birth control methods. The latter option was taken and synthetic pregnancy hormone capsules were implanted into the necks of 10 lionesses. Research showed that ovulation could be prevented for up to five years, but once the contraceptive was exhausted the lionesses returned to fertility.

Between 1981 and 1985 the population decreased from 500 to 250, mainly as a result of animals being shot when they strayed onto farms to the south of the park. In 1997 the numbers stood at 180 and it has been estimated that about 700 lions have been shot during the preceding 10 years.

To date, close to 400 bird species have been recorded in the park, which is one of only two breeding areas in southern Africa of greater and lesser flamingos. (See chapter 2 for bird-watching in other areas.) Breeding, however, only takes place when a sufficiently large area of the pan has been inundated, but when conditions are right, up to a million flamingos congregate on the pan. In June 1969 the pan dried up before the young flamingos were able to fly, forcing the adult birds to abandon their chicks. In the ensuing rescue operation 20 000 chicks were caught by hand and released at Fischer's Pan near Namutoni.

Two years later the pan once again dried up prematurely and an estimated 30 000 young birds marched 30 km to the nearest water at Poacher's Point. The marching chicks were fed by the adults, flying to and from the water. In August the chicks started on the second leg of their trek to the last remaining water in the Ekuma Delta. During the early stages of their march, the adult birds feeding them made a round trip of 100 km. By the end of August the majority of the 100 000 chicks hatched between May and August had reached the safety of the water in the Ekuma River. Flamingo rescue operations were also launched in 1989 and 1994.

Fischer's Pan offers good possibilities for waterbirds when the pan is flooded by the Omuramba Owambo. Up to 12 duck species are attracted to the pan, and marabou and yellow-billed storks, both species of flamingo and a variety of waders can be ticked here. Other interesting species to look out for include crowned crane, which are attracted to the tall grassveld of the Andoni Plains, and the black-faced babbler, a species occurring in the woodlands south of Namutoni. In the Halali area there is a possibility of ticking bare-cheeked babbler, Carp's black tit and violet wood hoopoe.

To date some 35 raptor species, including six types of vulture, have been recorded, among them white-backed and white-headed vultures, martial eagle, bateleur, steppe eagle, red-necked falcon and pygmy falcon.

Those interested in birdwatching will find *Birds of the Etosha National Park* a useful guide. In addition to colour photographs and details of the identification features, distribution, status and habitats of species likely to be seen, the guide contains a checklist and information on the park's five bird habitats. It is obtainable from shops in the rest camps.

The vegetation of the savanna surrounding the pan is dominated by mopane, which constitute about 90 per cent of the trees. Over much of the park the mopane grows as a shrub or small tree, but in the Halali area tall mopane woodlands occur. Conspicuous among the stands of mopane is the red bushwillow, or koedoebos.

South of Namutoni dense woodlands are dominated by tamboti and cluster-leaf trees, with the sandveld to the north of Namutoni characterised by Kalahari apple-leaf, purple-pod terminalia and the hairy lavender fever-berry.

A species that arouses the curiosity of many visitors is the moringa or phantom tree. It usually grows on rocky outcrops, but about 30 km west of Okaukuejo several hundred occur unexpectedly on the plains. Commonly referred to as the **Moringa**, or **Phantom Forest**, this is one of Etosha's major attractions and the weirdly shaped trees are a favourite subject for photographers. These squat trees owe their contorted shapes to the fact that their tender branches are browsed by elephant, giraffe and gemsbok.

The first recorded descriptions of Etosha were by the explorers Francis Galton and Charles Andersson, who camped near the Namutoni waterhole in 1851. Andersson described the pan as "covered with saline incrustations, and having wooded and well-defined borders. The surface consisted of a soft, greenish-yellow, clay soil, strewed with fragments of small sand-stone, of a purple tint."

The abundance of game attracted hunters and traders and in 1892 hunting regulations were promulgated to protect the animals. Following the 1896-97 rinderpest epidemic, large numbers of game were exterminated and veterinary control posts were established at Namutoni, Rietfontein and Okaukuejo to prevent stock movement. These were later converted to police posts.

On 28 January 1904 the fort at Namutoni was attacked by 500 Ndonga warriors. The garrison of four soldiers, later joined by three ex-servicemen, successfully held back the attack until late afternoon, when the attackers retreated. Under cover of darkness the soldiers and ex-servicemen escaped and the following day the fort was razed to the ground by the Ndonga.

Following the 1904 Herero Uprising it was decided to rebuild Fort Namutoni and an asymmetrical quadrangle, measuring about 60 m by 68 m, with a watchtower at the northeastern corner, was erected. The fort, however, lost its usefulness after the proclamation of Game Reserve 2 in 1907 and became dilapidated. In 1910 five police officers were stationed at the fort, but two years later it was closed. Toward the end of World War I, 190 German officers and troops surrendered at Fort Namutoni without a single shot being fired. In the years following, the condition of the fort deteriorated further but in 1951 funds were made available for its restoration. The restored fort was officially opened in 1958 to provide tourist accommodation.

Originally known as Game Reserve 2, Etosha was proclaimed in 1907 together with Game Reserves 1 and 3. The 93 240 km² conservation area comprised the Etosha Pan and the Kaokoland from the Kunene River in the north to the Hoarusib River in the south. In 1947 the Kaokoland portion of the reserve was demarcated for occupation by the Herero, while 3 406 km² of the Etosha portion was divided into farms.

In 1956, the size of the park was almost doubled to 99 526 km² on the recommendation of the Elephant Commission. The park was extended westward by incorporating state land between the Hoanib and Ugab rivers in exchange for the deproclamation of Game Reserve 1, northeast of Grootfontein.

The recommendations of the Odendaal Commission of 1962 resulted in a drastic reduction in the size of the park to 22 270 km², without any consideration of ecological boundaries or game migration routes. Three farms in the Otjovasandu area were, however, added to the much-reduced park, while the bergveld in the west and the sandveld north of Namutoni, originally earmarked for deproclamation, were fortunately retained.

The Etosha National Park has three rest camps. **Namutoni**, near the eastern entrance gate, **Halali** in the centre and **Okaukuejo** near the southern entrance gate. Accommodation at the rest camps ranges from rooms in the historic Fort Namutoni and de luxe rooms to bungalows and camp sites. Floodlit waterholes are situated on the perimeter of all three camps. Amenities at Namutoni and Halali include a restaurant, shop, kiosk, swimming pool and filling station. The main complex of Okaukuejo rest camp, comprising the restaurant, shop and kiosk, burned down in October 1997, and was re-opened at the beginning of 1999.

Hoba Meteorite

With a mass of 60 tonnes, the Hoba meteorite west of Grootfontein is the largest in the world and its cuboid shape makes it unique among meteorites. Its upper surface measures 295 cm by 295 cm, while its thickness varies from 75 cm to 122 cm. The meteorite consists of 82,4 per cent iron, 16,4 per cent nickel and 0,76 per cent cobalt, and with its relatively high nickel content is referred to as a nickel-rich ataxite.

It has been suggested that the meteorite broke up into several fragments before it collided with the earth about 80 000 years ago. Although much of the meteorite is below natural ground level, there is no evidence that a crater was formed on impact. Research has shown that the meteorite was subsequently covered by a layer of calcrete that was later eroded.

The meteorite first came to the attention of Europeans in 1920, when a farmer who was hunting in the area, Jacobus Brits, stumbled on it. The following year, the general manager of the South West Africa Company sent a letter and a photograph to the company's headquarters in London. In the letter he stated that the weight of the nickel was estimated at about 10 kg and that it was his intention to extract the metal by using a saw and an oxygen-acetylene torch.

The idea was fortunately abandoned, but over the years the meteorite has suffered periodically at the hands of vandals. In the mid-1980s Rössing Uranium Limited donated funds for an information wall, toilet facilities and a house for a full-time caretaker. The area surrounding the meteorite was also made more attractive and picnic sites with fireplaces were provided.

Lake Otjikoto

Lake Otjikoto, northwest of Tsumeb, is a well-known attraction *en route* to the Etosha National Park. It is a Herero name, translated as "deep hole" and is said to mean "the place which is too deep for cattle to drink water".

The first whites to see this natural phenomenon, Charles Andersson and Francis Galton, camped on the edge of Otjikoto in May 1851. Andersson described the lake as follows: "Otjikoto, one of the most wonderful of Nature's freaks, is situated at the northern extremity of those broken hills which take their rise in the neighbourhood of Okamabuti, and in the midst of a dense coppice. So effectually is it hidden from view, that a person might pass within fifty paces of it without being aware of its existence. Owing to its steep and rugged sides, cattle have no access to the water; and even a man can only approach this enormous well by means of a steep and slippery footpath."

Situated in an area of porous dolomite, the lake was formed when water seeped into fractures of the dolomite, dissolving it to form a large underground cavern. The cavern could not support the overlying roof of shales, which eventually collapsed to form an elliptical sinkhole of some 100 m by 150 m. During subsequent weathering, the shales were eroded away. The depth of the turquoise-coloured water fluctuates with the water table, but is generally taken to be 55 m.

The lake is home to Otjikoto tilapia, which can often be seen near the surface, close to the near-vertical cliffs of the sinkhole. This fish is classified as endangered; among the threats facing it are the larger Mozambique tilapia, introduced into the lake in 1980, and the extraction of water.

The Otjikoto tilapia is naturally endemic to the nearby Lake Guinas, from where it was introduced in the 1940s. With a length of up to 14 cm, this cichlid occurs in a variety of colours, ranging from olive green with dark stripes and black to combinations of yellow, blue, white, grey and black. These bright colours are thought to have developed because of the initial absence of predators, making camouflage unnecessary.

Owing to the depth of the lake, the Otjikoto tilapia cannot build their nests on the lake floor and have adapted their breeding habits by building nests on narrow shelves on the walls of the sinkhole. Nesting sites are vigorously defended by both parents.

Otjikoto is also of historical interest. In 1915 the retreating German force under Günther Wallbaum dumped weapons and ammunition into the lake to prevent them from falling into the hands of the South African Union Force.

Rumour had it that the Germans dumped between 300 and 400 wagon loads of ammunition, as well as 24 cannons, into the lake and in 1916 a salvage team was sent there to recover the weaponry. Five cannons, 10 gun carriages and three machine guns, as well as 85 725 Mauser and 4 684 cannon rounds, were brought to the surface. In 1970 a salvage operation was carried out and a Krupp ammunition wagon was uncovered in almost perfect condition, and can be seen in the Alte Feste Museum in Windhoek today.

Since 1977 several other weapons have been recovered, among them a Sandfontein cannon captured by the Germans from the Union Forces during a battle at Sandfontein in 1914. These armaments were restored with great care and can be seen in the Khorab Room at the Tsumeb Museum. Many more pieces are being conserved in their watery grave in an underwater museum.

Otjihaenamaparero Fossil Tracks

Several dinosaur tracks can be seen on the farm Otjihaenamaparero, southeast of Kalkfeld; the most striking are those of a three-toed dinosaur which left tracks over a distance of 25 m. The dinosaur probably resembled a kangaroo in build, with powerful hind legs and comparatively short forelimbs. Unlike the kangaroo, however, these reptiles did not leap, but ran like an ostrich, which possibly explains why there is no tail drag along the tracks.

The impressions were made between 150 and 180 million years ago when these prehistoric animals roamed across wet sand on the edge of an inland sea. The prints were preserved when the mud dried to form the Etjo Sandstone Formation, which in turn was covered by a layer of sediments that was less resistant to erosion than the mud below it. During subsequent weathering of this layer the track was exposed and eventually only the impressions remained.

Trails led by a San guide are conducted (tailored to suit the group), and overnight visitors can undertake horseback trips. Birding can be rewarding, with over 300 species recorded to date. Lunches are offered, but prior arrangements are necessary. Open throughout the year. Tel (067) 29-0153.

Waterberg Plateau Park

The Waterberg Plateau, west of Otjiwarongo, rises about 200 m above the surrounding plains and reaches its highest elevations in the west and the south. The plateau is an eroded relic of sedimentary sandstone deposited some 200 million years ago and is characterised by an undulating landscape of deep sand and sandstone rocks eroded into fascinating shapes. Several fountains surface at the base of the perpendicular cliffs; a feature that gave rise to the Afrikaans name, Waterberg.

The park was established to breed rare and endangered species, among them sable, roan, tsessebe and white rhino. It is also home to black rhino and the only population of foot-and-mouth disease free buffalo in Namibia. Other species to be seen here include eland, impala, giraffe, kudu, red hartebeest and blue wildebeest. Among the smaller animals are klipspringer, common duiker, Damara dik-dik, steenbok and lesser bushbaby.

Noteworthy among the park's more than 200 bird species are several Namibian "specials", among them Hartlaub's francolin, Rüppell's parrot, Bradfield's swift, Monteiro's hornbill, Carp's black tit, short-toed rock thrush and rockrunner.

Also of interest is the Cape vulture colony on the Okarakuwisa Cliffs – the only breeding colony of this species in Namibia. In the 1950s the colony numbered about 500 birds, but as a result of the indiscriminate use of poison by farmers and bush encroachment their numbers declined to less than 20 by 1980.

The vegetation on the plateau is a mosaic of tree and shrub savanna. The dominant trees, with an average height of 10 m, are wild seringa, silver cluster-leaf, Kalahari apple-leaf and several bushwillow species. The fountains support a lush vegetation dominated by the common cluster fig, weeping wattle, karree and several fern species.

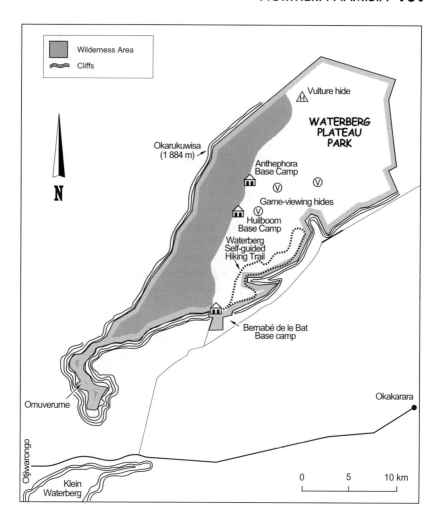

A Rhenish mission station was established at the Waterberg in 1873, but was destroyed seven years later during a clash between Damara and Herero forces and was only rebuilt in 1891. The ruins can be seen on the **Mission Walk** in the Bernabé de la Bat rest camp.

During the Herero Uprising of 1904 the deciding battle between the German colonial forces and the Herero took place at Waterberg. Reminders of this conflict can be seen in the **cemetery** near the resort office. The battle is still commemorated every year on the weekend either before or after

11 August by the Alte Kameraden, MOTHS, Pfadfinder, Boy Scouts and the Herero.

Private vehicles are not allowed on the plateau, but **guided tours** in open safari vehicles are conducted from the rest camp. Bookings must be made at camp reception. The tours usually include a stop at one of the hides overlooking the waterholes on the plateau, but the chances of seeing game are variable. Remember to take warm clothing along as it can get rather cold and windy on the back of an open vehicle.

A network of **nature walks** crisscross the Bernabé de la Bat rest camp, linking the chalets to other amenities and historical sites. Not to be missed is a late afternoon walk to **Mountain View**, a viewpoint on top of the plateau with magnificent vistas of the rest camp and the plains below.

Those seeking the excitement of tracking game on foot should consider joining a **guided wilderness trail**. The trails are conducted by an armed ranger in the park's 18 000 ha wilderness area. Although game viewing forms an integral part of the trail, the emphasis is on providing trailists with a total wilderness experience. Trails are conducted from April to November, starting at 14:00 on Thursdays and ending early on Sunday mornings. Namibia Wildlife Resorts, Private Bag 13267, Windhoek, tel (061) 23-6975 or 23-3845, fax 22-4900.

There is also a **50 km self-guided trail** which is hiked over four days. Because there is a possibility of encountering potentially dangerous animals, such as rhino and solitary buffalo, this trail should only be hiked by bushwise trailists. Except for the first day's ascent to the plateau, the terrain provides easy hiking, leaving ample time for birding and identifying some of the trees. Hikers are accommodated in overnight shelters without any facilities and must provide their own equipment and food. Namibia Wildlife Resorts, Private Bag 13267, Windhoek, tel (061) 23-6975 or 23-3845, fax 22-4900.

The park is open throughout the year. Overnight visitors may enter the camp up to 21:00, but day visitors must make prior arrangements (tel (067) 30-5001) and must leave the camp before 18:00.

Accommodation in the park's **Bernabé de la Bat rest camp** ranges from three- and four-bed bungalows to two-bed de luxe rooms and camp sites with communal ablutions. Amenities include a restaurant, shop, kiosk, filling station and swimming pool.

ROUTE 7

OKAHANDJA TO ETOSHA NATIONAL PARK VIA TSUMEB

DISTANCE: 565 km **TIME**: 6 hours **ROAD CONDITIONS**: Tar, except some deviations from the B1 **FUEL**: Okahandja, Otjiwarongo, Otavi, Grootfontein, Tsumeb, Etosha National Park **LINKING ROUTES**: Routes 8, 9, 10, 14, 15

This route starts at Okahandja (see route 1), 70 km north of Windhoek. On leaving Okahandja along the B1, you pass the turnoff to the **Okakango Wildlife Garden** and the **Ombo Ostrich Farm** (see route 1, p 79).

About 50 km north of Okahandja, the **Omatako mountains** come into view. Although the twin *inselberge*, or island mountains, resemble a woman's breasts, a woman's buttocks are far more important to Herero men and the name, Omatako, is translated as buttocks.

Rising 700 to 800 m above the surrounding plains, the northwestern peak has a height of 2 286 m. The peaks are capped by dolerite which intruded the sedimentary formations some 180 million years ago.

About 62 km south of Otjiwarongo is the signposted turnoff to one of Namibia's best-known and oldest lodges, **Mount Etjo Safari Lodge**. To reach the lodge, turn left onto the gravel-surfaced D2483 and continue for about 42 km to the lodge.

Named after the flat-topped Mount Etjo which dominates the scenery, the lodge lies within the Okonjati Wildlife Reserve, established in 1975 by world-renowned conservationist Jan Oelofse. Among the game to be seen are elephant, both species of rhino, giraffe and a variety of antelope, including sable, roan, kudu, gemsbok, blue wildebeest and red hartebeest. Predators include cheetah, leopard and lion. The lion are kept in an enclosure and for many visitors a highlight of their visit is watching, from the safety of a hide, the big cats being fed at close quarters. A pair of hippo inhabit the dam alongside the main lodge.

Mount Etjo is of historical significance and made world headlines when the **Mount Etjo Declaration** was signed in April 1989. Following fierce clashes between Swapo fighters and the South African military on the implementation date of

United Nations Resolution 435, representatives of Angola, Cuba and South Africa met there to get Namibia's independence process back on track.

Activities at Mount Etjo include morning and afternoon game viewing from an open safari vehicle and walks accompanied by experienced guides. Birdwatching can also be rewarding.

Accommodation at the main lodge is in luxury air-conditioned rooms with *en suite* facilities. The rooms face onto a well-kept garden and a waterhole, which is home to a pair of hippo. There is also a swimming pool, restaurant and bar.

Situated about 5 km from the lodge, the **Black Rhino bush camp** comprises eight rustic huts with *en suite* showers and a dining area. The camp is about a minute's walk from a waterhole overlooked by a game-viewing hide. Guests can also join game-viewing drives and other activities.

Continuing north along the B1, the turnoff to **Okonjima Guest Lodge** is signposted about 48 km south of Otjiwarongo. Turn left onto the D2515 and continue for about 25 km along a gravel road to the lodge.

Okonjima is a small family-run lodge, offering a variety of activities catering for every possible interest. Renowned for its hospitality, this is undoubtedly the best place in Namibia to get really close up views of cheetah and leopard.

Dominating the scenery are the Omboroko mountains, a relic of the Etjo sandstone formation that once covered large parts of northern Namibia. The mountains in the area are home to troops of chacma baboon and the name Okonjima appropriately means "place of the baboon" in the Herero language.

Among the more than 300 bird species identified to date are several Namibian endemics, including Hartlaub's francolin, Monteiro's hornbill, rockrunner and white-tailed shrike. A rewarding few hours can be spent in a hide overlooking a small artificial pond.

The lodge is well known for its leopard and cheetah that can be seen during the wild cat feeds that take place every evening. These animals are part of the projects of the **Africat Foundation**, a non-profit organisation dedicated to conserving Namibia's threatened cats, especially cheetah and leopard. The feeds are accompanied by an informative talk on the animals' habits and the work of Africat. Visitors keen to see both feeds must book a two-night stay.

In addition to the wild cats, guests can also meet at tea-time Cinga, Caesar and Chui, three tame cheetah, when they roam about the garden under supervision. Various other orphaned animals, such as caracal and warthog, also roam about, and are free to come and go as they please.

Another exciting activity is viewing nocturnal animals such as porcupine, caracal and badgers from a hide. Okonjima also offers sundowner walks and two guided walks; one focusing on the lifestyle of the San and the other on the indigenous people of Namibia.

Accommodation is offered in 10 rooms with *en suite* facilities. There is also a large thatched area where brunch and dinner is served, an outside fireplace and a swimming pool.

The turnoff to the **Waterberg Plateau Park** (see p 108) is signposted 29 km south of Otjiwarongo on the B1. Turn onto the C22 and continue for 41 km before turning left onto the D2512, which is followed for 19 km to the park entrance gate.

At **Otjibamba Lodge**, signposted on the B1, 3 km south of Otjiwarongo, guests are accommodated in comfortable chalets with *en suite* facilities. Among the game to be seen are giraffe, eland, gemsbok, springbok, blue wildebeest and impala. Facilities include a restaurant, lounge, bar, swimming pool and nine-hole golf course.

Otjiwarongo lies 174 km north of Okahandja. The **Tourist Centre** in Bahnhof Street, opposite the Hamburger Hof Hotel, provides information mainly on Namibia's northern region. P O Box 124, Otjiwarongo, tel (067) 30-3658, fax 30-3615. Open Monday to Friday, 08:00 to 13:00 and 14:00 to 17:00.

Originally known as Kanubes to the Herero, Otjiwarongo is said to mean "pretty place" or "place of the fat cattle" – an apt description, as the area is well known for its cattle ranches. A Rhenish mission station was established here in 1891 after an agreement was signed with the Herero chief, Kambazembi. In 1904 a military post was established at Okanjande, a few kilometres south of the present town.

On 2 April 1906 the first train steamed into the newly completed station at Kilometre 378 on the Swakopmund-Tsumeb line, which was built for the export of copper. One of the three **Henschel heavy-duty locomotives** used on the line can be seen in front of the town's railway station. Built in 1912, locomotive number 40 was used on the narrow gauge track until that was replaced by a 1,067 m track in 1960.

Worthwhile visiting is the **Crocodile Ranch**, the first and only one of its kind in the country. Crocodiles are bred here for their much sought-after hides, which are used to make high-quality handbags, and their meat, which is popular in Namibia. The ranch has a breeding population of about 47 crocodiles and breeding takes place from the end of September to mid-November. The eggs are then incubated at 32 °C and hatch after 88 to 90 days. The newly hatched crocodiles are reared in a nursery and are slaughtered when they are between 1,5 and 1,8 m long and their skins are about 30 cm wide. The ranch is open throughout the year and during a guided tour crocodiles of various ages can be viewed. Tel (067) 30-2121. Open Monday to Friday 09:00 to 16:00; Saturday, Sunday and public holidays 10:00 to 13:00.

Known for its efficient and friendly service, the **Hotel Hamburger Hof** in Otjiwarongo offers accommodation in comfortable rooms with *en suite* facilities. Excellent meals can be enjoyed in the restaurant.

Carstensen Bäckerei, on the corner of St George and Tuin streets, is well known for its German confectionery, bread, cakes, light snacks and coffee.

Otjiwarongo lies at the junction of the B1 to Tsumeb and the Namutoni rest camp in Etosha National Park, and the C38 to Outjo and Etosha's Okaukuejo rest camp (route 8). It is also the terminal point of route 9 linking Karibib and Otjiwarongo, which is an ideal connection route with the B1 when travelling to the Etosha National Park from the coast.

From Otjiwarongo, the B1 strikes northeast for 181 km to **Otavi**, where there is a choice of continuing for 63 km directly to Tsumeb, or taking the B8 to Grootfontein. It has been suggested that the Herero named the spring around which the town developed "Otavi", as they linked the sound of the spring with a calf pushing against a cow's udder.

North of the town, alongside the B1, an unobtrusive monument marks **Kilometre 500**, the spot where the capitulation conditions were signed on 9 July 1915 by the Commander of the Union Forces, Gen Louis Botha, the German Governor of South West Africa, Dr Seits, and the Commander of the German forces in South West Africa, Col Victor Franke. Although reference is often made to the Khorab Treaty and the Khorab Memorial, the treaty was signed here, and not some 30 km north at Khorab, where most of the German forces had assembled.

From Otavi, the B8 to Grootfontein traverses a valley between the Kupferberg and the Otavi mountains. The sudden change in the vegetation is obvious, with mountain seringa and phantom trees conspicuous on the rocky slopes.

The road passes Gross Otavi, where Damara miners are known to have smelted copper during the 1800s and possibly even earlier. **Kombat**, formerly known as Asis, is about 40 km beyond Otavi. Copper, lead and silver are mined at the Kombat mine, which was originally operated by the Otavi Minen- und Eisenbahn-Gesellschaft. The mine was reopened in 1960 by Tsumeb Corporation Limited, but was flooded in 1988 when an underground fissure was accidentally breached. Sealing off the area and dewatering the mine took nearly two years and full production was only reached in the middle of 1990.

With its fertile soil, and blessed with an annual rainfall that is about 100 mm higher than the surrounding area, the Otavi-Grootfontein-Tsumeb triangle is the maize basket of Namibia, producing a substantial percentage of the country's maize requirements during favourable years.

The turnoff to the **Hoba meteorite** (see p 105) is signposted 54 km east of Otavi along the B8. Turn left onto the D2860, which is followed for 19 km before you turn onto the D2859. The turnoff to the meteorite is signposted a few kilometres on.

A worthwhile detour from the meteorite can be made to the ostrich farm of the Unkel family, signposted on the D2859. Guided tours are offered and there is a restaurant (try their smoked ostrich platter) and curio shop. P O Box 652, Grootfontein, tel (06738) ask for 8-3130, fax (067) 24-2611.

Grootfontein, at the junction of the B8 to Rundu (see route 14, p 166) and the C42 to Tsumeb (see route 15), is an important centre for the maize and cattle farms of the district. Its streets are lined with lush green trees and the town is especially attractive in September and October, when blue jacarandas and red flamboyants create a blaze of colour.

The town owes its name to a fountain which provided water to game, as well as people, for thousands of years. The early Herero inhabitants knew the area as *Otjivandatjongue* or "hill of the leopard", while the Khoi named it *Geiaus* or "large fountain". The fountain can be seen behind the public swimming pool, in the Tree Park, established toward the end of the 1800s by the South West Africa Company.

In the mid-1880s, Grootfontein became the capital of the Republic of Upingtonia, after a group of Thirstland Trekkers settled here during their epic trek to establish a Calvinistic state. The republic was short-lived, however, and lasted only two years.

Of historical interest is the **old military fort** built in 1896 by the *Schutztruppe*. Between 1900 and 1905 the fort was enlarged several times and after 1915 it was occupied by a military magistrate. The limestone extension was added in 1922, after which the building was used as a boarding school until the late 1960s. The fort subsequently fell into disrepair but was saved from demolition after a public appeal for its restoration was launched in the early 1970s.

The fort was declared a national monument in 1975 and today serves as a museum. Exhibits centre on the early history of the area, including the Republic of Upingtonia. Also exhibited are a camera and typewriter collection and an excellent display of rocks and minerals. Especially worthwhile visiting are realistic reconstructions of a carpenter's workshop and a blacksmith's shop, with machinery that is still in working order. The turnoff to the museum in Eriksson Street is signposted on the B8 on the Rundu side of the town. Open Monday and Friday 16:00 to 18:00; Wednesday 09:00 to 11:00.

Other reminders of the German era are the graves of several *Schutztruppe* in the **cemetery** on the northern outskirts of the town.

A good place for a snack before continuing your journey is **Bäckerei and Café Jakob** in Okavango Street. The fare ranges from mouthwatering German-style confectionery and a variety of breads and cakes to light lunches.

The attractive and neat **Olea rest camp** in Grootfontein has fully-equipped bungalows and shady, grassed camp sites with communal ablutions. The municipal swimming pool and a restaurant are adjacent to the rest camp.

From Grootfontein the C42 winds through spectacular dolomite outcrops and mountain savanna vegetation to reach **Tsumeb**, administrative capital of the Oshikoto Region, after 60 km. The town lies at the centre of one of Namibia's richest mining areas and is one of the most beautiful towns in the country. It is the starting point of route 10 to Ruacana.

For the latest information on tourism in Namibia's northern region, be sure to call at **Etosha I in the Tourism Centre** in

Omeg Alee Street. The centre provides efficient and comprehensive information on tourism in the north of Namibia and also handles reservations, car hire and assists travellers with planning their trips. Open Monday to Friday 08:00 to 18:00; Saturday 08:00 to 13:00. Tel (067) 22-0728, fax 22-0916.

Iron Age smelting sites at Gross Otavi, Otjikoto and Tsumeb provide evidence of the exploitation of copper for hundreds of years by the indigenous people. The town developed around the rich copper deposits and the over 200 minerals (40 of which are specific to Tsumeb) which occur in the area.

A mining concession was granted to the South West Africa Company on 12 September 1892 and in January the following year an expedition visited Tsumeb to inspect the ore body. Commercial exploitation started in 1900 when the Otavi Minen- und Eisenbahn-Gesellschaft was founded. In August that year the company's chief engineer and 33 miners arrived at Tsumeb and on 28 December, 181 bags of copper, weighing nine tons, left for Walvis Bay by ox-wagon.

In May 1903, OMEG signed an agreement with the South West Africa Company to build a railway line to facilitate the export of ore. Work on a railway line between Tsumeb and Swakopmund started in November of that year and was completed on 24 August 1906.

Mining operations were adversely affected by World War I, which nearly brought production to a standstill. Full production was only reached again in 1921, when 85 000 tons of ore were mined, but the depression of the 1930s and World War II also disrupted the operations of the mine.

For many years the De Wet Shaft was the focal point of mining at the town, but by 1997 it had reached the end of its life and was closed. During its life span 25 million tonnes of ore were mined and the mine produced 2,8 million tonnes of lead, 1,8 million tonnes of copper and 900 000 tonnes of zinc. Despite the closure of the mine, Tsumeb's significance as a mining town has not diminished, due to the smelter which produces blister copper and refined lead.

Chief among the town's attractions and well worth visiting is the **Tsumeb Museum**, housed in the old German Private School in Main Street. Built in 1915, the school had hardly opened when it had to be evacuated to serve as a hospital for German troops. Between 1920 and 1950 the building once again served its original purpose.

The museum depicts the history and development of Tsumeb and its surroundings. Especially interesting are the display of German armaments, recovered from Lake Otjikoto, in the Khorab Room and a large collection of rocks and minerals from the Tsumeb area. Open Monday to Friday 09:00 to 12:00 and 15:00 to 18:00 (winter time 09:00 to 12:00 and 14:00 to 17:00); Saturday 09:00 to 12:00. Tel (067) 22-0447.

Several of the town's historic buildings serve as reminders of its mining history. The small but striking **Roman Catholic Church** on the corner of Main and Omeg Alee streets was consecrated in 1914 and named after the patron saint of miners, St Barbara. Particularly eye-catching is the unusual tower above the main entrance.

The **OMEG Minenburo**, in First Street, once dominated all other buildings and its prominent tower is easily mistaken for that of a church. Built in 1907 by Joseph Olbricht, the tower is symbolic of the importance and economic power of the OMEG company at the time.

The **Second Director's Residence**, just below the hospital in Hospital Street, dates back to 1912. Built as a second residence for directors of the OMEG company, it is characterised by turrets used for ventilation.

For visitors planning on staying over in Tsumeb there are a number of options. The **Makalani Hotel** in Fourth Road offers a homely atmosphere. The hotel has a restaurant and a private bar, Pierre's Pub.

The **Minen Hotel** in Tsumeb's Main Street is an owner-managed hotel offering bedrooms with *en suite* facilities and is well known for its excellent garden pub lunches and cuisine.

Punyu Tourist Park, on the southern outskirts of the town, caters for campers and caravanners. There are 21 grassed sites with electricity, braai places and ablutions.

From Tsumeb, the B1 to Etosha goes northwest to reach **Lake Otjikoto** (see p 106) after about 20 km. The turnoff to **Lake Guinas** is reached 7 km beyond Otjikoto. Although scenically more attractive than Otjikoto, this lake is often bypassed because of its distance from the B1. Despite the detour it is well worth a visit. Turn left onto the gravel-surfaced D3043, which is followed for about 19 km before turning onto the D3031. The turnoff to Guinas is signposted 4,6 km on.

Like nearby Otjikoto, Lake Guinas was formed when the roof of an underground cavern, formed when the dolomite rocks were dissolved by water, collapsed. It measures about 120 m in length by 60 m in width, and the depth of the dark, ink-coloured water ranges between 100 m and 130 m. Perched on the edge of the steep cliffs are numerous aloes, which are especially attractive in winter when their masses of flowers create a blaze of colour.

One of the many legends and theories surrounding the origin of these sinkholes claims that Lake Guinas and Lake Otjikoto are linked by an underground tunnel. No evidence for this has however been found, as Otjikoto's water level is about 8 m lower than that of Guinas. In addition it has been observed that the level of one lake rose significantly after rains, while the level of the other lake remained constant.

Guinas was the original home of the Otjikoto tilapia, a species thought to be derived from the banded tilapia (*Tilapia sparmannii*). It has been suggested that the banded tilapias were washed into the lake by flood waters and developed into a new species as a result of their isolation.

The lake is on private farmland and visitors must adhere to entry regulations. A pair of comfortable walking shoes is recommended due to the loose gravel on the pathway leading to the viewpoint.

About 74 km northwest of Tsumeb tùrn left onto the C38 to the Etosha National Park, which is reached 24 km further on. For those seeking accommodation outside the park there are two options. The **Etosha Aoba Lodge** is signposted 10 km east of the Von Lindequist Gate. Adjoining Etosha, the lodge offers accommodation in comfortable thatched cottages surrounded by 7 000 ha of bush. Amenities include a restaurant, thatched recreation area and swimming pool.

Mokuti Lodge, flagship of Namibia Resorts International, is situated on 4 000 ha of bush. It is 200 m from the Von Lindequist entrance to the Etosha National Park, just off the C38. Accommodation is in thatched bungalows, ranging from those with single and double rooms to family and luxury units. Facilities include a restaurant, bar and swimming pool. Guests can explore the reserve by way of nature walks, or join a guided horse trail. There is also a trim track and a reptile park.

From the Von Lindequist Gate at the eastern entrance to the Etosha National Park it is about 12 km on tar to Namutoni rest camp. For a detailed description of the Etosha National Park, see p 99.

ROUTE 8
OTJIWARONGO TO ETOSHA NATIONAL PARK VIA OUTJO

DISTANCE: 190 km **TIME:** 2 hours **ROAD CONDITIONS:** Tar
FUEL: Otjiwarongo, Outjo, Okaukuejo rest camp
LINKING ROUTES: Routes 7, 9, 11, 12

From Otjiwarongo (see route 7) the C38 branches off to the northwest to Outjo. The road traverses thornbush savanna which supports cattle and small stock. The mountain dominating the scenery to the west of the road, Groot Paresis, is volcanic in origin.

Outjo, 73 km northwest of Otjiwarongo along the C38, is the southern gateway to the Etosha National Park and Okaukuejo rest camp. It is also the starting point of route 11 to Sesfontein (see p 140) and route 12 to Epupa Falls and Sesfontein (see p 149).

The town developed around a spring where a trader, Tom Lambert, settled in 1880. In 1895 a German military force was stationed at Outjo and in the following year Hauptmann Ludwig von Estorff had a number of erven surveyed.

Work on the **windmill tower**, next to the Etosha Hotel in Otavi Road, began toward the end of 1900 and it was taken into use on 1 March 1902. The 9,4 m high tower was built from stone and clay. Power to pump water into a cement dam was generated by a wooden windmill mounted on the tower. From the 8 m dam a 620 m long pipeline distributed the water to the barracks, hospital and stables.

The **Naulila Monument**, in the old German cemetery adjacent to the Post Office, was erected in 1933 in memory of the German officials and soldiers murdered by Portuguese soldiers at the fort at Naulila in Angola on 19 October 1914. The monument also commemorates the soldiers who died or went missing during Major Victor Franke's punitive expedition against Naulila two months later.

Also worth a visit in Outjo is **Franke House**, which dates back to around 1899. It was one of the first houses in the town and is also sometimes referred to as the Kliphuis (stone house). It was built on the instructions of Major Von Estorff for the commander of the German troops stationed at Outjo. The historic building now serves as a museum depicting the history of the Outjo district.

The **Hotel Onduri** in Outjo's Etosha Street is perhaps best known for its extensive wine list, which features 125 South African and imported wines. Visitors can relax in the hotel's garden with its green lawns and shady trees. There is a restaurant and bar, and a swimming pool nearby.

The **Etosha Garden Hotel** in Otavi Street is a small hotel surrounded by a lush garden. Facilities include two restaurants, beer garden, swimming pool, shop and snooker table.

From Outjo, the C38 continues north to Okaukuejo, the westernmost of Etosha's three rest camps.

Visitors have a choice of two accommodation establishments outside the park. **Toshari Inn**, 27 km south of Andersson Gate, offers accommodation in comfortable chalets in a setting of natural vegetation. Amenities include a restaurant, boma, bar and swimming pool. P O Box 164, Outjo, tel (06548) 3702.

The turnoff to **Ongava**, one of Namibia's most luxurious lodges, is signposted close to Andersson Gate. From the turnoff it is about 7 km to the lodge. The magnificent thatched central area comprising reception, lounge and dining area is perched on a hill, affording guests far-reaching views. Accommodation is in tastefully furnished thatched bungalows.

Alternatively, visitors can opt for the **Ongava Safari Camp** – a small camp in a secluded section of the reserve. The camp overlooks a floodlit waterhole and guests are accommodated in safari tents with *en suite* facilities. There is also a dining area and bar.

Game roaming the plains of the 35 000 ha private game reserve include white rhino, elephant, giraffe, roan, springbok, Burchell's zebra, gemsbok, lion and leopard. Guided game drives are undertaken to Etosha, and guided walks and night drives are conducted on request at Ongava. Travel Shop, P O Box 6850, Windhoek, tel (061) 22-5178, fax 23-9455.

From the Von Lindequist Gate the C38 continues for 17 km to Okaukuejo rest camp. For a detailed description of the Etosha National Park, see p 99.

ROUTE 9

KARIBIB TO OTJIWARONGO

DISTANCE: 197 km **TIME:** 2 hours **ROAD CONDITIONS:**
Tar, except detours off C33 **FUEL:** Karibib, Otjiwarongo
LINKING ROUTES: Routes 7, 8

The C33, linking Karibib (see route 1) and Otjiwarongo (see
route 7), provides convenient access to Omaruru, which can
alternatively be approached along the gravel C36 from
Wilhelmstal. It is also a convenient connecting route for those
travelling from the coast to the Etosha National Park.

The C33 is joined 2 km east of Karibib and heading toward
Omaruru, the scenery is dominated by the looming hulk of the
Erongo mountains (see p 83).

Omaruru is reached 58 km after turning off the B2 and is
also on the route followed by travellers approaching the
Brandberg (see route 13) from Windhoek via Okahandja and
Wilhelmstal. The Herero name is translated as "bitter thick-
milk" – a reference to milk produced by cows grazing on the
bitterbush (*Pechuelloeschae leubnitziae*). These bushes remain
green long after most other vegetation has become unpalatable
and the meat and milk of animals that feed on them have a
bitter taste.

In 1870 the Swedish traveller and hunter, Axel Eriksson,
made Omaruru the headquarters of his trading ventures. In the
same year a **mission station** was established on the banks of
the Omaruru River and the mission house in Wilhelm Zeraua
Street is the oldest house in the town. Built from raw clay
bricks, it was completed in 1872 for the Rhenish missionary
Gottlieb Viehe, who translated the New Testament, the liturgy,
prayers and catechisms into Herero in the house in 1874. In
the years following the house served as a temporary military
post, and the special envoy of the Cape Government, W C
Palgrave, and Captain Curt von François, held meetings with
local chiefs here.

The municipality has turned the mission house into a museum with photographic displays of the early missionaries, an
antique cooldrink machine and farming implements. Also on
display are household effects, including the table on which

Viehe translated the New Testament into Herero. The keys are obtainable from the municipal offices in Main Street (Monday to Friday, 08:00 to 13:00 and 14:15 to 17:00), or by making prior arrangements, tel (064) 57-0028 during office hours.

Opposite the mission house is a **graveyard** where a number of Germans and Herero Chief Wilhelm Zeraua have been buried. On the weekend preceding 10 October each year, the Herero pay homage to their leader and the colourful procession from the Ozonde residential area to the cemetery is worth seeing if you are in the area. The followers of Chief Zeraua unite under the White Flag and the women taking part in the procession dress in white.

Other reminders of the town's history include the **Franketurm**, or Franke Tower, and the adjacent battlefield. Access is either along Ian Scheepers Road on the southern outskirts of the town, or by turning off Wilhelm Zeraua Street into Hospital Street. The tower was erected in 1908 by residents to honour Captain Victor Franke, who relieved the town from a seige by Herero. While suppressing a Bondelswarts uprising in Gibeon in January 1904, Franke learnt that Okahandja and Omaruru were being besieged. After gaining permission from Governor Leutwein, his company marched north and after 19 days and roughly 900 km, they relieved both towns. The relief of Omaruru proved to be difficult, though, as the German troops were greatly outnumbered. On 4 February 1904 Franke led a cavalry charge, causing the Herero chief, Manasse, and his followers to flee. After this battle, the highest German military honour, the *Pour le Merite*, was bestowed on Franke.

In front of the tower is a cannon used during the battle, in which about 100 Herero and nine Germans were killed. Part of the battlefield, adjacent to the tower, was declared a national monument in 1972. The tower is locked, but a key can be obtained from the nearby Hotel Staebe.

The **Hotel Staebe** on the eastern outskirts of the town has a distinctly German atmosphere and a reputation for friendly and personal attention. Amenities include a swimming pool. The **Omaruru rest camp** on the northern outskirts of the town offers accommodation in five-bed chalets (non self-catering) and camp sites with communal ablutions. There is also a heated swimming pool, restaurant and bar, as well as an arts and crafts centre. With 53 bird species recorded in a 2,6 ha area, it offers excellent opportunities for birding.

There are a number of options if you are looking for a place to have a snack or a meal. In addition to the Hotel Staebe there is **Errol's Pub and Steakhouse**, in the Omaruru rest camp.

Breakfast and à la carte lunches and dinners with gemsbok steak specialities are served; tel (064) 57-0516. The **Omaruru Souvenirs and Kaffeestube**, at the northern end of Wilhelm Zeraua Street, serves breakfasts, light lunches and cakes; tel (064) 57-0230. For freshly baked bread and cakes, try the **Omaruru Dampfbäckerei**, also in Wilhelm Zeraua Street.

Heading north from Omaruru along the C33, the turnoff to the luxurious **Epako Game Lodge** is signposted after about 22 km. Renowned for its personalised service and excellent cuisine, which combines traditional Namibian ingredients and French cooking, it is well worth a stopover. A dining terrace overlooking a nearby waterhole, which is floodlit at night, enables you to watch the passing parade of animals while enjoying your meal. This is also one of the best places in Namibia to get really close-up views of white rhino.

Comprising 11 000 ha of thornbush savanna, undulating hills and mountains, the farm is home to a large variety of game such as white rhino, elephant, leopard, cheetah, giraffe, warthog and Burchell's zebra. Among the 11 antelope species to be seen are eland, gemsbok, kudu, wildebeest, springbok, impala and black-faced impala. To date some 180 bird species have been recorded.

On the afternoon game drive sundowners are enjoyed on a mountain overlooking the surrounding valleys and mountains. The morning game drive includes visits to rock engraving and painting sites. Guests can also undertake guided walks, tailored to suit their interests.

Accommodation is in two-bedroom units with *en suite* bathrooms. Other amenities include a spacious lounge, restaurant, swimming pool and tennis court.

Continuing through thornbush savanna, the turnoff to the village of Kalkfeld is reached about 67 km beyond Omaruru. A worthwhile detour here is to the **dinosaur tracks on the farm Otjihaenamaparero** (see p 107). Take the D2483 from Kalkfeld for 19 km and turn right onto the D2414, continuing for 10 km to the signposted turnoff. A few minutes' walk from the parking area is a sloping rock slab where several fossil tracks can be seen. A camp site with hot water ablutions and flush toilets is available on the farm; tel (067) 29-0153.

Backtrack to the C33 and continue for about 68 km to Otjiwarongo, where you can either link up with route 7 to the Etosha National Park via Otavi, Grootfontein and Tsumeb, or route 8 to the park via Outjo.

ROUTE 10
TSUMEB TO RUACANA

DISTANCE: 475 km **TIME**: 6 hours **ROAD CONDITIONS**: Tar
FUEL: Tsumeb, Ondangwa, Oshakati, Ruacana (unreliable)

From Tsumeb the B1 heads in a northwesterly direction, passing Lake Otjikoto, Lake Guinas and the turnoff to the Etosha National Park (see route 7). About 100 km out of Tsumeb is the veterinary control gate at Oshivelo, the gateway to what was formerly known as Owambo.

Nowadays referred to as the four northern regions (Oshikoto, Oshana, Omusati and Ohangwena) the area is characterised by an exceptionally flat plain that forms part of the Kalahari basin, with altitudes ranging between 1 090 and 1 150 m.

Prior to independence this area was largely inaccessible to tourists, as it was a flashpoint in Swapo's liberation struggle. Although security is no longer a concern, the area is not visited by many tourists, except those using the B1 as an access route to the Kaokoveld via Ruacana.

The four regions are the traditional home of eight cultural groups, the largest being the Kwanyama people who also live in southern Angola. Most of the people are subsistence farmers and the small fields of *mahangu* (pearl millet) and sorghum surrounding the *egumbo*, or traditional homesteads, are a familiar sight. Cattle, goats and pigs are also reared, while donkeys are popular as pack animals. This is the most populated part of Namibia and nearly 40 per cent of the country's inhabitants live here.

There is a well-developed informal sector and the large number of cuca shops, with names like "Cape to Cairo", "Face to Face", "Funky Town Bar" and "Happy Bar Generation", are unlikely to escape your attention. These informal bars and liquor outlets took their name from a brand of Angolan beer which used to be widely sold in the north of the country. There are also roadside markets where fruit, vegetables, clothing and other commodities are sold, as well as open-air butcheries.

There are no major towns between Tsumeb and Ondangwa along the B1. However, be on the lookout for livestock and donkeys crossing the road. A few kilometres east of Ondangwa you cross from the Oshikoto Region into the **Oshana Region**, named after the network of shallow watercourses that criss-cross the area. Locally known as *oshanas*, these seasonal watercourses are filled by *efundjas*, or floods, the extent of which is determined by the rains in the Cuvelai River basin in Angola.

The landscape is characterised by *oshanas*, with scattered marula and fig trees interspersed by clumps of real fan palms. With their straight trunks and fan-shaped leaves, these palms are especially attractive in the late afternoons, when they create a picture not easily forgotten.

As one approaches Ondangwa the traffic and the number of people increase markedly and one tourist aptly dubbed Ondangwa "Anarchy City". Be especially wary of taxis, as their drivers tend to disregard all traffic rules. **Ondangwa** served as the administrative centre of the former Owamboland, before the headquarters was moved to Oshakati. During Namibia's liberation struggle it was an important base for the South African Defence Force. The town's inhabitants of military personnel and government officials lived within the confines of a fortified village.

Also of interest are the early Finnish missionary buildings in the village of **Olukonda**, 10 km southeast of Ondangwa. Follow the D3605 from Ondangwa for 5 km, turn onto the D3606 and continue for another 5 km. Dating back to the early 1870s, **Nakambale House** was built by the Finnish missionary Martti Rautanen, who was also known as Nakambale – a name meaning "the person with the hat". It was the first mission house built in the region and is the oldest major building in northern Namibia. In this house Rautanen translated the Bible into Ndonga, one of the Oshiwambo dialects.

Nakambale Church, the oldest church building in northern Namibia, was built in 1889 by the first Christians of the Olukonda parish and Reverend Rautanen. It was later extended twice, but fell into disrepair after a new church was built in the early 1970s. In 1991 it was restored with funds and technical support from the Finnish government. About 100 000 bundles of hay and 25 km of binding wire were used for the thatch roof.

Also of interest is the adjoining **cemetery**, where Rautanen, members of his family, the Ondonga king Elifas, and prominent parishioners were buried.

The **Nakambale Museum rest camp** offers accommodation in traditional Owambo huts, a historic mission cottage and camping or caravaning sites with ablution facilities. There is also a shop and kiosk on site.

At Ondangwa the B1 goes northward for 60 km to **Oshikango**, where there is a border post providing access into southern Angola. The C46 continues in a northwesterly direction and after about 25 km reaches **Ongwediva**, the educational centre of the north. Dominating the town's buildings is the steep-pitched roof of the Teachers' Training College hall. Among the town's other educational institutions are the Valombola Technical School and the Eluwa Special School for the Disabled.

Of interest in the town is the **Oshana Environment and Art Association's centre**. Art from the northwest region is sold here and among the work on sale (depending on the supply) are traditional handmade clay pots, baskets, woodcarvings, jewellery and paintings. The centre's original building was constructed from beer bottles to encourage the community to recycle waste materials. It can also be worthwhile to pop into the **Oshiko Traditional Shop**.

Oshakati, the administrative capital of the Oshana Region, is reached after a few more kilometres. During Namibia's liberation war the town was a key military base of the South African Defence Force and its core was a fortified residential area for military personnel and government officials. Each house had a bomb shelter and many of these can still be seen; some of them have found use as storerooms.

Since independence the town has developed rapidly and now has a variety of shops, trading stores and a modern shopping complex. Not to be missed, though, is a visit to the market stalls on the western outskirts of the town, where just about everything is sold, including dried mopane worms.

There are a number of accommodation options in Oshakati, among them **Oshandira Lodge**. Formerly an officers' club of the South African Air Force, the lodge lies adjacent to the airfield. It offers comfortable accommodation, a restaurant, lively bar and a swimming pool. The **Santorini Inn** has rooms with *en suite* facilities, a restaurant, bar, swimming pool, pool table and braai facilities.

From Oshakati, the C46 to Ruacana takes a northwesterly direction, passing through the **Omusati Region**, which takes its name from the Oshiwambo word for the mopane tree, the most dominant tree in the west of the region. The region's population is distributed in 35 settlements and villages, the most important town being Uutapi, which has been earmarked as the regional capital.

After passing through Oshikuku and Ombathi, the settlement of Ombalantu is reached. A 30 km detour on the D3612 leads to Tsandi, the region's commercial centre. Of great historical significance in the area is **Ongulumbashe**, where the first shots in Namibia's liberation struggle were fired on 26 August 1966. In a clash between members of the South African Police and combatants of the People's Liberation Army of Namibia, two PLAN members were killed and nine captured. A further 36 PLAN members were captured in follow-up actions. In the 23-year armed struggle that followed more than 7 700 PLAN members lost their lives. The site of the first clash is marked by a monument which is the focal point of Namibia's Heroes' Day celebrations, held on 26 August each year. The turnoff is signposted just east of Tsandi in central Omusati Region.

Continuing along the C46, Mahenene is passed, followed by the turnoff to the village at Ruacana. Then, quite unexpectedly, you look over Angola and the diversion weir upstream of the hydro-electric scheme.

After forging its way southward from its headwaters near Huambo in Angola for several hundred kilometres, the Kunene River suddenly splits into several fingers and ravines at Ruacana. Here the river plunges some 120 m down a series of gorges and cliffs along a 700 m wide face and then swings sharply west, carving its way through a 2 km long gorge before continuing its journey to the Atlantic Ocean. It has been suggested that the name Ruacana is derived from the Herero word *Orua hakahana* , which means "the hurrying of the waters".

During the early 1900s the border between Namibia and Angola was disputed for many years, but in 1926 it was agreed that the falls would be in Angolan territory and the boundary was fixed below them.

A 320 MW hydro-electric power station was built at Ruacana during the 1970s, but since the complex is underground except for a few buildings next to the surge bayhead, there is little to suggest that there is a power station here. To build the tunnels and shafts, as well as the caverns housing the machine, transformer and surge chamber halls, 415 000 m³ earth had to be excavated.

From the intake structure the water is transported along a 1,5 km pressure tunnel (with a diameter of between 7,4 m and 8,3 m), to the surge bayhead, which is connected to the powerhouse complex via four 140 m high penstocks. After passing through the surge chamber, the water is discharged into the river via a 675 m long tailrace tunnel.

Since the flow of the river is controlled by the Calueque Dam, 40 km upstream, and to a lesser degree by the diversion weir, about 1 km upstream, the falls are dry except during flood peaks, usually in April.

Hippo Pools community camp site at the western end of Ruacana Gorge offers rather basic facilities. The camp site is reached 16 km west of the turnoff to Ruacana on the C46; continue 600 m past the turnoff to Nampower's hydropower plant to the end of the tar road.

From Ruacana a rough 4x4 track continues close to the river to the Epupa Falls (see p 152), 120 km further west. At least 10 hours should be allowed if you plan to use this route.

WESTERN NAMIBIA

Covering some 96 000 km², the arid western and northwestern reaches of Namibia are a sanctuary to desert-dwelling elephants and offer some of the most dramatic scenery in the country – rugged mountains, expansive gravel plains and sweeping river valleys. It is also home to the Himba people, one of Africa's few cultural groups that largely still pursue their traditional way of life.

This region covers the former ethnic homelands of Damaraland, which now falls partly in the Erongo and the Kunene regions, and Kaokoland, which lies in the northern Kunene Region. The name Kaokoland refers to the area between the Kunene River in the north and the Hoanib River in the south, with the Kaokoveld extending further south to the Ugab River.

Brandberg

The Brandberg lies about 20 km west of Uis, as the crow flies, and about 85 km from the coast. Its most popular attraction is the so-called **"White Lady" frieze** in the Tsisab Ravine in the northeast of the massif. The best time to visit the site is during the cool early morning hours. From the car park it is about an hour's walk and it is wise to take a sunhat and water along.

Following its "discovery" in 1918, early interpretations attributed the central figure to Egyptian, Cretan and Mediterranean origins. Subsequent research has, however, led archaeologists to believe the "White Lady" is neither a female, nor white. It has been suggested that the frieze portrays indigenous people, with the white colour representing body paint, commonly used by shamans, or medicine men. Furthermore, careful examination of the painting showed that the "White Lady" has a penis, no breasts, and is depicted with a bow – sufficient evidence that the "White Lady" is a male!

A steel frame has been erected at the overhang to the frieze to prevent vandalism, but other paintings in the area do not enjoy this protection. *No paintings should be touched or*

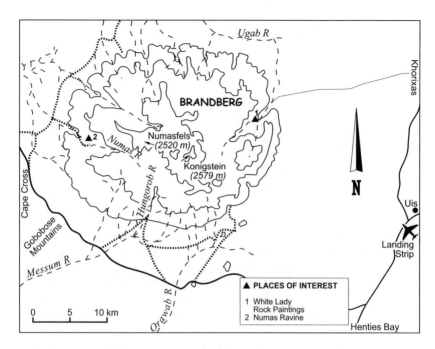

sprayed with liquids under any circumstances. The Brandberg is likely to be declared Namibia's first World Heritage Site.

The Brandberg is home to one of the largest concentrations of rock paintings in the world. Although the "White Lady" site is the best-known, over 43 000 other paintings have been identified to date, making the rock art of the Brandberg the most intensively studied in the world.

The name Brandberg means "Burning Mountain", a reference to the glowing reddish-orange colour of the granite in the early morning and late afternoon. This, combined with the black basalt at its base, gave rise to its descriptive name.

The Brandberg is an oval-shaped massif, measuring about 30 km in an east-west direction and 23 km from north to south. It rises nearly 2 000 m above the surrounding plains to the 2 579 m high Königstein, the highest point in Namibia. The Brandberg consists of a granite core rimmed by Karoo sediments. The original volcano was active during Karoo times, about 180 million years ago, and following the volcanic activity large amounts of magma intruded the Karoo sediments. Over millions of years the sediments were eroded, laying bare the granitic core and carving a number of deep valleys into the massif, the most dramatic being the Tsisab in the northeast and the Numas in the west.

Herds of springbok and gemsbok, as well as ostriches, are attracted to the plains surrounding the Brandberg after good rains. The rocky areas are the habitat of klipspringer, Hartmann's mountain zebra, rock dassies and dassie rats. Leopard, black-backed jackal and aardwolf occur, but are seldom seen because of their nocturnal habits.

To date, some 120 bird species have been recorded in the Brandberg. Two colourful birds to keep an eye out for are the rosy-faced lovebird and Rüppell's parrot, which flies noisily between trees. Species you are likely to spot include red-eyed bulbul, mountain chat, pririt batis and dusky sunbird. Rock pigeon and pale-winged starlings are abundant. Look out for Herero chat, which only occurs in a narrow belt from the Naukluft mountains to southwestern Angola. On the gravel plains you chance ticking Rüppell's korhaan, Gray's lark and tractrac chat, while lappet-faced vultures sometimes soar overhead.

Pastoralists too were attracted to the Brandberg. One of the most dense concentrations of stone-walled sites associated with pastoral people in the central Namib is situated on the southern aspect of the mountain. There is clear evidence that these people retreated to the mountain plateau as the plains grasses began to wither. Archaeologist John Kinahan estimated that while 100 sheep would need 500 ha of grazing to survive on the plains for six months, the same herd could, in principle, be maintained for a similar period on 10 ha on the grassy plateau.

Another attraction of the Brandberg is the backpacking opportunities it presents. Since the terrain is extremely rugged and without designated footpaths, any extended trip into the mountain should only be tackled by extremely fit and experienced backpackers. Groups should ideally be led by someone with knowledge of the mountain and where to find water (see chapter 2 under the appropriate heading). Depending on the route taken, three to four days should be set aside for a return trip to Königstein.

Kaokoland

Covering some 48 982 km², the area between the Hoanib and the Kunene rivers is generally referred to as Kaokoland. The name "Kaoko" is Herero in origin and refers to the mountainous terrain. It is a tract of unspoilt wilderness, uniquely adapted wildlife and home to the Himba.

Although some of the roads are proclaimed district roads, most are nothing more than tracks that are hardly maintained, necessitating a four-wheel drive vehicle. A two-vehicle party is recommended on account of the rugged terrain and the lack of facilities.

Visitors must be self-sufficient in respect of all supplies, including water, as the water of many springs is brackish. Fuel is available only at the veterinary control gate near Palmwag, Sesfontein and Opuwo, and you should have sufficient fuel to cover at least 800 km. Also remember to take emergency spares, as there are no garages other than at Opuwo.

A good map is essential – the 1:500 000 topographical map (Opuwo) shows most of the major tracks, springs and settlements and is useful when planning your trip. Do not count on covering too great a distance in a day as progress is often painfully slow, with an average of 25 km per hour possible on a fairly good track.

Be aware of the risks of camping in the wild, where potentially dangerous animals are sometimes present. The tranquillity of the Kunene River should not be taken for granted – take care of crocodiles. A mosquito repellent, as well as precautions against malaria, are essential in summer.

The area north of the Hoarusib River originally formed part of Game Reserve No 2, which was proclaimed in 1907, but in 1947 deproclaimed and set aside for occupation by Herero-speaking people. In terms of the recommendations of the Odendaal Commission, Kaokoland became a homeland in 1970, and nothing came of subsequent undertakings that a new game reserve would be created. Attempts to give conservation status to western Kaokoland during the mid-1980s and in 1992 were unfortunately also unsuccessful.

Until the mid-1970s Kaokoland was a wildlife paradise, but a devastating drought and large-scale poaching resulted in a dramatic decline in animal numbers. Virtually all the black rhinos were wiped out, and the elephant population was reduced significantly. The adjoining Damaraland suffered a similar fate, but fortunately action was taken before game numbers were affected to the same extent as those of Kaokoland. World-renowned conservationist Garth-Owen

Smith initiated a community-based conservation programme, and the Save The Rhino Trust, under Blythe Loutit, played a major role in creating an awareness of the plight of the area's wildlife and in combating poaching. By the mid-1980s poaching had been brought under control and there have only been isolated incidents of poaching since then, while game numbers have increased steadily.

The elephants of Kaokoland are one of the major attractions of the area, but their existence is now threatened by the ever-increasing number of tourists. Camps are often made at springs in the riverbeds, thereby preventing the animals from obtaining much-needed water, often at the end of a long journey. The animals are then forced to find another waterhole, which could be 30-40 km away. When elephants are spotted, tourists invariably try to get as close as possible to take photographs. As the elephants often have no way of escaping from the rugged river valleys, they are placed under severe stress and some elephants are becoming increasingly aggressive.

Giraffe are often seen along the river courses, which also offer food and shelter to kudu. Springbok, gemsbok and ostrich inhabit the plains, with the more mountainous areas the habitat of herds of Hartmann's mountain zebra.

The Himba, Herero-speaking pastoralists, live in small settlements dotted throughout the area. They have a striking physical appearance and the men are often said to resemble the Masai of East Africa. Boys and young men wear a plait or *ondatu*, which is split into two when permission is granted to marry and the hair is then covered with a cloth headdress.

To protect their skin against the harsh climate, Himba women cover their bodies with a mixture of butterfat, powdered oxides and herbs, giving their skin a rich, gleaming ochre colour. Married women can be distinguished by their leather headdresses and other adornments, including necklaces, belts and wide copper bracelets. A conspicuous adornment worn around the neck is the *ohumba*, a large white shell which is passed on from mother to daughter.

Their beehive huts are made from saplings, usually mopane, which are covered with a mixture of mud and cattle dung. The homesteads are often deserted, as the Himba continuously move with their herds of cattle and goats in search of grazing. Do not remove anything from seemingly abandoned homesteads.

Palmwag Concession Area

Visitors are attracted to Palmwag mainly by the possibility of catching a glimpse of the rare **desert-dwelling elephants and black rhinos** living in the area. Situated among real fan palms, the lodge overlooks a spring in a tributary of the Uniab River which is often visited by elephants. The black rhino are far more elusive, though, and more often than not it is a case of being at the right place at the right time. Other animals you might see are giraffe, kudu, springbok, gemsbok, Hartmann's mountain zebra, steenbok and ostrich.

Another attraction of Palmwag is the spectacular scenery, which is dominated by boulder-strewn plains interrupted by clumps of *Euphorbia* bushes. Table-top mountains and conical peaks form an impressive backdrop to the rocky plains. Among the sites worthwhile visiting are **Van Zylsgat**, a deep pool in the Uniab River, and the **Auob Canyon**.

The lodge is the base of Desert Adventure Safaris and unlike the Damaraland Wilderness Camp and Etendeka Mountain Camp, the tariff for self-drive visitors does not include activities such as game drives, or walks. Although the lodge is accessible by sedan car, the tracks crisscrossing the area are negotiable by four-wheel drive vehicle only. Palmwag's concession stretches from the D3706 westward to the Skeleton Coast Park, with the Torra Bay-Khorixas road forming the southern boundary, and the Hoanib River the northern boundary. The area (including the Hoanib River) may only be entered once the necessary permit has been obtained at the lodge.

Accommodation is in three- and four-bedded reed huts with *en suite* showers. Cooking is not permitted in the huts because of the fire hazard, but braai places are provided. Breakfast and à la carte lunches and dinners are served in the rustic restaurant, where there is also a bar. For those who prefer to rough it, a camp site with hot water ablutions is available. There are also two swimming pools and a small shop, with fuel available at the veterinary control gate.

Petrified Forest

The well-known Petrified Forest, west of Khorixas, is exposed on a small, sandstone rise on the northern bank of the Aba-Huab River, and covers about 800 m by 300 m. The trees are embedded in sandstone of the Ecca Group, a subdivision of the Karoo Sequence, and are about 260 million years old.

The name Petrified Forest is somewhat of a misnomer, as the absence of roots and branches has given rise to the theory that the trees did not grow here. It has been suggested that the trees were uprooted and transported to their present site by floodwaters following warmer climatic conditions after the Dwyka glaciation. This theory is supported by the parallel orientation of many of the trunks.

After they became stranded on sandbanks and shoals the trunks were embedded in sand carried down by the rivers. Ideal conditions for petrification existed, as the trunks were deposited in an oxygen-depleted environment, preventing decay of the organic material. Silica-rich water penetrated the logs, filling the cells, bark and other parts, and precipitated silica. This long process was accompanied by the hardening of the sediments into sandstone.

Nearly 200 million years later, after the uplifting of the area, the overlying rocks were stripped away by erosion in a warm, often arid climate. The remains of at least 50 trees, some partially exposed and others completely exposed, can be seen. A good indication of their size is a partially exposed trunk with a length of more than 30 m and an estimated circumference of 6 m. The growth rings and bark texture are so well preserved that the petrified trees can easily be mistaken for logs.

The trees belong to the *Gymnospermae*, a group of cone-bearing plants which flourished between 300 and 200 million years ago. Present-day members include the cycad order and the yellowwood, pine, cypress and welwitschia families.

The Petrified Forest can be visited daily from 08:00 to 17:00 throughout the year. Although the entrance gate is staffed, entry is free. Covered parking and picnic places are provided at the entrance gate. *The site is a national monument. Tempting as it might be, you should not remove even the smallest piece of petrified wood!*

Spitzkoppe

The imposing Spitzkoppe, also known as the Matterhorn of Namibia, is a well-known landmark between Usakos and the coast. Rising some 700 m above the flat surrounding plains, the Gross Spitzkoppe has a height of 1 728 m. Immediately to the east are the Pondok mountains, which owe their Afrikaans name to their resemblance to African huts. About 10 km south-west is the 1 572 m high Klein Spitzkoppe.

Geologically the area correlates with the Damara Sequence, which dates back some 750 to 700 million years, and the younger Karoo Sequence, of about 350-150 million years ago. During the breakup of the Gondwana superconti-nent in Karoo times, large parts of southern Africa were affect-ed by volcanic activity. Vast amounts of lava were extruded through the Spitzkoppe, Brandberg and Erongo volcanoes, with subsequent intrusion of granitic magma forming the Spitzkoppe, Brandberg and Erongo complexes. Erosion has since exposed the granitic cores to form typical *inselbergs*, or island mountains.

The Gross Spitzkoppe was first ascended in 1946, up the northwest face, and then remained inviolate for 10 years before the second successful attempt. In 1960 a three-man

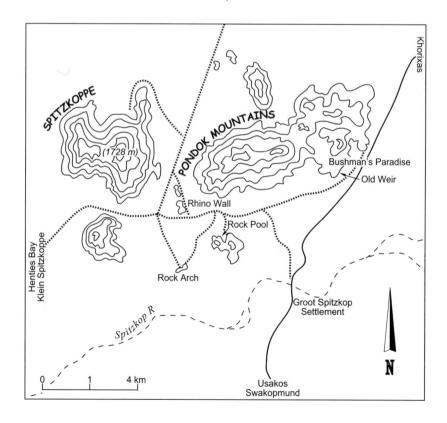

party pioneered a route up the precipitous west face. The mountain, sections of which are E-grade, remains popular with local as well as overseas mountaineers. There are numerous fascinating rock formations in the area – one resembles a shark's mouth, another a natural rock arch – so consult the map and do take time to explore the area thoroughly.

As with other mountains in the arid areas of the country, early humans found refuge here and there are several rock painting sites. One such site, **Bushman's Paradise**, is reached by following a track along the base of the Pondok Mountain in an easterly direction. Along the way you will see a **small stone dam**, which is filled by runoff from the smooth boulders when the area occasionally gets meagre rainfall. The dam was built near the turn of the century, when the Deutsche Kolonial-gesellschaft für Südwestafrika set up a farm here in 1896.

Further along, a chain handhold helps you to scale the steep smooth slope to the **Bushman's Paradise**. From the top there are good views of the usually barren plains below and after a short scramble to the right you look down into a sur-prisingly vegetated amphitheatre. From here make your way to the large overhang at the head of the amphitheatre. Despite

being declared a national monument as long ago as 1954, the paintings have unfortunately been extensively damaged by vandals. However, a visit is still worthwhile and you are sure to agree that a better name than Bushman's Paradise would have been hard to find.

If you have time, you can take an alternative return route which winds down to the floor of the amphitheatre, allowing you to have a close look at the vegetation, in a setting resem-bling a natural rock garden. The route takes you through a nar-row cleft where caution should be exercised. From the base of the mountain it is a walk of about 10 minutes back to your car.

The **Spitzkoppe Community Tourist Camp** is a community project aimed at preserving this popular tourist attraction. Basic camping facilities are provided, with accommodation in traditional thatched two-bed huts also available. Because water is extremely scarce in this area, visitors are advised to bring their own supplies. Tourmaline and other semi-precious stones found in the vicinity can be purchased at the craft shop at the entrance gate, as well as locally made crafts. Local guides can be hired to locate rock art sites.

Twyfelfontein

With more than 2 400 rock engravings, Twyfelfontein is one of the most precious open-air rock art galleries in the world. Unidentifiable antelope and animals are depicted in more than 20 per cent of the engravings, with giraffe (13 per cent), ostrich (11 per cent), zebra (7 per cent) and rhino (6 per cent) also represented. Animal tracks are shown in 15 per cent of the engravings, and abstract engravings make up 7,6 per cent of the total.

Some rock slabs have as many as 70 engravings, with a rhino measuring 92 cm by 55 cm and an elephant measuring 57 cm by 73 cm among the largest.

An engraving that attracts considerable attention is that of a lion with an unusually long, L-shaped tail, with a track at the tip of its tail and spoor instead of paws. An interesting aspect of this engraving is that the lion appears to have an antelope in its mouth. Closer inspection, though, will reveal that the antelope has been superimposed. There are at least 30 other engravings on this slab, including those of snakes, giraffe, rhino and zebra.

To prevent vandalism, visitors must be accompanied by a guide, but before setting off, pay a visit to the information centre with its excellent displays on the geology, vegetation and archaeology of the area. From the information centre a trail meanders up the main valley past several sites, including the elephant and rhino sites described above. The lion panel will also be seen on this route, which takes about an hour to complete, but can be extended by about 40 minutes by continuing on the second circular route.

Especially interesting on the longer route are one of the few rock painting sites at Twyfelfontein and the "Dancing Kudu" panel. In contrast with many of the other petroglyphs that have a rough texture, this engraving was rubbed and polished to give it a shiny appearance. Surrounding the kudu are numerous abstract shapes – circles, some concentric, others with dots or rays.

Because of the heat and the difficulty of seeing the engravings in direct sunlight, early morning and late afternoon are the best times. Comfortable walking shoes, a sunhat and a water bottle are advisable and you should allow at least two hours at Twyfelfontein. An entry fee is payable.

Vingerklip

Also known as the Kalk Kegel (limestone skittle), this column of limestone conglomerate is situated atop a small hill west of Khorixas. It has a circumference of roughly 44 m at its base and points skyward for some 35 m. The conglomerate of which the formation is composed was laid down an estimated 15 million years ago, giving it the same age as the Sesriem and Kuiseb Canyon conglomerates.

The Vingerklip is situated on the floodplain north of the Ugab River and once formed part of a plateau which stretches for some 80 km in an east-west direction. Incision of the plateau dates back about 50 million years, when the Ugab River began carving a broad valley. During the course of a drier period, some 30 million years ago, the valley filled with fine sand and conglomerate as a result of the weaker flow of the river. Erosion of the valley was accelerated when the climate became wetter, resulting in the incision of three terraces. The Vingerklip is an erosional relic of the main terrace.

The first recorded ascent was in 1970, by an American climber named Tom Choate, and was probably one of the earliest climbs in the country with mechanical aids. The first free climb was made three years later, when a party led by Udo Kleyenstuber ascended the eastern face.

Seemingly guarded by the famous rock formation, **Vingerklip Lodge** has 10 comfortable bungalows, as well as a spacious restaurant under thatch, sundowner venue and swimming pool.

ROUTE 11
OUTJO TO SESFONTEIN

DISTANCE: 410 km **TIME**: 5 to 6 hours **ROAD CONDITIONS**: 131 km tar; 279 km gravel, usually good, but can be corrugated **FUEL**: Outjo, Khorixas, veterinary fence near Palmwag, Sesfontein **LINKING ROUTES**: Routes 12, 13, 17

From Outjo (see route 8) take the C38 toward Okaukuejo and turn left onto the C39 about 700 m after leaving the town.

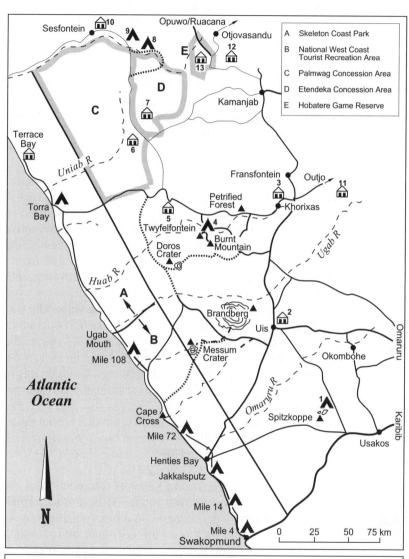

A	Skeleton Coast Park
B	National West Coast Tourist Recreation Area
C	Palmwag Concession Area
D	Etendeka Concession Area
E	Hobatere Game Reserve

KEY FOR NUMBERED CAMP SITES AND REST CAMPS

1 Spitzkoppe
2 Brandberg rest camp
3 Khorixas rest camp
4 Aba-Huab
5 Damaraland Wilderness Camp
6 Palmwag Lodge
7 Etendeka Mountain Camp

8 Khowarib
9 Warmquelle (Ongongo)
10 Fort Sesfontein Lodge
11 Vingerklip Lodge
12 Kavita Lion Lodge
13 Hobatere Lodge

Heading westward through a landscape characterised by hills, plains with hills and low mountains, the sudden change of vegetation from thornbush to mopane savanna is particularly noticeable.

About 28 km after turning onto the C39, a signpost indicates the turnoff to the **Munsterland Caves**. From the turnoff it is 2 km to the farmhouse of Mr Hartung, who conducts tours.

Although the smaller of the two caves does not have any stalactites or stalagmites, a visit is still worthwhile. From the large entrance chamber visitors follow a narrow passage and descend by two wooden ladders to smaller chambers deep in the cave system.

The cave complex on the adjoining farm is far more spectacular, with numerous stalactites and stalagmites. The roof of the main cave is about 6 to 7 m high and the cavern has a diameter of roughly 25 to 30 m. The tour, including the drive to the cave and back, takes from one and a half to two hours.

A strong torch, comfortable walking shoes and casual clothing are essential. Tours must be booked in advance with Mr Hartung. Telephone (067) 31-2020.

Continuing along the C39, the turnoff to the **Vingerklip** (see p 140) is signposted 50 km further on. From here it is a further 19 km along the D2743. Situated conveniently close to the Vingerklip, **Omburo Ost** offers visitors an opportunity to view well-preserved rock paintings and engravings. Guided tours in open vehicles are conducted to the sites in the picturesque Ugab Valley.

The farm is signposted on the D2351, about 5 km southeast of Vingerklip Lodge. Advance reservations are essential. E Reitz, P O Box 271, Outjo, tel (06532) ask for Epupa 3311, fax (0654) 31-3000 (indicate P O Box 271).

About 8 km before entering Khorixas the junction of the C35 from Uis to Khorixas (see route 13) is reached. **Huab Lodge**, an upmarket lodge situated on a private game reserve, is reached by turning right onto the C35 and then travelling toward Kamanjab for 46 km. Turn left onto the D2670 and follow it for 30 km. Accommodation at the lodge is in thatched bungalows on a fully inclusive basis. Amenities include a swimming pool, and among the activities offered are guided drives and walks.

Khorixas is reached 131 km west of Outjo. Formerly known as Welwitschia, Khorixas is said to be a Khoekhoen name for a tree with edible berries resembling currants, a possible reference to the mustard bush. There is little of interest in this rather rundown and depressing town other than the **Khorixas Community Craft Market** in the centre of the town. Among the items for sale at the craft market are carvings from corkwood trees, carved makalani nuts, seed necklaces and Himba dolls made from leather.

Accommodation at **Khorixas rest camp** comprises self-catering chalets, with equipped kitchen and fridge. Camp sites with communal ablutions are also available. Facilities include a restaurant, lounge, bar, swimming pool and curio shop. There is also a short nature trail. The turnoff to the rest camp is signposted about 2 km west of the town, from where it is another 1 km.

The C39 from Khorixas to Torra Bay follows the Aba-Huab River valley, passing through numerous river courses, which should be approached with caution following rains, as the road could be washed away. The turnoff to the **Petrified Forest** (see p 135), where petrified tree trunks can be seen alongside welwitschias (a "living fossil plant"), is signposted 43 km west of Khorixas.

Following the course of the Aba-Huab River, the road winds past interesting sandstone rock formations. Perched on the top of the hills flanking the valley are occasional stands of *Acacia robynsiana*, with their long, slender branches.

The turnoff to Twyfelfontein is signposted about 72 km west of Khorixas. Turn left onto the D3254 and keep an eye out for a track leading off to the right after about 11 km. A short detour along this track leads to the **Wonder Hole**. It has been suggested that this deep hole was created when a subterranean river swallowed a chunk of earth. On one side it is possible to scramble onto a ledge to have a better view into the hole. Take care, however, of the loose gravel around the edges.

Return to the D3254 and turn right, continuing for 3 km before turning right onto the D3214 (signposted Twyfelfontein/Verbrandeberg). After about 3 km you cross the Aba-Huab River. The delightful **Aba-Huab Campsite** on the southern bank of the river is situated conveniently close to Twyfelfontein, the Burnt Mountain and Organ Pipes. It has camp sites with communal ablutions and a bar. The desert-dwelling elephants are frequently seen in the area, even passing through the camp at night!

The turnoff to **Twyfelfontein** (see p 139) is signposted a few kilometres beyond Aba-Huab Campsite and after 5 km the road ends at a parking area.

Also worthwhile visiting in the area are the Organ Pipes and the Burnt Mountain. Returning to the D3254, you turn right, travelling along a wide valley, with the Burnt Mountain to the right. The **Organ Pipes** are reached about 3 km beyond the turnoff. Leave your car at the parking area to the left of the road and take one of the paths leading to the Organ Pipes, a mass of perpendicular dolerite pillars.

The Organ Pipes are exposed in a gorge roughly about 100 m long and with a maximum depth of 5 m. They were formed by the intrusion of a dolerite sheet into the shales of the Karoo Sequence some 120 million years ago. When the dolerite cooled down it shrunk and split into angular columns. It was subsequently exposed by the river cutting its way through the dolerite sheet.

From the Organ Pipes parking area you have an excellent view of the **Burnt Mountain**, part of a 12-km long range lying generally east-west, and rising some 200 m above the surrounding landscape. During the heat of the day the mountain is stark and uninviting, but in the early morning and late afternoon it presents a kaleidoscope of colour.

The Karoo shales and limestones which formed the mountain were deposited some 200 million years ago. About 80 million years later, doleritic lava intruded these rocks, causing wide-ranging contact metamorphism. Hydroxides and oxides were released, giving the rocks an amazing variety of colours – red, orange, black, grey, white and purple. An interesting feature at the eastern end of the mountain is a heap of shale that underwent drastic changes when it was intruded by dolerite and now resembles ash and clinker.

Because the area is extremely susceptible to compaction, please heed the request not to walk about in the area.

From the Burnt Mountain, backtrack to the C39 and turn left. The road continues along a spectacular valley, crosses the Huab River and then winds through breathtaking scenery dominated by table-top mountains and cone-shaped peaks. About 32 km after rejoining the C39 you reach the turnoff to **Damaraland Camp**, an upmarket location offering guests an opportunity to experience the wilderness atmosphere of Damaraland.

From the signposted turnoff it is about 11 km along a four-wheel drive track to the camp, which is also conveniently situated for motorists travelling from Swakopmund to Etosha National Park via the Skeleton Coast Park (see route 17). Guests travelling in sedan cars can leave their vehicles in a secure parking area, from where they are transferred to the camp.

One of the main attractions of the area is the superb scenery, which alternates from gravel plains and table-top mountains to hidden valleys. Another attraction is the possibility of seeing desert-dwelling elephant and black rhino, both of which occur in the area. As their movements are dictated by the availability of food and water, sightings cannot be guaranteed, but there is always a possibility of chancing on them. Other game species roaming the area include springbok, gemsbok, kudu, Hartmann's mountain zebra and giraffe.

Opened in 1996, the camp is a unique joint venture between Wilderness Safaris Namibia and the local Bergsig-De Riet community. The camp is owned and operated by Wilderness Safaris for an initial 10-year period. Financial benefits to the community accrue from the lease of the land, a percentage of turnover, salaries and payments for services such as laundry and road maintenance. After the 10-year period the residents' trust will acquire 20 per cent of the shareholding a year and the camp will, therefore, be wholly owned by the community after 15 years. At that stage they can decide whether they want to retain Wilderness Safaris to manage and market the camp. It was this approach which won the camp second place in the Silver Otter Awards of the Guild of British Travel Writers in 1997.

The staff are motivated, friendly and helpful, and the camp has a reputation for outstanding service. Combined with the superb scenery and the sense of isolation, Damaraland Camp offers guests an unforgettable experience.

The camp comprises eight spacious safari tents with twin beds and an *en suite* shower, hand basin and toilet. Amenities include a dining area under canvas, a curio shop and a small pool, which is surrounded on three sides by cliffs.

Activities include scenic and nature drives, as well as a guided walk to the summit of a mountain overlooking the camp. During the walk the indigenous uses of various plant species are explained to guests. Trips to the rock engravings at

Twyfelfontein are available and, depending on rainfall, the desert-dwelling elephants can sometimes be seen in a riverbed close to Twyfelfontein. The clear night sky offers ideal opportunities for stargazing through the camp's telescope.

From the turnoff to the Damaraland Camp, the C39 continues westward for 11 km to the small settlement of Bergsig. At the junction travellers following the optional leg of route 17 from Swakopmund to Terrace Bay join and can either continue to Sesfontein or follow this route in reverse to Outjo.

At the T-junction, take the D2620 (signposted Kamanjab) for 39 km and then turn left onto the D3706 to Sesfontein, continuing for about 5 km to the veterinary control gate, where fuel is available. The turnoff to **Palmwag Lodge** (see p 135) is reached less than 1 km after passing through the gate.

Etendeka Mountain Camp lies in a concession area immediately to the east of the D3706 to Sesfontein. The camp is accessible only by four-wheel drive vehicle and guests arriving by sedan car are transferred to the camp from a parking area at the veterinary fence. Visitors travelling by four-wheel drive vehicle can travel to the camp, but must allow one to one and a half hours for the 18 km trip from the D3706.

The camp derives its name from an OvaHimba word meaning "a place of flat-topped hills", a reference to the range of mountains dominating the scenery to the east of the camp. These mountains were formed some 135 million years ago when lava flowed in successive layers over sandstone beds.

Although several species of game, including desert-dwelling elephant and black rhino, occur in the concession area, concessionaire Denis Liebenberg considers any sightings of game a bonus. Other species seen from time to time are gemsbok, kudu, Hartmann's mountain zebra and giraffe.

Etendeka has a fine reputation for personalised service. It aims to provide a wilderness experience and guests are exposed to the scenic beauty of the area and its many interesting facets. On guided nature walks and drives visitors are introduced to uniquely adapted smaller creatures and plants, as well as aspects of nature that are often overlooked.

Guests are accommodated in safari tents with beds, a wash basin, water jug and drinking water. As water has to be transported from a spring several kilometres away, the tents do not have facilities *en suite*. Reed-enclosed bucket showers, with only the sky as a roof, are provided instead. The camp's dining area and railway-sleeper made bar are under canvas. Lodge and Guest Farm Reservations, P O Box 21783, Windhoek, tel (061) 22-6979, fax 22-6999.

From Palmwag, the D3706 heads north to Sesfontein, passing the turnoff to the Khowarib Schlucht after about 70 km.

The **Khowarib Schlucht** is a spectacular 25-km long gorge cut through the rugged mountains of Kaokoland by the Hoanib River. With a width of up to 500 m, the mountains tower some 450 m above the riverbed in places.

During the German administration, the Schlucht was used as a transport route between Outjo and Sesfontein. It is negotiable by four-wheel drive vehicle only and after meandering through the gorge for 23 km, the track traverses extensive plains covered in mopane woodland. It takes about five hours to cover the 85 km between the Sesfontein road and the C35. The track crosses the river several times, necessitating four-wheel drive, and numerous stretches of axle-deep silt, which throws up clouds of fine powdery dust, have to be negotiated. Elephants are sometimes encountered in the Schlucht. The track joins the C35 54 km north of Kamanjab (see route 12).

Perched on the cliffs overlooking the Hoanib River, the **Khowarib Community Tourist Camp** is at the western end of the Khowarib Schlucht. In the riverbed below the camp, water surfaces as springs, creating an oasis in a harsh, barren, arid environment. Accommodation is in traditional Himba or Damara huts, but camp sites with basic ablution facilities are also available. The camp is signposted on the D3706, 70 km north of Palmwag, and is reached 2 km further on.

Remaining on the D3706, you reach **Warmquelle**, a German name meaning "hot springs", about 11 km beyond the Khowarib Schlucht turnoff. As you enter the settlement, turn right to the school and follow a track, which bears left after about 100 m, for about half a kilometre to the large, shady fig trees surrounding the springs.

The first gardens were laid out below the springs by Dr C A Schlettwein, who purchased the 4 000 ha farm Warmbad in 1900. Schlettwein bought the farm on the assumption that the young German colony would eventually build its own harbour, as Walvis Bay was already a British possession. He was convinced that the harbour would be built in the north of the country, but his plans were thwarted by the cost of building a connecting railway line and World War I.

Schlettwein grew vegetables, tobacco, maize and lucerne, which were sold to the German *Schutztruppe* stationed at Sesfontein. The land under cultivation was gradually extended, necessitating better irrigation methods, and in about 1910-11 an aqueduct was built from the spring to the lands. The remains of this aqueduct can still be seen today.

After World War I Warmquelle was acquired by the government in exchange for a farm in the Kamanjab district, in order to enlarge the reserve created for the Topnaar Khoikhoi.

Also worthwhile visiting in the Warmquelle area is the **Ongongo Waterfall**. Approaching this scenic spot, it is hard to imagine an oasis tucked away in the folds of the wastelands surrounding it.

The falls can either be reached by continuing past the school, or taking the turnoff indicated by a makeshift signpost on the D3706 and continuing for about 6 km to the community camp site. Sedan cars can drive to the camp site gate, but the track leading down to the camp site is negotiable by four-wheel drive vehicle only.

Also known as Blinkwater (Shiny Water), the falls cascade over a tufa formation – evidence that the area experienced a much wetter phase during the recent past – into a 2 m deep pool. The water is so clear that even at this depth the pebbles can clearly be seen. The water is lukewarm and the pool is especially welcome after a long, dusty day's drive. Remember not to use soap in the water. The area above the falls is worth exploring.

The **Warmquelle Community Campsite**, established at Ongongo in conjunction with the Save the Rhino Trust, consists of a number of camp sites, shaded by mopane trees, and basic ablution facilities.

Heading west from Warmquelle along the D3706, **Sesfontein** is reached after about 20 km. The settlement owes its name to the springs originating in the area, where green, irrigated fields and date palms create an oasis in an otherwise barren landscape.

The focal point of the settlement, the historic **German fort**, is a few hundred metres from the road, but is clearly signposted. Following the outbreak of rinderpest (cattle plague) in 1896, the German authorities established several control posts in the north of the country; Sesfontein was the most westerly. It was also used as a base for combating poachers and gunrunners from Angola. The construction of a road between Outjo and Sesfontein in 1901 made it possible to transport building material to Sesfontein for the construction of a military station. In 1905-6 it was converted into a fort, which accommodated 40 soldiers and had a stable for 25 horses. A 5 ha garden where wheat and dates were cultivated was laid out and some of the original palm trees can still be seen today. The gardens were irrigated by an extensive system of furrows fed by a spring a few hundred metres from the fort.

In 1909 Sesfontein ceased to be used as a military post, but continued to be occupied by three policemen until it was abandoned in 1914, without having seen any military action. It subsequently fell into disrepair.

After many years of neglect, the historic fort received a new lease on life a few years ago when it was restored and turned into **Fort Sesfontein Lodge**. Its comfortable rooms front onto a central courtyard planted with palm trees. The officers' mess now serves as a restaurant, bar and lounge. There is also a swimming pool. Camp sites with communal ablutions are available. *This is also the last refuelling stop before Opuwo in Kaokoland.*

From Sesfontein travellers in four-wheel drive vehicles can follow route 12 in reverse back to Outjo, while those in sedan cars can backtrack to the D2620 and then travel via the scenic Grootberg Pass to Kamanjab, where the tar road is joined. From Kamanjab follow route 12 in reverse to Outjo.

ROUTE 12
OUTJO TO EPUPA FALLS AND SESFONTEIN

DISTANCE: 1 200 km. **TIME**: minimum 5 days. **ROAD CONDITIONS**: 155 km tar; 1 045 km varying from good gravel to rough 4x4 tracks. **FUEL**: Outjo, Kamanjab, Opuwo, Sesfontein. **LINKING ROUTES**: Route 8, 11

From Outjo (see route 8), take the C38 north for 8 km and then turn onto the C40 which goes in a northwesterly direction. A worthwhile detour for good views of tame and wild cheetah is to the **Otjitotongwe Lodge and Cheetah Guest Farm**. Activities include guided game drives, guided walks and cheetah feeds. Of interest are the fossil algae dating back 600-700 million years. Accommodation is in thatched bungalows with *en suite* facilities. Take the turnoff from the C40 onto the F(P)2683, about 24 km east of Kamanjab. The farm is a further 8 km on.

About 4,5 km before reaching Kamanjab, keep an eye out for an inconspicuous track which turns off to the right. After about 2 km the track ends at the parking area below **Peet**

Albert Koppie, Namibia's second-largest rock engraving site.

Here Later Stone Age artists carved over a thousand engravings into the bluish-grey granite rocks. The quality and detail of

these engravings are generally not as good as those of Twyfelfontein though. Animals are depicted in more than 60 per cent of the engravings, followed by abstracts (22 per cent) and animal tracks (7,5 per cent).

The small farming settlement of **Kamanjab** is reached 155 km after leaving Outjo. It is the last stop en route to Kaokoland and it is advisable to stock up on any supplies you might have forgotten.

From Kamanjab head north along the C35 toward Ruacana. A guest farm in the area with an excellent reputation for service and a homely atmosphere is **Rustig Guest Farm**. Guests at

this 6 000 ha cattle and game farm can undertake guided game drives, walk about the farm, or participate in farm activities. Accommodation is in comfortable rooms with *en suite* facilities. Turn right onto the D2763 about 8 km north of Kamanjab, continuing for 14 km before taking the D2695 for 6 km.

About 34 km north of Kamanjab, a signboard indicates the turnoff to **Kavita Lion Lodge**. Situated on the farm Karos, which shares a common boundary with the Etosha National Park, the lodge is owner-managed by Uwe and Tammy Hoth. The farm

is home to a variety of game, including giraffe, blue wildebeest, the rare black-faced impala, gemsbok and Hartmann's mountain zebra. A diversity of birds can also be seen.

Karos is home to the **Afri-Leo Foundation**, a non-profit organisation aimed at protecting Namibia's declining lion population. In September 1997 five lions were obtained from the Ekongoro Zoo in Rundu and after being held in holding camps, they were released into three 1 ha camps at the end of January 1998. As it will not be possible to return them to the wild, it is planned to release the lions in a 150 ha camp once the necessary funds have been obtained. Only when this has been achieved will it be possible to accommodate wild lions leaving the Etosha National Park.

Guests can undertake game-viewing drives and guided nature trails, or learn more about the customs of the Himba people by joining an early morning two-hour trail to Ohorongo, a Himba demonstration village. Also on offer are day excursions into western Etosha, day trips to Himba villages at Opuwo and three-day trips to the Epupa Falls.

Accommodation consists of five double rooms with *en suite* facilities on a full board basis. There is also a swimming pool. **Otjombungu Camp** consists of five camp sites with five thatched A-frame shelters, tapped water, hot and cold water showers and flush toilets.

Beyond the turnoff to Kavita Lion Lodge, the road skirts the western boundary of the Etosha National Park and about 69 km north of Kamanjab reaches the turnoff to **Hobatere Lodge**. The lodge is reached 15 km beyond the turnoff.

The lodge lies in a 32 000 ha game park characterised by large granite outcrops separated by deep river valleys and plains. It is a sanctuary to a large variety of game, including elephant, gemsbok, eland, giraffe, kudu, springbok, black-faced impala and Hartmann's mountain zebra. Predators include lion, leopard, cheetah, as well as a variety of smaller carnivores.

Guests are accommodated in thatched-roof rondavels with *en suite* shower and toilet. The lounge, dining area and bar are under thatch and there is a boma and outside braai area, as well as a swimming pool. For those seeking more secluded accommodation there is a tree house for two people. Built in an enormous leadwood tree, it overlooks a waterhole frequented by game. Guests are dropped off in the late afternoon with dinner packs and a light breakfast and are collected the following morning.

Activities include game drives in open vehicles and guided walks, tailored to suit the group. Night drives are conducted after dinner to enable visitors to see some of the nocturnal animals of the area. Trips last about an hour and a spotlight is used to search for animals. Also on offer are guided trips to western Etosha, an area that is closed to casual visitors.

Continuing northward along the C35, the Werda veterinary control gate is reached 10 km beyond the turnoff to Hobatere. After another 122 km the C35 meets the C41 to Opuwo.

Opuwo, the administrative capital of the Kunene Region, is another 60 km from there.

The town owes its name to an incident that took place in the mid-1500s, when a group of Herero people migrated from Angola southward into Kaokoland. On reaching a spring they decided to settle and named their new home Opuwo, a Herero word meaning "far enough". Early white travellers and explorers corrupted the name to Ohopuho and Ohopoho, but the original name was eventually recognised.

The settlement developed around what was known as the Native Affairs office, which was opened on 12 April 1939. It later became the administrative seat of Kaokoland and following independence the regional capital of the Kunene Region. Despite its status, it has the atmosphere of a frontier settlement – an assortment of government buildings, a few shops and Himba women in traditional dress.

It is the last refuelling stop before venturing further into Kaokoland. Ensure that you have sufficient fuel to cover the 800 km journey to Sesfontein.

Okahane Lodge in Opuwo offers well-appointed rooms with *en suite* facilities, a restaurant, boma, bar facilities and swimming pool.

From Opuwo the **Epupa Falls** are reached by taking the D3700, which initially winds north. The road then swings in a northwesterly direction, flanked by the Steilrand mountains to the southwest and the Ehomba mountains to the northeast. Okangwati, a former South African Defence Force base, is about 104 km beyond Opuwo and from here it is another 73 km to the Epupa Falls.

After the harsh landscape of Kaokoland, the spectacular view of **Epupa Falls** that greets one from the viewpoint about 500 m before reaching the falls comes as a complete surprise. Stately makalani palms line the river as its wends its way through the arid landscape to tumble over a multitude of cascades into a deep gorge.

Except at the **Enyandi and Ondorusso rapids**, upstream of Epupa Falls, the gradient of the Kunene River is generally gentle. At Epupa, however, a rock shelf extends at an angle of 45° across the river for 457 m, causing the river to split into several channels.

The main fall, close to the southern bank, is about 36 m high and is the only fall with a direct drop. It plunges into a narrow, 6 m wide gorge and carries an estimated third of the water. A multitude of further cascades tumble at various intervals over the rock shelf. Adding to Epupa's allure is the abundance of real fan, or makalani, palms growing on the banks of the river and on the islands separating the channels. Baobabs cling to the steep cliffs of the gorge. The falls are especially attractive in April, when the flow of the Kunene peaks. The river usually reaches its lowest level in November.

A spectacular view of the falls can be obtained about 1 km downstream by following a footpath along the slopes of the hills towering above Epupa.

Visitors to Epupa have a choice of three places to stay at. The **Epupa camp site**, operated by Kaokohimba Safaris in conjunction with the local Himba community, who receive part of the income generated, comprises camp sites with braai places, cold showers and flush toilets.

Adjacent to the Epupa camp site is **Omarunga Camp**. Accommodation is in luxury tents with *en suite* facilities. There is also a restaurant and bar. Visits to nearby Himba villages, and rafting trips when the level of the water is high, are offered. The camp only caters for guests.

Epupa Camp is a luxury tented camp upstream of the falls. Guests are accommodated in safari tents with *en suite* facilities on a fully inclusive basis. Facilities include a rustic reed and thatch restaurant and bar. Prior reservations are essential.

From Epupa, backtrack to Okangwati and take the road via the settlements of Etengwa and Otjihanda, a particularly bad stretch of road. Named after a former "Bantu" Commissioner, the 13 km long **Van Zyl's Pass** snakes down the escarpment. Over the last 1,7 km the pass descends steeply, dropping over 400 m in altitude.

The road then continues to the spectacular **Marienfluss**, one of the most popular attractions in western Kaokoland. Stretching northward for 50 km to the Kunene River, the Marienfluss valley is up to 15 km wide. To the west it is bounded by the spectacular Hartmann's mountains, with the Otjihipa mountains rising over 800 m above the valley floor to the east.

For much of the year the red sands of the valley are devoid of any vegetation, but after rains it is transformed into a swathe of breathtakingly beautiful waving grasslands. During such periods, large herds of gemsbok and springbok migrate to the valley. As the grazing diminishes the herds break up into smaller groups and individuals. Among the smaller inhabitants you may spot are bat-eared foxes and suricates.

Especially conspicuous when there is grass cover are the fairy circles, circular patches of barren soil, ranging from two to five metres in diameter. Several theories about their origin have been advanced, but so far no conclusive evidence has been found for any of them.

Over the last few years the number of visitors to the valley has grown, and their vehicles have disturbed the sensitive sandy plains and created unsightly new tracks. *Please remain on existing tracks and do not be tempted to blaze your own!*

A camp site is reached about 3 km beyond **Otjinhungwa** at the northern end of the Marienfluss. Run by the local Himba community in conjunction with Kaokohimba Safaris, the camp site is on the banks of the Kunene River. Only basic facilities are provided.

Backtrack up the Marienfluss for 50 km from Otjinungwa and bear right at the Van Zyl's Pass junction, continuing for 28 km to Rooidrom (Red Drum), a well-known landmark. The route then continues to **Orupembe**, a semi-permanent Himba settlement, from where you head in a southwesterly direction before the road swings southeast to Purros. Dominating the scenery to the interior are the flat-topped Etendeka mountains, consisting of layers of sandstone interbedded with basalt that was extruded about 135 million years ago.

About 110 km beyond Orupembe the settlement of **Purros** is reached. The strong springs surfacing in the otherwise dry bed of the Hoarusib River here have attracted people for thousands of years. On the eastern bank of the river is a small settlement of Herero families and semi-permanent Himba nomads.

Game, too, are attracted to the springs and elephants are frequently seen in the area. In 1990, 29 gemsbok and 10 giraffe were released near Purros in an effort to build up the once prolific game population, which was almost wiped out by drought and poaching. The resettlement project enjoyed the support of all the headmen, who undertook to be the custodians of the animals.

Excellent camping facilities, run by the Purros community, are available a few kilometres from the settlement. The **Ngatutunge Pamwe Campsite** was established in 1987 as a pilot project by renowned conservationist Garth Owen-Smith and anthropologist Margie Jacobsohn, to enable the community to benefit from tourism.

It comprises four shady camp sites with fireplaces, hot showers and ablutions. Guides can be hired for drives to track down the desert-dwelling elephants living in the area. There is also an interesting guided walk, focusing on the many indigenous uses of the plants growing in the area.

From Purros the D3707 heads in a southeasterly direction to Sesfontein. The road initially follows the Gomatum River valley to Tomakas, where there is a semi-permanent Himba settlement. It then crosses the **Giribes Plains**, a flat expanse stretching for more than 20 km in all directions, and reaches Sesfontein after about 105 km from Purros.

At Sesfontein the route joins up with route 11 from Outjo to Sesfontein.

ROUTE 13

USAKOS TO SPITZKOPPE AND KHORIXAS

DISTANCE: 260 km **TIME**: 4 hours **ROAD CONDITIONS**: 32 km tar; 228 km gravel district and minor road route (variable) **FUEL**: Usakos, Uis, Khorixas **LINKING ROUTES**: Routes 2, 11

This route provides a convenient link between the coast, Damaraland and further afield, Etosha. It incorporates two of Namibia's best known landmarks, Spitzkoppe and Brandberg.

From Usakos (see route 2) take the B2 towards Swakopmund for 23 km and turn right onto the road signposted Henties Bay-Uis. The road forks after 1 km; take the D1918 toward Henties Bay for 17 km and then turn onto the D3716. The **Spitzkoppe** (see p 136) turnoff is reached 10 km on.

Continue along the D3716 from Spitzkoppe to the D1930. At the junction, turn left, continuing for 55 km to the junction with the C36 from Omaruru. Turn left and after a short distance you will arrive at the former mining village of **Uis**.

The Khoekhoen name Uis is said to mean "place of brackish water". The presence of tin in the area was confirmed as early as 1911 and in 1922 Mr Etemba Schmidt erected a mining plant in the Kartoffel River. However, it was only in 1951, with the establishment of the Uis Tin Mining Company (SWA) Ltd, that large-scale mining was carried out. ISCOR, the South African iron and steel giant, acquired the mining rights in 1958 and its subsidiary, IMEX, took over the mine. In 1966 IMEX became known as IMCOR.

Although there are extensive ore reserves in the area, the ore body is of extremely low grade and the mine was one of the lowest grade tin mines in the world. Following the collapse of world prices in the mid-1980s, mining became uneconomical and the mine was closed in November 1990.

The closure of the mine left the small-scale Damara miners, who used to sell their manually produced tin to it, destitute. A small-scale tin mining project was set up in 1991 and the first shipment of 3 tonnes of high grade tin concentrate produced by the miners left Uis in March 1997.

The **Brandberg rest camp** at Uis is an ideal base for those wishing to explore the Brandberg at leisure. Accommodation is available in four-bedded flats and family houses. Camp sites are also available. Facilities include a restaurant, bar, swimming pool, snooker room and tennis court.

The **Messum Crater**, a geologically interesting formation, is reached by taking the C35 from Uis toward Henties Bay for 14 km and then turning onto the D2342 (signposted Brandberg West), which is followed for 40 km. Keep an eye out for a fairly indistinct track that turns south as you are about to cross the Messum River. From here a track leads in a southerly and southwesterly direction for about 23 km to the outer rim of the crater. It then follows a tributary of the Messum River to reach the junction with the Messum River after 4,5 km. About 2,8 km further on the track leaves the river to ascend the northern rim of the crater.

With a diameter of 21 km, the crater consists of an inner core, surrounded by gravel plains, and an outer ring of concentric hills. The crater is the remains of a volcano that was active in Late Karoo times, some 120 million years ago. Vast quantities of lava were extruded through the volcano, which could have towered 2 000 m above its surroundings. During one of the volcanic phases, the cone subsided, while magma intruded into the volcano.

The substrate of the crater floor is extremely sensitive to disturbance and tracks can remain visible for decades. Please help to preserve this sensitive environment by remaining on well-defined tracks.

To reach the "**White Lady**" (see p 130), take the C35 north toward Khorixas for 14 km and then turn left onto the D2359 and follow it for 21 km.

About 32 km beyond the D2359 turnoff the C35 crosses the Ugab River and 19 km on you reach the D2612, which provides a short cut to **Twyfelfontein** (see p 139), the **Burnt Mountain** and **Organ Pipes** (see route 11). On reaching the C39, 47 km on, turn left and continue along route 12 to Khorixas.

10

NORTHEASTERN NAMIBIA

*With its magnificent woodlands and perennial boundary rivers, the northeast of Namibia contrasts sharply with the arid western regions of the country. Here can be found vast swathes of tall woodlands, riverine forests, floodplains and reed-lined channels. A stunning variety of birds is attracted to this diversity of habitats, and several animal species that occur here are found nowhere else in Namibia. It is also home to the last of the San people, who supplement their traditional economy with subsistence farming and small herds of cattle. **This is a high risk malaria area and precautions are advisable.***

Bushmanland

Covering 18 468 km², Bushmanland was set aside in the 1960s as a "homeland" for the San people on the recommendation of the Odendaal Commission. Since the demarcation of Namibia's 13 regions it has been referred to as the Tsumkwe district.

Bushmanland shares its eastern border with the international boundary between Namibia and Botswana, with the veterinary fence, or Red Line, forming the western border.

Western Bushmanland is covered by deep Kalahari sands dominated by tree savanna and woodlands comprising silver cluster-leaf, bushwillow, Kalahari apple-leaf, wild seringa and lavender fever-berry. A number of San communities live at former military bases and small settlements. These San people have not lived in the area traditionally, but are Vasekela San, originally from Angola, and San from northwestern Kavango. They were relocated in the late 1970s when the South African Defence Force established a combat unit of primarily San people in Bushmanland.

Eastern Bushmanland, also referred to as the Nyae Nyae area, stretches from about 40 km west of Tsumkwe, the administrative centre of the area, eastward to the Botswana border.

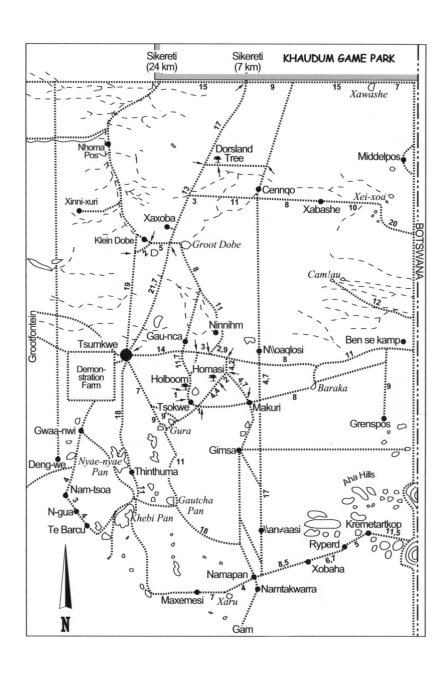

Sikereti
(24 km)

Sikereti
(7 km)

KHAUDUM GAME PARK

15 9 15 7

Xawashe

17

Nhoma
Pos

Dorsland
Tree

Middelpos

Xinni-xuri

Cennqo

3 11

8

Xabashe 10

Xei-xoa

20

Xaxoba

Klein Dobe

5 ○*Groot Dobe*

13

8

Cam!au

12

19

21,7

11

Grootfontein

Gau-nca

Ninnihm

Tsumkwe

14 3 2,9

N\\oaqlosi

Ben se kamp

Demon-
stration
Farm

11,7

Homasi

8

11

7

Holboom

1

4,2

4,7

4,4

4,7

Baraka

9

Tsokwe

Makuri

8

18

9 9

Gura

Grenspos

Gwaa-nwi

Gimsa

Deng-we

Nyae-nyae
Pan

Thinthuma

11

17

Aha Hills

Nam-tsoa

11

Gautcha
Pan

N-gua

Te Barcu

Khebi Pan

18

\\an≠aasi

Kremetartkop

11,5

Ryperd 5

8,5

6,7

Xobaha

Namapan

4

Namtakwarra

Maxemesi 7 *Xaru*

N

Gam

BOTSWANA

The name Tsumkwe is believed to mean "the feather of the Pleiades" – a reference to the constellation Pleiades. An administrative post was established here on Christmas Day 1959 by the first Bushman Commissioner, C V McIntyre. Today it still has the atmosphere of a frontier settlement, consisting of a conglomeration of government buildings.

Covering about 890 000 ha, the eastern part of the Tsumkwe district is the ancestral home of about 2 000 Ju'/hoan San, a subgroup of the !Khu-San. Their ancestral area once stretched from Rundu southward to the Eiseb Omuramba, eastward across the Aha mountains to Botswana, beyond Tsau Kuri, to Lake Ngami, and from there in a northwesterly direction to the Kavango River. Like the San elsewhere in southern Africa, the Ju'/hoan have been affected by numerous changes, and contrary to popular belief, they do not walk around in loincloths with bows and arrows slung over their shoulders. They live in several small settlements, practising a subsistence economy of dryland crop production and cattle farming, and supplement their diet with veld foods.

The tree savanna and woodland vegetation of the area is characterised by Lowveld cluster-leaf, red and russet bushwillows, leadwood and a variety of *Acacia* species.

Although a variety of game occur in the area, including elephant, several antelope species, lion, hyaena and wild dog, wildlife is not abundant and the animals migrate freely. During the rainy season, when the panveld area becomes inundated, the animals move to the more sandy areas west of Nyae-Nyae and a belt north of Tsumkwe. As the surface water dries up, the animals return to the panveld. Game viewing is hence not the main attraction, which is rather the wilderness atmosphere and sense of isolation.

The Bushmanland pan system, comprising Nyae Nyae, the "Pannetjiesveld" (named after the numerous small pans in the area) and the southern pans of Khabi and Xae-Sca, is one of Namibia's most important wetlands.

After good summer rains **Nyae Nyae**, the largest pan, covers several square kilometres and attracts upward of 11 000 wetland-associated birds, including 6 000 lesser flamingos, over 1 500 ruffs and 1 000 wood sandpipers. The red-billed teal is the most common waterfowl, while Cape teal, Cape shoveller and southern pochard are also well represented. Two wader species considered rare in southern Africa, are the black-tailed godwit and the great snipe. Breeding populations of slaty egret and wattled crane have also been recorded.

The "Pannetjiesveld" is an important breeding area for several heron and egret species. Among the waterfowl found here are white-backed and yellow-billed ducks, spur-winged goose, maccao duck, and African and Baillon's crakes.

Khaudum Game Park

Situated north of Bushmanland, this park covers 384 000 ha of woodlands. Although wildlife is not as abundant as in Etosha, its remoteness and wilderness atmosphere ensure a very special experience for visitors. The park lies within the Kalahari system and is characterised by sand dunes that have been stabilised by vegetation. The three major *omiramba*, a Herero word meaning poorly defined drainage line – the Khaudum and Cwiba omiramba in the north and the Nhoma in the south – are conspicuous features. A network of sandy tracks, negotiable only by four-wheel drive, crisscross the park.

The vegetation type in the south of the park is open savanna, characterised by red umbrella thorn, bushwillows, trumpet thorn (*Catophractes alexandri*), Lowveld cluster-leaf and Kalahari apple-leaf. The northern half is characterised by tall dry woodland comprising species such as wild seringa, Zambezi and wild teak, and manketti tree. Copalwood, sometimes referred to as bastard or false mopane, also occurs, and from a distance is easily confused with the mopane. Extensive reedbeds and grasslands occur in the omiramba.

Khaudum is a stronghold of Namibia's roan population and these rare antelope are usually seen in the Khaudum Omuramba in the north of the park. Other antelope species to be seen include kudu, blue wildebeest, gemsbok, steenbok and common duiker, as well as small numbers of tsessebe, eland, red hartebeest and reedbuck.

It is also home to Namibia's second-largest lion population and a refuge for the last few packs of wild dogs. Other predators include leopard, spotted hyaena and black-backed and side-striped jackals.

Elephants are common during the dry winter months only, while giraffe are abundant, but extremely difficult to spot, as they blend in well with the wooded landscape. The dry winter months are generally the best season for game viewing, as the

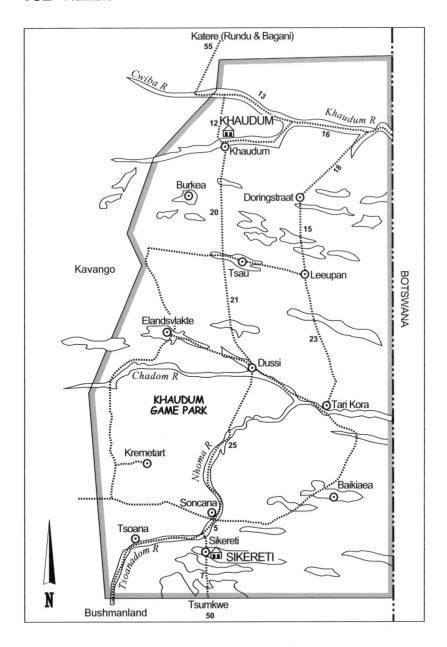

animals then congregate around the waterholes. After the first summer rains, however, the game disperse widely throughout the park and adjoining areas.

The park is rich in raptors and among the species to be seen are white-backed, lappet-faced and white-headed vultures, martial eagle and bateleur. Among the interesting species to keep an eye out for are Bradfield's hornbill, rufous-bellied tit, Arnot's chat and sharp-tailed starling. October to April is generally the most rewarding time for birding, as there is an influx of several migrant species into the area.

Due to the park's inaccessibility and the rough tracks, travelling in the park is restricted to a minimum of two four-wheel drive vehicles per party. You must take sufficient food and water for at least three days' travelling. The sandy tracks in the north of the park require constant use of four-wheel drive, so ensure that you have sufficient fuel for at least 800 km, bearing in mind that consumption can be considerably higher in four-wheel drive. During and after the rainy season, which extends until March, the southern part of the park and the omiramba (river courses) can be very muddy.

Accommodation at **Sikereti** in the south, and **Khaudum** in the north, comprises four thatch and wooden bungalows at each camp and camp sites. Amenities include braai places, tapped water and communal ablutions. Beds with mattresses, but no bedding, are provided. The camps are unfenced and animals such as spotted hyaena pass through occasionally.

Mahango Game Park

Bordering on the Kavango River in the east and Botswana in the south, this 24 462 ha park is a mosaic of woodlands, floodplains and reed-lined waterways. Tall jackal berry, mangosteen, waterberry and apple-leaf grace the floodplain margins, with a few large baobab trees and wild date palms also conspicuous. Away from the water's edge, the deciduous woodlands are dominated by wild seringa, copalwood, wild and Zambezi teak, and a variety of *Acacia* species.

One of the park's main attractions is its prolific birdlife, with over 450 species recorded. Specials to keep an eye out for include slaty egret, finfoot, coppery-tailed coucal, white-rumped babbler and swamp boubou. Among the noteworthy woodland specials are Bradfield's hornbill, white-breasted cuckooshrike and sharp-tailed starling. Topping the list of more than 20 raptors recorded for Mahango are the western banded snake eagle and Dickinson's kestrel.

Large numbers of elephant are attracted to Mahango during the dry winter months, but once the summer rains set in they disperse widely. You will be surprised how well these gigantic animals can melt away in dense vegetation, so keep an eye out for herds making their way to the river.

Animals associated with the river and the floodplains include hippo, crocodile, red lechwe and reedbuck. Sitatunga inhabit the papyrus swamps, but the chances of seeing this elusive antelope are slim. Mahango is also an important habitat for roan and sable, two species limited to northeastern Namibia, the Waterberg Plateau Park (see p 108 and a few farms with suitable habitat.

Other game you might spot include blue wildebeest, buffalo, kudu, gemsbok, tsessebe, bushbuck, impala, steenbok and common duiker. Also to be seen are warthog, vervet monkey, baboon and ostrich. Predators are represented by leopard, and lion and wild dog occasionally move through the park.

The road network consists of a riverside loop and a route traversing the dunes to the west of the proclaimed road that dissects the park. The riverside loop is accessible to sedan cars during the dry season, but could be difficult to negotiate during rainy periods. After following the Mahango Omuramba for a short distance, the road winds along the edge of the Kavango River floodplains to reach a cluster of baobabs after 10 km. The

nearby **picnic spot at Kwetche** suggests itself as a good stop and offers good views over the backwaters of the Kavango River. From here the road winds back to the main road.

Visitors travelling in a four-wheel drive vehicle have the option of a 29 km route through the dune landscape between the Mahango and Thinderevu omiramba. There is a hide overlooking a waterhole equipped with a pump along this route – a good place to spend a few hours game viewing during the dry season. The route is especially attractive in midsummer, when the pinkish-mauve flowers of the Zambezi teak create an attractive display.

The park is open throughout the year from sunrise to sunset to day visitors only.

Popa Falls

This delightful rest camp on the southern banks of the Kavango River is popular with those travelling between Rundu and

Katima Mulilo, and is an ideal base for exploring the nearby Mahango Game Park.

The name Popa Falls conjures up images of a raging waterfall, so little wonder that first-time visitors are disappointed when the "falls" turn out to be nothing more than a series of rapids. The rapids are created by a quartzite ledge that obstructs the flow of the river across its 1,2 km width. Here, the river splits into numerous channels, separated by small islands, to form a series of cascades with a total drop of about 4 m. The "falls" are best viewed when the level of the river is low, usually September and October, as the cascades are virtually "drowned" when the water level is high.

To view the cascades, take the metal bridge over the stream running past the picnic sites for day visitors and follow the well-trodden footpath to the banks of the river. With a bit of rock hopping you can jump across the first channel when the level of the river is low and find yourself surrounded by rushing channels of water. Alternatively, a short upstream stroll along the river bank will provide an impressive view over the river before it splits up.

The vegetation is characterised by magnificent riverine forests comprising jackal berry, mangosteen, buffalo thorn and wild pear, with Kalahari apple-leaf and bushwillows occurring away from the river. The birdlife is rich and varied and includes rarities such as rock pratincole (July-January), Narina trogon, swamp boubou and coppery-tailed coucal. Among the more commonly seen birds are several kingfisher and bee-eater species, as well as noisy flocks of arrow-marked babblers.

Anglers can try their hand and luck for tigerfish, threespot and greenheaded tilapia, nembwe and green happy, to mention but a few of the species occurring in the Kavango River. Permits are obtainable at the rest camp office.

When **Popa Falls rest camp** was built, the vegetation was disturbed as little as possible and the rustic teak wood and thatch bungalows, served by communal ablutions, nestle unobtrusively among the riverine trees. Each hut has a braai place and there is also a central braai and field kitchen area, but no restaurant. Although a limited range of non-perishables, cooldrinks and liquor can be purchased at a small shop in the park office, visitors are advised to be self-sufficient. Camp sites with fireplaces, a field kitchen and communal ablutions are also available. The camp is open from sunrise to sunset.

ROUTE 14
GROOTFONTEIN TO KATIMA MULILO AND IMPALILA ISLAND

DISTANCE: 640 km **TIME**: 7 hours **ROAD CONDITIONS**: Tar, except 60 km scheduled for completion by March 2000; Mudumu and Mamili national parks 4x4 only **FUEL**: Grootfontein, Rundu, Divundu, Omega, Kongola, Katima Mulilo **LINKING ROUTES**: Routes 7, 15

From Grootfontein (see route 7) on the B8, the road heads in a northeasterly direction. After about 40 km the vegetation begins to change markedly, with real fan palms, also known as makalani palms, conspicuous among the woodlands.

About 55 km out of Grootfontein, the turnoff to Tsumkwe (see route 15) is passed. Continuing along the B8, the turnoff to **Roy's Rest Camp** is signposted 500 m further on. Accommodation is in rustic wood and thatch bungalows with *en suite* facilities and there are also camp sites with hot water ablutions. Facilities include a restaurant, bar, swimming pool and curio shop. Among the activities offered are bird and game

watching and a 30 minute bush walk through the game camp, where there is a possibility of spotting eland, kudu, Burchell's zebra, blue wildebeest and ostrich.

Back on the main road, after another 72 km the Mururani veterinary control gate is reached. Here you pass from the commercial farming area into the Kavango Region, passing numerous small settlements as you head northeast to Rundu. Along the roadsides are the makeshift stalls of craftspeople selling their wares.

Rundu, the capital of the Kavango Region, is 248 km northeast of Grootfontein. Situated on a high bank, the town overlooks the Kavango River and the derelict settlement of Calai in Angola.

The **Tourism Centre** in the central business district provides information on attractions and accommodation in the region and also handles reservations for accommodation and tours. Tel (067) 25-5909, fax 25-5910.

Most visitors use Rundu as an overnight stop *en route* to Katima Mulilo, or are attracted by the Kavango River. Activities on the river include sundowner cruises, canoeing and angling for bream, nembwe and tigerfish. The riverine vegetation offers excellent opportunities for birding.

The Kavango people are renowned for the handicrafts fashioned from teak wood. Handicrafts range from a variety of household implements to furniture and the **Mbangura Woodcarvers' Cooperative shop** is well worth a visit.

In April each year the Kavango River becomes a kaleidoscope of colour when literally anything that floats participates in the **Rundu Float Carnival**. The event takes place over a 16 km stretch of the river and prizes are awarded for sportsmanship and for the most original float. Races in traditional *watus*, or dugout canoes, are also held.

Rising in the central highlands of Angola, the **Kavango River** forms the boundary between Namibia and Angola for some 400 km. It is a lifeline to the region's inhabitants, the greatest proportion of whom live in a narrow belt along it. The river reaches its peak at Rundu in February or March, inundating the fertile floodplains, which are planted with sorghum, millet (*mahangu*) and maize.

The river is home to some 73 fish species, and they are an important source of protein. Although commercial fishing equipment, and even mosquito nets, are increasingly being favoured, traditional methods are still applied. Among these are spearing fish and the use of funnel-shaped fishing baskets and fish weirs.

The river is also a highway for the Kavango people, who ply the waterway in their *watus*. The trunks of Zambezi teak, copalwood and wild teak trees that are still green are generally favoured for making these dugouts.

There is a choice of several accommodation establishments in Rundu, among them the **Kavango River Lodge**, which overlooks the river. The lodge offers comfortable accommodation in self-catering bungalows. Included in the tariff are the contents of a fridge, stocked for breakfast or a snack. Activities include canoeing, boat trips, sightseeing and sunset cruises and fishing trips.

Another option in Rundu is the **Omashare River Lodge** in Usivi Road. It also overlooks the Kavango River and offers luxury accommodation with river views. Amenities include a restaurant, ladies bar and swimming pool. Activities catered for include boat trips on the Kavango River, nature walks and safaris to Caprivi and Botswana.

There are also several lodges in the vicinity of Rundu; all of them are on the banks of the Kavango River and all are well signposted.

Set among shady trees, **Sarasunga River Lodge** is 4 km from Rundu. Accommodation is in reed-walled and thatch bungalows with *en suite* shower and toilet. Facilities include a restaurant, bar and swimming pool and among the activities offered are canoeing, angling and birding. There is also a grassed camp site with communal ablutions.

Kaisosi River Lodge lies 7 km east of Rundu. Accommodation is in thatched chalets and camp sites are available. Amenities include a restaurant, bar and swimming pool. Boat trips are offered.

A little further out of Rundu is the delightful **nKwasi Lodge**. It offers accommodation in teak and thatch bungalows tucked away among riverine forest. Facilities include a restaurant and bar, and boating, angling, sundowner trips and horseback trails are offered. Good birding can be enjoyed in the riverine forest. The turnoff is signposted 11 km east of Rundu on the B8 to Katima Mulilo; it is a further 9 km to the lodge.

From Rundu, you head east along the B8, passing through magnificent woodlands, to reach the northern approach to the **Khaudum Game Park** (see route 15 and p 161) after 112 km. Continuing for another 106 km, the turnoff to the Popa Falls rest camp is at Divundu. Turn right here onto the gravel D3403 and continue for 5 km to the signposted turnoff to **Popa Falls** (see p 164).

Popa Falls rest camp is an ideal base for undertaking day trips to **Mahango Game Park** (see p 163), 21 km further southeast along the D3403.

There are a number of accommodation options in the area other than Popa. **Suclabo Lodge**, adjacent to Popa Falls, is situated on a high bank overlooking the Kavango River. The turnoff is signposted 700 m east of Popa. Accommodation is in reed and thatch bungalows and there is a restaurant, bar and swimming pool. Boat trips on the river are offered.

The turnoff to **Ngepi Camp** is signposted 5,7 km east of Popa on the D3403. From the turnoff it is another 4 km to the camp, which offers grassed camp sites on the banks of the Kavango River. Facilities include a bar, meals, canoe and fishing trips on the river, and day excursions to nearby Mahango Game Park.

Ndovhu Lodge, also on the banks of the Kavango River, offers accommodation in safari tents with *en suite* facilities. A spacious, thatched restaurant-bar-lounge complex overlooks the river. Drives to Mahango Game Park, birding and fishing are among the activities offered. The lodge is signposted 3 km west of Mahango Game Park.

From Popa, backtrack to the B8 and turn right to cross the Kavango River by way of a single-lane bridge. On passing through a police checkpoint, you enter the **Caprivi Strip** and the **Caprivi Game Park**. Sandwiched between Angola and Zambia in the north, Botswana in the south and Zimbabwe in the east, the strip has an interesting international history. It projects eastward from Divundu for 500 km to Impalila Island at the confluence of the Chobe and Zambezi rivers, and has a width ranging between 30 and 50 km.

This geographical curiosity was created in terms of the Anglo-German Treaty of 1 July 1890. Britain gained control over the island of Zanzibar and the northwestern part of Botswana, while Helgoland and the Caprivi Strip became German possessions. Originally named the German Zambezi Territory, the strip was renamed after the Imperial Chancellor at the time, Count George Leo Von Caprivi Capra di Montecuccoli and became known as the Caprivi Zipfel.

German administration was established only in 1907, when the German flag was hoisted at Schuckmannsburg. Following Britain's declaration of war on Germany, Schuckmannsburg was attacked by a British force in 1914 and remained under military control until 1929. It was subsequently administered as part of the British Protectorate of Bechuanaland (now Botswana) until South Africa took over its administration in 1935.

Except for the Golden Triangle along the Kwando River, western Caprivi has enjoyed conservation status since 1963. The **Caprivi Game Park**, a 40 km wide strip of land, extends eastward from Divundu for 190 km to the Kwando River.

During the dry winter months, large herds of elephant congregrate along the Kavango River. At times over 1 500 elephant gather in the area, forming herds of between 300 and 500 animals. You are, therefore, well advised to heed the road signs warning you of elephants.

Covering 600 000 ha, the conservation area was initially set aside as a nature reserve, but was later proclaimed a game park. During Namibia's liberation struggle it was an operational zone controlled by the South African Defence Force and movement was restricted to travelling on the proclaimed road between Divundu and Kongola.

Even today, access is restricted to the **Golden Triangle** in the east of the park, partly because there are no facilities for visitors. Another reason is that the area is the ancestral home of the Barakwena San, although large numbers of Vasekele San fled to the Caprivi Strip during the Angolan civil war. Many were conscripted into the SADF during Namibia's liberation struggle and had nowhere to go when Namibia became independent. The status of the park still has to be decided and it has been suggested that core conservation areas be established along the Kavango and Kwando rivers and the remainder of the park be deproclaimed and managed on a multiple land-use basis, incorporating conservancies. The animals tend to congregrate along the Kavango and Kwando rivers, except during the rainy season, when the seasonal pans allow them to disperse. After rains there is a large-scale migration of elephants from Caprivi to Botswana and Angola.

During the dry winter months **Horseshoe Bend** on the Kwando River is a particularly good vantage point for elephants. Other animals to be seen include hippo, giraffe, kudu, Burchell's zebra, impala, tsessebe, sable and eland. A visit is most rewarding toward the end of the dry season, when the Kwando River is the only source of water. After the first summer rains, however, the numerous clay pans in the bush are filled with water and the animals disperse.

West Caprivi has an impressive bird list, with over 339 species recorded to date, while a further 71 species recorded in neighbouring Kavango and east Caprivi are likely to occur there. Species of special interest to birders include slaty egret, western banded snake eagle, Dickinson's kestrel, wattled crane, red-winged pratincole, greater swamp warbler, swamp boubou and brown firefinch.

A four-wheel drive vehicle is essential to negotiate the rough tracks' hazards – loose sand during the dry winter months and patches of mud during the rainy season. Permits to enter the area can be obtained from the Susuwe office, situated a few kilometres north of the B8. The turnoff is signposted just west of the Kongola Bridge over the Kwando River. Visitors must report to the office before entering the park.

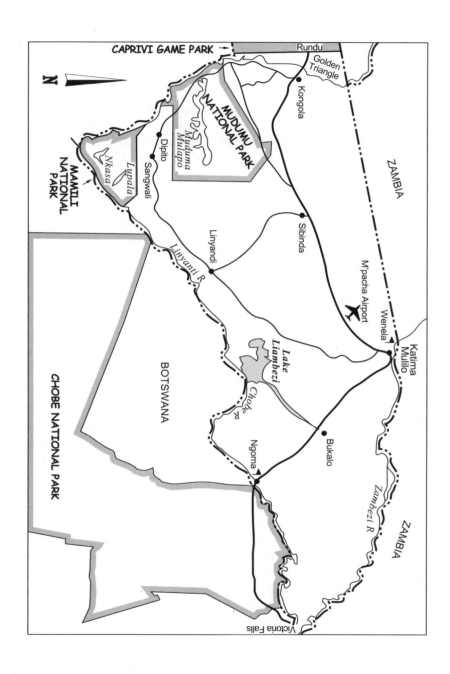

The only amenity is a camp site, without any facilities, at **Nambwa**, south of the B8. Shaded by tall trees, it is situated on a small termitaria island and overlooks a side channel of the Kwando River. Visitors must be totally self-sufficient.

About 190 km east of Divundu Bridge, the Kwando River marks the eastern boundary of the Caprivi Game Park and the Caprivi Strip fans out into **eastern Caprivi**, which resembles the fist of an extended arm. A well-watered region with an average rainfall of over 700 mm, it is bounded by perennial rivers, except in the north. In the northeast the Zambezi River forms a natural boundary with Zambia, with the Kwando-Linyanti-Chobe system forming the western, southern and eastern boundaries with Botswana.

Shortly after crossing the Kwando River you pass through a police checkpoint and about 7 km later you reach Kongola village. If you are heading for Katima Mulilo, continue along the B8 for 114 km. Traditional crafts, including baskets and bowls, can be bought at **Mashi Crafts** at the Kongola junction

However, if you are planning to explore the Mudumu and Mamili national parks, turn right onto the D3511. Both parks are best explored in four-wheel drive vehicles and, owing to their isolation, parties should consist of at least two vehicles. Also bear in mind that because there are no facilities whatsoever, visitors have to be self-sufficient in all respects.

After travelling for about 7 km along the D3511, a turnoff to the right leads for 3 km to the **Kubunyana camp site** on the banks of the Kwando River. Established with the assistance of the nearby upmarket lodge, Kubunyana is a community initiative in the Mayuni Conservancy. Facilities include camp sites with communal ablutions and three dome tents under thatch with their own kitchen and ablutions.

From Kubunyana transfers can be undertaken to a luxury island lodge catering for discerning travellers (scheduled for completion in November 1999). Situated on the western side of an island in the Kwando River, the lodge lies about 2,5 km west of Kubunyana. Activities offered include game drives in the Caprivi Game Park, birding, and boat and sundowner cruises on the Kwando River. The thatched main complex with its teak decks comprises a reception area, dining room and bar. Nestling among dense riverine vegetation, the six two-bed chalets overlook the river. Natural materials (thatch, wood and rock) have been used and each chalet has its own plunge pool.

The lodge is run by the owners of Impalila Island Lodge which has established itself as one of Namibia's foremost lodges. Bookings can be made with the reservations office of Impalila Island Lodge.

The **Open Sky African Safaris camp** is signposted 22 km south of Kongola village. Situated on the banks of the Kwando River, amenities include safari tents, communal ablutions and a thatched dining area and bar.

Lizauli Traditional Village is signposted 31 km after the turnoff from the B8 onto the D3511. Opened in 1993 as a living open-air museum, the focal point of the reed-enclosed village is the *khuta* (or meeting place). Other buildings include the headman's (induna) house, the houses of his eldest son and grandmother, the boys' and girls' houses, a grain store and a chicken coop.

During a guided tour of the village, visitors will gain an insight into the social customs, beliefs and origins of the Caprivi people. The uses of a variety of household implements are explained, and the pounding of millet by two women is demonstrated. Toward the end of the tour there is a performance by a witchdoctor to the beat of traditional drums.

Continuing along the D3511, the northern boundary of **Mudumu National Park** is reached 4 km on. Covering almost 101 000 ha of mainly woodlands, this little-known park is centred around the Mudumu Mulapo, a fossil river course. The Kwando River forms a natural boundary in the west for about 15 km, and the park extends eastward for 40 km.

Much of the vegetation is dominated by mopane woodlands, interspersed with patches of silver cluster-leaf and *Acacia* woodlands. Lush riverine forests of forest waterwood, fig trees, African mangosteen, mahogany and sausage trees line the Kwando River – a world of reed-lined waterways, quiet backwaters and forested islands.

The Kwando River is not only a source of water for the Kwando-Linyanti wetlands, but also a source of confusion, as its name changes no less than six times along its course. In Angola it is known as the Cuando, but where it cuts through the Caprivi Strip it is the Kwando. Further downstream, where it forms the boundary between Namibia and Botswana, the Batswana call it the Mashi. Once the river takes a sharp northeasterly turn it is known as the Linyanti and east of Lake Liambezi the Batswana refer to it as the Itenge and the Chobe.

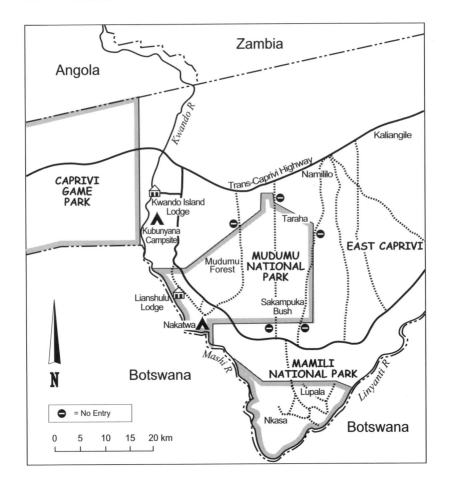

Proclaimed in 1990 as a sanctuary to the region's dwindling wildlife, game numbers are still relatively low. Among the species to be seen are elephant, buffalo, kudu, roan and impala. Mudumu is the best place in Namibia to see oribi, small antelopes favouring open grasslands. The river and adjacent habitats are inhabited by hippo, crocodile, a small population of red lechwe and sitatunga, a species confined to papyrus swamps.

One of the park's main attractions is the excellent birding it offers, with a checklist exceeding 400 species. One of the best places in southern Africa to see the brown firefinch is at Lianshulu Lodge, where the brown-throated weaver can also readily be seen. Other interesting species include western banded snake eagle, racket-tailed and broad-billed rollers (the latter from September to April), white-rumped babblers and Arnot's chat, as well as coppery and purple-banded sunbirds.

The area along the Kwando River is crisscrossed by a network of tracks, with the woodlands traversed by three running north-south. A four-wheel drive vehicle and a sense of direction are essential, as the tracks are rough and unmarked. During the summer rainy season, the clayish soil tracks are often impassable.

The turnoff to **Lianshulu Lodge** and **Lianshulu Bush Lodge** is signposted 3 km after entering the park. Situated on a concession within the park, the lodge comprises thatched reed and wood chalets and a large thatched reception area, lounge, bar and dining room overlooking Lianshulu lagoon, a quiet backwater of the Kwando River. There is also a swimming pool. Accommodation is on a full board basis and activities are aimed at providing a wilderness experience, rather than focusing on game viewing. Visitors can go on nature drives in open safari vehicles, guided walks in the park, boat trips or a sundowner cruise on the Kwando River.

The only other amenity in the park is the **Nakatwa camp site** of the Ministry of Environment and Tourism. It is signposted 4,7 km south of the Lianshulu turnoff and is 4 km from there. Note that there are no facilities, and visitors must be totally self-sufficient.

Continuing along the D3511, you leave the park 8,3 km beyond the Nakatwa turnoff and after another 20 km the turnoff to Sangwali is reached. Turn right here and continue through the village until the road deteriorates into a track, taking care to take the right-hand fork where the road splits. The northern boundary of **Mamili National Park** is reached after 7,5 km and the Shishinze office is just a further 600 m.

Although game is not as abundant as in some of Namibia's other game parks, the Mamili National Park offers visitors a true wilderness experience. There are no facilities and very few people have discovered this wild tract of land.

Cradled by the V-shaped arms of the Kwando-Linyanti River, the 32 000 ha park was set aside in 1990 to conserve Namibia's largest wetland, the Linyanti Swamps. From its origin in the highlands of Angola, the Kwando River flows in a southeasterly direction for nearly 1 000 km. It then quite unexpectedly makes a 90° turn to the northeast to follow the Gomare Fault and becomes known as the Linyanti River.

The annual floodwaters of the Kwando-Linyanti reach the area in August or September, inundating the floodplains and flooding the relic channels. During exceptionally high floods, such as those of 1958 and 1978, up to 80 per cent of the park is flooded and the area is turned into a mosaic of narrow reed-lined channels, oxbow lakes and reedbeds, a microcosm of the famed Okavango Delta. During such floods the two large tracts of termitaria forest become inaccessible, hence the names Nkasa and Lupala islands. For more than two decades, however, the floodplains have received very little overflow from the Linyanti.

Mamili is home to one of the largest concentration of buffalo in Namibia. Totalling over 1 100 animals a few years ago, large numbers had to be shot in 1997 and 1998 after the animals were burnt by underground fires. Large herds of elephant congregate on Nkasa and Lupala islands during the dry winter months, but after the first summer rains they migrate out of the park within a matter of days. Other species to be seen include red lechwe, reedbuck, impala, kudu, roan and common duiker. Large predators are represented by lion, leopard and spotted hyaena, while hippo and crocodile abound in the river. There is also a large hippo population at Shimbu Pool in the Sishika Channel. The success rate for game viewing varies, but June to November is generally the best time to see game.

The park, however, offers excellent opportunities for birding and species of interest to birders include slaty egret, coppery-tailed coucal, swamp boubou, chirping cisticola and long-tailed starling. In summer large numbers of migrants move into the park, among them squacco heron, yellow-billed kite, white and open-billed storks, several bee-eater species, hooded kingfisher and broad-billed roller.

A four-wheel drive vehicle is essential to explore the rough tracks, especially from December to February (depending on the start of the rainy season) when the tracks are often impassable. Groups should consist of at least two vehicles.

Facilities in Mamili National Park are limited to two demarcated **camping areas** without any amenities, requiring visitors to be self-sufficient. One of the camp sites, in the southeast of the park, is situated among shady trees on the banks of the Linyanti River, but can be difficult to access after rains. A nearby alternative camp site has good views over the floodplains, but lacks shade. Another camp site, on the edge of the Rudobe Forest, has good shade but no views. It lies about 18 km west of the Linyanti River camp site, close to Shimbu Pool.

You can rejoin the D3511 by travelling from the park to the village of Malegalenga and then continuing to Linyandi, the tribal seat of the Masubia people. From Linyandi the road goes in a northeasterly direction, passing the turnoff onto the D3514, leading to the northern point of **Lake Liambezi**, before rejoining the B8, about 8 km from Katima Mulilo.

The lake is fed by the Kwando-Linyanti and Zambezi rivers, which spill onto the eastern floodplains when the level of the river rises more than 6,8 m at Katima Mulilo.

Between 1958 and 1980, Liambezi received a sufficient inflow of water along the Bukalo and Kalengwe channels to counteract the evaporation of water, estimated at about 2 m a year. However, in the following five years there was no inflow and the lake dried up in 1985, a phenomenon known to have occurred earlier this century. It remained dry for 14 years, until the waters of the Zambezi River fed it once more in June 1998.

When full, the lake covers about 10 000 ha and has an average depth of 3-5 m. During such years the fish in the lake are an important source of protein for the people living in the area and up to one tonne of fish is caught daily.

On rejoining the B8, turn right and continue for 8 km to **Katima Mulilo**, the administrative capital of the Caprivi Region. Situated on the banks of the Zambezi River, Katima Mulilo is a Lozi name which means "to quench the fire" and there are two interpretations of it. According to one version it used to be an old practice on long journeys to take burning embers along in canoes. This eliminated the problems of lighting fires at night, but in rapids, such as the Mpwanda Rapids at Katima Mulilo, there was always a chance of the embers being extinguished by splashing water. Another explanation is that travellers could wade across the river at the Mpwanda Rapids, which at times are no deeper than crotch height, but the long wade was enough to douse any fires of passion amorous travellers might have had.

Caprivi was initially administered from Schuckmannsburg and later as part of the former British Protectorate of Bechuanaland, now Botswana. It was not until the mid-1930s that Katima Mulilo became the administrative centre of the region. Following the demarcation of Namibia into 13 regions after independence, it became regional capital of the Caprivi Region, but despite this status Katima Mulilo has the atmosphere of a frontier town. The streets are crowded with people and cars and at the **open-air market** goods ranging from chickens in coops and dried fish to colourful material from Zambia and fresh scones can be bought.

At the adjoining **Caprivi Art Centre** soapstone and wood carvings, handicrafts and printed material are sold. Some of the crafts are manufactured locally, while others are from nearby Zambia and Zimbabwe. The centre is well worth a visit.

Also of interest is a large **baobab**, which was hollowed out and fitted with a toilet by Major Lyle Trollope, who became Commissioner of the region in 1939. The tree can be seen behind the Caprivi Regional Council building.

Katima's most popular landmark is without doubt the **floating bar** of the Zambezi Lodge. In the late afternoons the river is transformed by a golden glow and there are few places in Namibia as idyllic for sundowners as this.

The **Zambezi River** provides ample opportunities for picnicking, boating, angling and birdwatching. Do not become complacent, however, as a number of people have been killed by crocodile and hippo.

Well over 70 fish species have been recorded in this water-rich region and the Zambezi offers excellent opportunities for angling. Tigerfish, western bottlenose, sharptooth catfish, banded tilapia (bream) and brownspot largemouth are among the most common species landed.

Birdlife is prolific and you might spot several species which in Namibia occur only in the northeast of the country. Among these are the honey buzzard, black-cheecked lovebird, racket-tailed roller, bearded robin and broad-tailed paradise whydah.

Along the Zambezi River you could see African fish eagle, white-crowned plover, half-collared kingfisher, white-fronted bee-eater and little bee-eater. Keep an eye out for African finfoot, which favour the quiet reaches of the river.

Birds associated with the riverine forests and mixed woodlands include green-spotted dove, pied barbet, fork-tailed drongo, white-browed robin, three-streaked tchagra, white helmetshrike and blue waxbill.

The **Zambezi Lodge**, on the eastern outskirts of Katima Mulilo, comprises chalets, some of which overlook the

Zambezi River, and has a camp site with communal ablutions. Amenities include a thatched terrace where breakfast and lunch are served, a restaurant for dinner, swimming pool and nine-hole golf course.

Katima Mulilo is a convenient stopover for travellers heading to Zambia. The Wenela border post is reached by turning left at the T-junction where the B8 joins the main road through Katima. The border post is reached 6 km on along a gravel road, and from there you can either continue to Mongu in western Zambia, or take the ferry across the Zambezi River to Sesheke. It is planned to build a bridge across the Zambezi River as part of the Trans-Caprivi Highway.

The town is also a convenient stopover *en route* to Botswana's famed Chobe National Park, Impalila Island and the Victoria Falls in Zimbabwe. Continuing along the B8, the turnoff to **Kalizo Lodge** is signposted 14 km out of Katima Mulilo; it is a further 25 km to the lodge.

Situated 40 km downstream of Katima, the lodge specialises in freshwater angling safaris and also offers excellent opportunities for birding. Angling on this stretch of the upper Zambezi is exceptional and tigerfish of up to 9 kg have been landed. Other popular species include nembwe and threespot tilapia. Accommodation is in reed, wood and thatch chalets on the banks of the Zambezi River, and camp sites with ablutions are also available.

The tar road beyond the Kalizo turnoff is in the process of being tarred and is scheduled for completion in March 2000. The Ngoma border post is reached 69 km out of Katima Mulilo and after crossing Ngoma Bridge and clearing customs and immigration with the Botswana authorities you enter Chobe National Park.

Although situated in Namibia, access to **Impalila Island** in the far northeastern corner of Namibia is either by air or via the border town of Kasane in Botswana. The reason for this logistical headache is that the eastern floodplains of Caprivi are at best difficult to negotiate, and totally impossible when the floodplains are inundated. Also referred to as "The One Island in Africa Where Four Countries Meet", Impalila is sandwiched between Namibia, Botswana, Zambia and Zimbabwe at the confluence of the Zambezi and Chobe rivers. West of the island, which is 11 km long and 4 km at its widest, lie the vast eastern Caprivi floodplains.

From Katima Mulilo, take the B8 to Ngoma border post and then travel through Botswana's famed Chobe National Park to the border town of Kasane. Guests of **Impalila Island Lodge** are met in Kasane and after clearing immigration facilities they are transferred by boat to the lodge, situated among beautiful riverine forest on the northwestern corner of the island. One of Impalila's main attractions is the outstanding birding that can be enjoyed in the area. Among the noteworthy species are Pel's fishing owl, western banded snake eagle, coppery sunbird, swamp and tropical boubous, brown firefinch and Narina trogon. Also to be seen are rock pratincole (July to January) and African skimmer (April to December), as well as pygmy goose, lesser gallinule and rufous-bellied heron. The summer months are the most rewarding time for birdwatching.

Angling is superb and tigerfish of up to 8 kg have been caught. Pink happy, bream and Upper Zambezi yellowfish are also taken. Angling can either be done from motor boats or from a *mokoro* (dugout canoe) in the rapids. The lodge actively encourages catch and release.

Bordering on Chobe National Park in Botswana, the lodge offers excellent game-viewing opportunities from the Chobe River. Game likely to be seen during a boat trip include puku, a species which reaches the southern limit of its distribution at Chobe, red lechwe, Chobe bushbuck, giraffe, kudu, hippo and crocodile, as well as large herds of elephant. Lions are seen regularly and wild dogs occasionally, while a few fortunate visitors have also spotted the elusive sitatunga. The dry winter months, when the animals congregate along the Chobe River, are best for game viewing.

The lodge comprises six luxury chalets, built from wood, rock, thatch and reeds, overlooking the backwaters of the Zambezi River. Centred around an ancient baobab is an open-air central lounge and dining area, built on raised decks. There is also a swimming pool.

Activities offered include boat trips, exploring the waterways in a *mokoro* with a guide, guided walks on islands in the area, self-guided trails, visits to nearby traditional villages and sunset cruises. Angling enthusiasts are well catered for.

Impalila is indisputably Namibia's finest lodge in terms of the standard of service and the range of activities offered.

ROUTE 15

GROOTFONTEIN TO KHAUDUM GAME PARK (SIKERETI CAMP)

DISTANCE: 345 km **TIME:** 6 hours **ROAD CONDITIONS:** 55 km tar, 221 km fair gravel, 68 km 4x4 track **FUEL:** Grootfontein, Farm Hieromtrent, Rundu, Divundu **LINKING ROUTES:** Route 14

Completely off the beaten track, this route explores the tracks of Bushmanland and the Khaudum Game Park. Although accessible by sedan car, a four-wheel drive vehicle is essential to explore the area beyond Tsumkwe. Groups should consist of at least two vehicles and must be self-sufficient.

From Grootfontein (see route 7) the B8 heads in a north-easterly direction to reach the turnoff to Tsumkwe after 55 km. **Roy's Rest Camp** (see route 14) is 500 m further north along the B6. Turn right onto the gravel C44 and continue for 72 km to the signposted turnoff to the farm Hieromtrent. As fuel supplies are unreliable at Tsumkwe, the well-signposted 12 km detour to Hieromtrent, where fuel is available, is advisable.

Continuing along the C44, the veterinary control fence marking the western boundary of Bushmanland (see p 158) is reached 3,3 km beyond the D2893. About 13 km after passing through the veterinary control gate, you will reach the turnoff to the **Omatako Valley rest camp**, a project of San communities living in the area. Visitors can see how veld food is gathered and cooked by San women, undertake guided bush walks, village tours and bush rides on horseback. There is also a craft shop where traditional San crafts can be purchased. Facilities include camp sites and basic thatched huts with communal ablutions.

Continuing in a southeasterly direction, **Tsumkwe**, the administrative centre of Eastern Bushmanland, is reached about 133 km further on. Among the things to see in eastern Bushmanland are two large baobabs that have long served as landmarks. Particularly well known is **Holboom**, an enormous baobab named after a cavity in its trunk. Another beacon is **Grootboom**, which justifies its Afrikaans name (Big Tree) with a circumference of 30 m at its base. To reach the Holboom, continue west along the C44 from Tsumkwe for 11,2 km and then turn right onto a track which is followed for about 12 km to the enormous baobab. From here, head for the San settlement at Tsokwe where you turn left and after about 1 km left again to reach the Grootboom a few kilometres on. Continuing in a northeasterly direction from the Grootboom, you will reach a junction where you keep left and after 4,2 km you will link up with the C44. Turn left here, continuing for 17 km to Tsumkwe.

Other attractions include the numerous pans and the **Aha mountains**, a range of low hills extending into Botswana.

Accommodation in Tsumkwe is limited to the **Tsumkwe Lodge**, which has thatched bungalows, a restaurant and bar. Four-by-four vehicles with guides can be hired, and safaris to Khaudum Game Park arranged.

Khaudum Game Park is reached by turning north at the four-way intersection in Tsumkwe. Although the track's surface is generally hard, patches of soft sand necessitate a four-wheel drive vehicle. Keep an eye out for a track turning to the right after 36,6 km. Turn right and continue for 2,7 km to the **Dorslandboom**, an enormous baobab that served as a camping site when the Thirstland Trekkers (Dorslandtrekkers) passed by during their epic trek to Angola in the 1880s.

Backtrack to the main track and continue for 17,7 km to the unfenced southern boundary of the **Khaudum Game Park** (see p 161). Sikereti Camp, a further 7,6 km on, is an ideal base for exploring the southern part of the park.

From Sikereti visitors have the option of travelling to Khaudum Camp via Tari Kora, Leeupan and Doringstraat or via Dussi and Tsau. Although much shorter, the latter route passes through very thick sand, necessitating constant use of low range four-wheel drive.

The track from Khaudum Camp to the B8 is extremely sandy and you should allow four to five hours to cover the 58 km stretch; much of it will be covered using low range four-wheel drive. On reaching the B8, you have a choice of continuing on route 14 to Popa Falls, the Mahango Game Park and Katima Mulilo, or travelling back to Rundu and Grootfontein in the other direction. Travellers heading for Rundu along the B8 can take the Shitemo turnoff if they need fuel. For travellers continuing to Popa, fuel is available at Divundu, 88 km after joining the B8.

NAMIB DESERT

Covering some 16 per cent of the country's surface, the Namib Desert is a landscape of infinite variety and ever-changing moods. It is a harsh, arid land where years can go by without a single drop of rain to quench the parched earth. Yet, it is one of the most spectacular and fascinating areas in Namibia, with scenery ranging from the magnificent dune sea of the central Namib to the seemingly endless gravel plains between the Kuiseb and Swakop rivers. It is home to many small creatures that are uniquely adapted to their seemingly inhospitable environment, and occur nowhere else in the world. To protect this unique tract of land two conservation areas, the Namib-Naukluft Park and the Skeleton Coast Park, with a combined area of over 6,6 million hectares, have been set aside.

Cape Cross Seal Reserve

Situated in the National West Coast Tourist Recreation Area, Cape Cross is home to Namibia's largest breeding colony of Cape fur seals. It is the most important of the three mainland breeding colonies along the Namib coast and, with an estimated population of 250 000 foraging seals, it supports nearly a third of Namibia's foraging seal population. It is also of historical significance.

Although the seals are present throughout the year, their numbers fluctuate considerably, depending on marine conditions. Males have an average mass of 187 kg; the average female weighs 75 kg.

The colony becomes a hive of activity in mid-October, when the bulls arrive to establish their territories, which are vigorously defended against would-be intruders. Cows have a gestation period of eight months, but birth only takes place after a full year, as the development of the embryo is delayed by four months. About 90 per cent of the pups are born in a 34-day period, beginning late November and early December. The pups congregrate in dense "pods" while their mothers feed at sea, and are vulnerable to predation by black-backed jackal and brown hyaena, which are responsible for up to 25 per cent of mortalities. On returning from the sea, cows locate their pups by a combination of scent and call.

Research has shown that seals can eat the equivalent of 8 per cent of their body mass. Roughly half of their diet consists of pilchards and maasbankers, with octopus, squid and other cephalopods constituting about 37 per cent. Rock lobster and other crustaceans make up the balance.

The seals at Cape Cross have been exploited for their skins and other products since 1895, when 2 500 skins were exported. Since then the industry has experienced mixed fortunes, but the harvesting has continued to this day. After reaching a peak in the early 1980s, the demand for pelts crashed in 1983, as a result of the stand taken by animal rights groups. Harvesting continued on a small scale at some colonies and despite the protests the Ministry of Fisheries sets an annual quota for harvesting of pups and bulls.

Toward the end of the 1800s, guano, the mineral-rich dried excrement of sea birds, was collected from the "islands" in the salt pans south of Cape Cross. In 1895 6 000 tonnes of guano were collected, but the Damaraland Guano-Gesellschaft faced numerous problems. By 1902 production had decreased to 500 tonnes and the operation closed down the following year.

The rocky promontory is also of historic interest, as it was here that the first European, Diego Cão, set foot on the Namibian coast in 1486. He erected a limestone cross, or padrão, just over 2 m high and weighing about 360 kg, and in time the site became known as Cape Cross.

For over four centuries the padrão withstood the ravages of nature, until it was removed in January 1893 by Captain Becker of the German cruiser, *Falke*, and taken to Germany. A granite replica was made in 1894 on the instructions of Kaiser Wilhelm II and erected at Cape Cross on 23 January the fol-

lowing year. The replica bore the German coat of arms and an inscription in German, in addition to the Portuguese and Latin inscriptions on Cão's cross. The inscription reads: "Erected at the command of the German Kaiser and King of Prussia Wilhelm II in 1894 on the site of the original which was weathered by the years."

Visitors are often surprised to see two crosses at Cape Cross. In 1974 the area around the site was landscaped and paved circles and semi-circles, representing the Southern Cross (symbolic of the direction in which Cão sailed), were built on different levels.

Facing the terraces, the German replica is to your left (the highest level). The star-shaped pattern on the terrace is symbolic of the importance of stars to early navigators. The cross on the terrace to the right is an authentic replica of Cão's padrão. It was commissioned by the National Monuments Council and unveiled in 1980 on the exact spot where the original padrão stood. Based on a plaster cast of the original, the cross was cut from Namib dolerite; the same hard rock which forms the outcrop at Cape Cross. The Cão family crest and the wording of the original padrão in Latin and Portuguese, English, Afrikaans and German can be seen on the other levels.

Cape Cross is open daily from 10:00 to 17:00. Picnic facilities are provided (if you can stomach the smell of the seals), but not accommodation.

Namib-Naukluft Park

Covering nearly 5 million hectares, the Namib-Naukluft Park is the third largest game park in Africa. It is a spectacular mosaic of landscapes, ranging from the orange dunes of the dune sea and the vast gravel plains between the Swakop and Kuiseb rivers to the wetlands of Sandwich and the rugged mountains of the Naukluft massif. It comprises several sections, each with its unique landscapes, atmosphere and attractions.

Namib

This section of the park lies between the Swakop River in the north and the Kuiseb River in the south. Its stark and barren landscape is characterised by vast gravel plains, isolated *inselberge* (island mountains), the spectacular Moon Landscape of the Swakop River Valley and the badlands of the Kuiseb Canyon.

To date nearly 60 mammal species have been recorded in the area; the most commonly seen larger species are gemsbok, springbok and Hartmann's mountain zebra. The mountain zebra occur mainly in the eastern part of the park, especially in the vicinity of the Kuiseb and Swakop canyons. Gemsbok are fairly widely distributed after the summer rains, but during

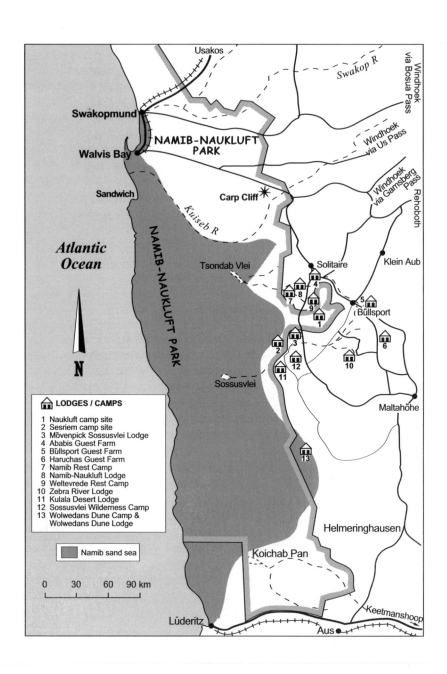

the dry season they concentrate in large numbers on the southeastern plains and in the Kuiseb River area. Springbok are also
widely distributed.

Klipspringer occur in suitable rocky habitats, especially the
rocky canyons in the upper reaches of the Swakop, Khan and
Kuiseb rivers. The Kuiseb Canyon is also home to three troops
of chacma baboon and the westernmost troop have been
observed to go without water for up to two weeks.

Among the predators the black-backed jackal is the most
widely distributed. Leopard occur in the Kuiseb and Swakop
canyons and the mountainous areas of the northeast. Spotted
hyaena inhabit the eastern part of the park and along the coast
brown hyaena patrol the beaches in search of food.

The Namib section of the park has one of the highest densities of lappet-faced vulture in Africa. Among the other
species to be seen are ostrich, Ludwig's bustard, Rüppell's
korhaan, Namaqua sandgrouse, Stark's lark, grey-backed
finchlark and tractrac chat.

The vegetation is sparse, except in the Kuiseb and Swakop
rivers, where a variety of trees and shrubs grow. Among these
the camel thorn, ana tree, ebony tree and real mustard tree are
the most conspicuous.

The gravel plains are often bare for years, except for camel
thorn trees and shrubs growing in the shallow river washes.
However, after good rains the plains are transformed into waving grasslands. Along the coast the vegetation is characterised
by dwarf shrubland, dominated by brakbos (*Salsola*) and ink-
bos (*Arthraerua leubnitziae*). A rich diversity of lichens is also
found here, but the most fascinating plant is without doubt the
welwitschia (see p 12).

The **Tinkas Nature Walk** initially follows the course of the
Tinkas River, before winding back across the deeply dissected
plains to the starting point. Along the way there are fascinating
geological formations, and natural water seeps and rock over-
hangs through which one has to scramble. The walk takes four
to five hours and you should take at least 2 ℓ of water along.
No permit (except the park entry permit) is required.

A permit is not required when travelling on the proclaimed
roads, but once you turn onto the park roads one is necessary.
Permits can be obtained from the tourist offices at Hardap and
Sesriem, or Ministry of Environment and Tourism (MET) offices
in Swakopmund, Windhoek and Lüderitz. Entry and camping

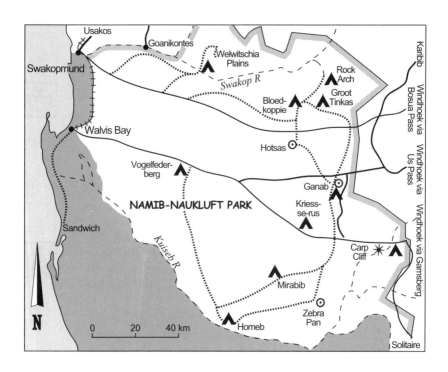

permits are obtainable over weekends from filling stations in Swakopmund and Walvis Bay.

Facilities in this section of the park are limited to **camp sites** with braai places, picnic tables, refuse bins and field toilets. These are at Kuiseb Bridge, Kriess-se-Rus, Homeb, Mirabib, Vogelfederberg, Ganab, the Swakop River and Bloedkoppie. The Groot Tinkas camp site is accessible only by four-wheel drive vehicle.

Naukluft

Originally proclaimed as a sanctuary for the Hartmann's mountain zebra in 1968, the Naukluft mountains are home to a variety of other mammals, including kudu, gemsbok, springbok, klipspringer and steenbok. Among the smaller mammals are chacma baboon, black-backed jackal, rock dassie and dassie rats. The rugged kloofs support a healthy population of leopards, with cheetah and spotted hyaena occurring from time to time.

To date some 204 bird species have been recorded in the area. Birding can be rewarding, as the complex lies at the southern limit of several species typical of northern Namibia, such as Rüppell's parrot, Monteiro's hornbill, Herero chat, white-tailed shrike and chestnut weaver. At the same time, it is the northern limit of distribution of a number of Karoo species, including the Karoo robin and the cinnamon-breasted warbler. Among the species requiring specialised habitats (such as krantzes) for breeding are black eagle, augur buzzard, lanner falcon and Bradfield's swift. Species you might spot in kloofs with pools include hamerkop, pied barbet, pririt batis, brubru and common waxbill. Be on the lookout for mountain chat, Layard's titbabbler and dusky sunbird on the slopes. The rock-runner is restricted to northern and eastern slopes. The plateau is the habitat of species such as Ludwig's bustard, sabota lark, bokmakierie (whose loud onomatopoeic call is often heard) and the uncommon long-billed lark. The gravel plains surrounding the Naukluft support ostrich, Rüppell's korhaan, spike-heeled and Stark's larks, tractrac chat and sociable weavers.

The vegetation of the Naukluft complex is classified as Semi-desert and Savanna Transition (Escarpment Zone) type. Characteristic trees and plants include various corkwoods (*Commiphora*), thorn trees (*Acacia*), *Euphorbia* species and quiver trees. A mosaic of five main plant communities has been identified and the one visitors are most likely to encounter is the gorge community. These communities are confined to gorges with springs, of which there are about 10 in the complex. They have a rich diversity of species and in the Naukluft River more than 150 species have been recorded. A characteristic tree of the river valleys is the common cluster fig, which attracts large numbers of birds when it bears fruit.

The other communities are those of the plateau, mountain areas, gravel plains surrounding the complex, and the sandy plain transitional community.

The massif is part of the high-rising escarpment that marks the western edge of Namibia's interior highlands. The flat, tri-angular plateau of the mountain complex is separated from the adjacent highland plateau to the south by the impressive near vertical Johann Albrechts Felsen (cliffs). In the northwest and west its highest peaks loom almost 1 000 m above the Namib plains.

The plateau consists mainly of dolomite and limestone for-mations. Dissolution of these formations by ground water over many millennia has given rise to karstification of the plateau and an extensive underground drainage system. In some of the deeply incised kloofs discharge from this underground water reservoir creates crystal-clear springs and streams.

Tufa, also known as fountain stone or waterfall limestone formations, are associated with these springs and streams. These soft, or semi-friable, porous limestone deposits are formed by the evaporation of calcium carbonate-rich stream water that filters through the dolomite rocks. The widespread distribution of these deposits throughout the Naukluft mountains attests to a considerably wetter period during the recent past. A particularly impressive tufa formation with delightful pools is reached after a 20 minute walk from the Naukluft camp site.

In the geological history of this part of the country the Naukluft mountains are of particular interest. The Rehoboth-Sinclair Basement Complex, found mainly on the western side of the massif, consists of metasedimentary and volcanic rocks, gneisses and granites, varying from 1 000 to 2 000 million years in age. The overlying sediments of the Nama Group consist mainly of black limestone, deposited about 600 million years ago when the southwestern corner of southern Africa was covered by a shallow tropical sea. The Naukluft "nappes" forming the upper part of the mountains are very large, sheet-like units of sedimentary rocks, which were emplaced along low-angle fault- or fracture-planes, known as thrusts, some 500 to 550 million years ago.

The rugged Naukluft mountains are ideal walking country and visitors have a choice of two day walks or an overnight hiking trail. The 17 km **Waterkloof Trail** starts at the camp site and can be completed in six hours, while four to five hours should be set aside to hike the 10 km **Olive Trail**. Remember to take sturdy walking shoes, a hat, sunscreen cream, a day-pack, trail snacks and at least 2 ℓ of water per person. No permits are required for these walks.

The more adventurous can tackle the **Naukluft Hiking Trail**, an eight day, 120 km circular route traversing the mountains, with an option of a four-day trail. Hikers are rewarded with dramatic views, but the steep inclines demand a high level of fitness. Along the route, hikers are accommodated in basic overnight shelters. Owing to high summer temperatures, the route is only open from 1 March to 31 October. Groups must

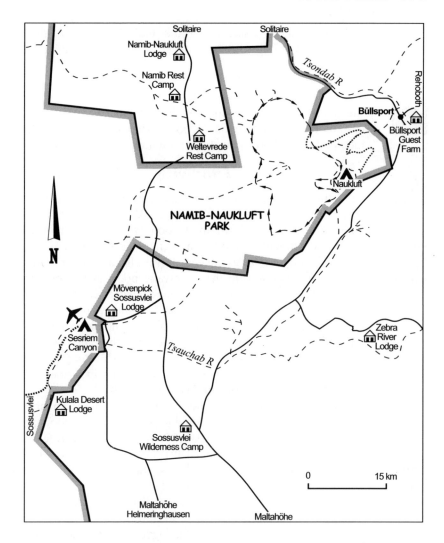

consist of at least three people and are limited to a maximum of 12. Namibia Wildlife Resorts, Private Bag 13267, tel (061) 23-6975 or 23-3845, fax 22-4900.

The **Naukluft 4x4 Trail** is an exciting off-road trail that provides the ultimate challenge to driving skills. Covering 72 km, the route traverses a variety of terrains, ranging from steep inclines to rock-strewn descents. At the end of the first day's leg, accommodation is provided in a rustic overnight camp high up in the mountains. There are several vantage points with magnificent vistas along the trail. Namibia Wildlife Resorts, Private Bag 13267, tel (061) 23-6975 or 23-3845, fax 22-4900.

Naukluft is open all year from sunrise to sunset.

Accommodation at **Naukluft** is limited to four shady camp sites with cement tables and benches, fireplaces and communal ablutions. It is essential to book camp sites prior to your intended visit. There is no shop, restaurant or filling station.

Sandwich

Until the late 1980s Sandwich lagoon was one of the most scenic spots along the Namibian coast. With a length of 10 km and a width of up to 3 km, the lagoon was a mosaic of freshwater pools fringed by reeds, water channels and salt marshes, flanked by high dunes to the east. It was also a haven for large flocks of flamingos, and the freshwater pools at its northern end attracted a variety of freshwater-associated wetland birds.

Since the mid-1980s the lagoon has undergone dramatic changes following the formation of a sandspit, which separated the lagoon from the ocean. At the same time the northern sandspit moved landward, smothering the freshwater ponds at the northern end of the lagoon, which resulted in a dramatic decrease in the numbers and diversity of birds.

Despite the changes to the lagoon, the Sandwich area remains a wetland of international importance and among the 180 bird species recorded to date 30 are migratory. During the first full bird count in February 1991 the total number of birds was estimated at 179 000. Curlew sandpiper, little stint, and common and Arctic terns constituted more than 75 per cent of this number, while greater and lesser flamingos were almost equally represented and totalled 30 200. Most of the waders occur on the mudflats south of the lagoon, an area not accessible to visitors.

The area north of Sandwich is popular with anglers, but angling is prohibited along this stretch of coast from 25 January to 15 April. The lagoon is, however, out of bounds to anglers throughout the year.

Originally named Ponta do Ilheo, the bay was once used as a deep-water anchorage for sailing vessels, hence the reference to Sandwich Harbour on some maps. The name Sandwich is said to be derived from the original Dutch name Zandvisch, but a more likely explanation is that it owes its name to the 195 ton whaler *Sandwich* – the first known vessel to drop off anchor here in 1789.

Over the past two centuries Sandwich has served various purposes. Whalers took shelter in the bay during storms and in the mid-1800s De Pass, Spence and Company established a trading station here. Cured fish, shark liver oil, seal skins and guano were exported to Cape Town and Mauritius. Toward the end of the 1890s the South West Africa Company established a meat canning factory at Sandwich. Cattle were obtained from the pastoral Khoikhoi, but the venture was soon forced to close down. Between 1904 and 1906 Sandwich was used as a back door for gunrunning to the Herero and Nama, who rose against the German administration.

Between 1910 and 1947 guano was collected from the natural sand islands in the lagoon. Land was reclaimed to enlarge one of the islands and by 1943 the "island" covered 8 ha. After numerous problems the collection of guano ceased in 1947 and in 1956 the concession was cancelled. In the years following the sea and the dunes reclaimed their rightful place, destroying almost all evidence of human activities here.

Sandwich is open throughout the year between 06:00 and 20:00. Overnight camping is strictly prohibited in the Sandwich section of the park. A wide choice of accommodation is, however, available in Swakopmund and Walvis Bay.

Sesriem

Situated on the edge of the vast sand sea of the Namib, Sesriem is a base for exploring two of the Namib's most spectacular features: Sesriem Canyon and Sossusvlei. The delightful camp site owes its name to a nearby canyon which holds water for several months after good rains. To draw water from the pools, early travellers had to tie a bucket to six (*ses*) ox thongs (*rieme*) lashed together; hence the name.

The canyon lies about 4 km south of the camp site and from the parking area a track leads down into the canyon. As you make your way down, you are transported 15-18 million years back in time when alternating layers of gravel, sand and pebbles were deposited during a wetter phase. These layers were later cemented into calcrete conglomerate. Some two to four million years ago continental uplift caused the incision of the Tsauchab River and over time the river carved a gorge up to 30 m deep and about 1 km long.

Sesriem has camp sites with fireplaces, tapped water and communal ablutions. The sites are shaded by age-old camel thorn trees. Amenities include a small shop selling a limited range of non-perishables, cool drinks and liquor, a filling station and swimming pool.

Mövenpick Sossusvlei Lodge, adjacent to Sesriem, comprises 45 *en suite* units, open-air dining terrace, bar and swimming pool. The walls and ceilings of the bedrooms are made from canvas, and the sloping walls of the bathroom and the foyer-dressing room recreate the adobe-style walls characteristic of an Arab village.

Sossusvlei

From Sesriem it is possible to travel to within 5 km of Sossusvlei in a sedan car. The road is being tarred and is expected to be completed in 1999. From the parking area where sedan cars are left, four-wheel drive vehicles can continue to the parking area at the vlei, but remember that the area is ecologically sensitive and you should not deviate from the main track. It is advisable to deflate tyres to avoid getting bogged down.

An early start is advisable, as the dunes are at their best just after sunrise, when the orange colour of the slopes, catching the first rays of the sun, contrast sharply with the jet black colour of the shaded slopes. Confirm the gate opening and closing times at the tourist office, as they vary with sunrise and sunset.

About 24 km from Sesriem a viewpoint is reached and after crossing the Tsauchab River the road continues along the broad river valley, flanked by high dunes. **Dune 45**, one of the most photographed Namib dunes, is about 45 km from Sesriem and the parking area for sedan cars is reached after a further 15 km.

Sossusvlei marks the end of the Tsauchab River's journey to the sea. Tens of thousands of years ago the river flowed into the Atlantic Ocean, but the ever-encroaching dunes swamped its course. Over thousands of years the Tsauchab River has, nevertheless, managed to keep open part of its course, which ends in twin pans.

The pans can be dry for as long as a decade and are inundated only in years of exceptional rains. Such an event is rare, but when it does take place, water spills over into the northern arm of Sossusvlei. This pan has appropriately been named **Nara Vlei**, on account of the large numbers of naras, a plant endemic to the Namib, growing on its perimeter. When the Tsauchab reached the pans during January 1997 floods, the water dammed up for nearly a kilometre and the main Sossusvlei pan retained water for 15 months.

Also worthwhile exploring is **Dead Vlei**, which was cut off from the course of the Tsauchab River an estimated 500 years ago. The grotesque skeletons of camel thorn trees and the cracked, stark white floor of the pan present a scene of utter desolation, reminiscent of the devastation after an atomic explosion. The vlei is reached after a 30 minute walk from the signposted parking area near Sossusvlei.

One of the main attractions of Sossusvlei are the spectacular dunes with their sinuous crests. These are known as star dunes and are usually formed where low energy, multidirectional winds blow. In the Sossusvlei area, the dunes north of the Tsauchab River reach up to 325 m, while freestanding dunes to the south of the river attain heights of about 220 m.

West of Sossusvlei is a 60 km wide belt of linear dunes, lying north-south. With a length of up to 50 km and heights ranging between 60 and 100 m, they lie diagonally to the prevailing southwesterly winds. Dune streets of up to 1,5 km wide separate them.

Closer to the coast is a 10-20 km wide belt of crescentic dunes, including transverse and barchan types. These dunes lie roughly perpendicular to the southwest wind which is dominant along the Namib coast.

The sand covering the Namib was washed into the Atlantic Ocean by the Gariep (Orange) and Fish rivers millions of years ago. This material was subsequently transported northward and deposited on the shore by the ocean currents.

One of the most fascinating aspects of the Namib dune sea is the way in which the creatures living there have adapted to survive in their inhospitable environment. In fact, the Namib's almost entirely barren dune environment is the only area of its kind in the world where a fauna has evolved.

The dunes are the habitat of several species of tenebrionid beetles, lizards, spiders and other small creatures which derive their water requirements from dew, light rain and fog which, on average, penetrates for 100 days a year up to 50 km into the desert.

Among the unusual animals is the nocturnal web-footed gecko (*Palmatogecko rangei*), which has webbed feet that enable it to move rapidly over the soft sand. It feeds on small insects and is, in turn, preyed on by the "dancing white lady" spider (*Carparachne arenicola*). "White lady" spiders live in tunnels in the sand dunes and to prevent their homes from collapsing, the tunnels are lined with spider webs when they are being dug.

Another interesting dune inhabitant is the shovel-snouted lizard (*Aporosaura anchietae*). It is also referred to as the "clown of the Namib" – a name which refers to the thermal "dance" it performs when lifting its feet off the hot sand.

Also living in the dunes is the *Comicus* cricket, which takes shelter in the cool, moist, deeper layers of sand during the day. Lobed feet allow it to move with ease over the sand when it emerges at night to feed.

An interesting reptile of the dunes is the side-winding adder (*Bitis peringueyi*), which has an average length of 20-25 cm. For the greater part of the day it conceals itself, with only its eyes and tail exposed. This is not only done to protect itself from extremes of temperatures, but also to ambush geckos and other small reptiles.

One of the fascinating small mammals of the dunes is Grant's golden mole (*Eremitalpa granti namibensis*), which was first recorded in 1837 by the explorer Captain James Alexander. No further specimens were obtained until 1962, when a skull fitting its description was discovered in owl pellets in 1962. In 1963 a specimen was collected in the Kuiseb River. By day the golden mole is dormant, usually at the base of a grass tuft or hummock dune, emerging at night to feed on insects and their larvae.

Sossusvlei on Foot walks are conducted at Sossusvlei by Nubib Adventures. Lasting about three hours, the walks provide an ideal opportunity to learn more about the many fascinating aspects of the Namib and to experience the desert. Nubib Adventures also conducts guided overnight **Sossusvlei Hikes** (April to October) to the Witberg, an island mountain surrounded by dunes, south of Sossusvlei. The two-day trail covers about 35 km and provides a unique opportunity to experience the solitude and the magnificent dune landscape. P O Box 186, Maltahöhe, tel (06638) 5713, fax (063) 29-3231.

NamibRand Nature Reserve

Covering over 150 000 ha, the NamibRand Nature Reserve is one of the largest private nature reserves in southern Africa. The reserve shares its western border for about 120 km with the Namib-Naukluft Park, with the rugged Nubib mountains forming a backdrop to the east. With landscapes ranging from orange windswept dunes and rocky outcrops to extensive gravel plains, the main attraction of NamibRand is its scenic beauty, wide open spaces and silence. This vast desert sanctuary is host to a variety of game, among them gemsbok, springbok, ostrich, red hartebeest and Burchell's as well as Hartmann's mountain zebra. No less interesting though are the smaller mammals and the multitude of creatures that are specially adapted to survive in this inhospitable environment.

To generate income for the reserve a number of exclusive concessions have been granted to tour operators. Balloon flights are undertaken from **Camp Mwisho** on the farm Kwessiegat in the north of the reserve. The balloons take off just after sunrise and during the one hour flight you can enjoy a bird's-eye view of the desert dunes and plains. A champagne breakfast is served at the landing spot. Guests are accommodated in safari tents with *en suite* facilities at Camp Mwisho on the night before the flight. Namib Sky Adventure Safaris, P O Box 5197, Windhoek, tel (063) 29-3233, fax 29-3241.

At **Wolwedans Dune Camp**, which is spectacularly situated in the dunes, guests are accommodated in comfortable tents with *en suite* facilities. Built on raised decks, each tent has expansive views of the surrounding desert. The main complex is likewise built on a raised platform and comprises a lounge, dining room, open-plan kitchen and a sundowner deck. Guided nature drives led by experienced guides enable visitors to explore this fascinating desert.

Another option at NamibRand is the upmarket **Wolwedans Dunes Lodge**, situated a few kilometres from the Wolwedans Dune Camp. The lodge, comprising a lounge, dining room, bar and sundowner deck, is built on wooden platforms and stilts in the dunes. Each of the eight accommodation units comprise a double room with *en suite* bathroom and a sundeck with spectacular vistas of the surrounding desert. A combination of split-poles and canvas give the impression of a classic camp. Activities include scenic morning and afternoon guided drives and there is also a possibility of walks.

On the farm Die Duine, in the south of the reserve, guided desert walking trails are conducted by the husband-and-wife team of Marc and Elinor Durr. Their **Tok Tokkie Trails** are tailored to suit participants, and last from one to four days. To ensure personal attention, groups consists of two to six trailists, although larger groups are catered for on request. The trails lead through spectacular and varied scenery, ranging from mountains to dunes and vast plains. Along the way trailists will have a close-up view of the desert life and gain an insight into the many fascinating aspects of the Namib Desert. The rates are inclusive of all equipment (only bring your own boots) and meals. Other activities include duneboarding and kite flying. Families with children are welcome and are well catered for. P O Box 162, Maltahöhe, tel (06638) ask for Namgorab 5230, or (061) 23-5454.

Skeleton Coast Park

The Skeleton Coast Park is renowned for its excellent fishing, the solitude it offers those seeking to escape from everyday life and its spectacular landscapes. The 1,6 million hectare park is divided into a southern section, between the Ugab and Hoanib rivers, and a northern section, between the Hoanib and Kunene rivers. The latter is managed as a wilderness area and access can only be gained by joining a fly-in safari operated by the concessionnaire.

The landscape of the southern section consists mainly of flat gravel plains interrupted by rocky outcrops and several large ephemeral rivers. North of Torra Bay, the landscape is characterised by transverse dunes of the northern sand sea of the Namib Desert.

The vegetation is sparse; the most common species being dollarbush (*Zygophyllum stapfii*), brakspekbos (*Zygophyllum simplex*), occasional stands of gannabos (*Salsola*) and a variety of succulents.

Mammals are not represented in large numbers and are mainly limited to black-backed jackal and brown hyaena. Springbok and gemsbok are attracted to the springs in the Uniab Delta. Lions occasionally migrate down the river courses to the coast.

Birdlife is far more prolific and to date over 203 species, excluding 23 offshore and 10 extralimital species, have been recorded in the park. Large numbers of sea- and shorebirds are attracted by the nutrient-rich ocean, and Palaearctic migrants occur along the coast and at coastal wetlands from July or August to April. At least 17 Palaearctic migrant species have been recorded, among them grey plover, turnstone and sanderling.

The coast is an angler's paradise and attracts thousands of anglers each year. The most eagerly sought-after species are cob and galjoen, while steenbras and blacktail are also popular. Galjoen and blacktail are usually caught in turbulent surf off rocky areas. Cob and steenbras favour water off sandy and pebble beaches, but are also taken from rocks in deeper water. Angling areas have been set aside at Torra Bay and Terrace Bay and it is prohibited to deviate from demarcated roads.

Not to be missed is the **Uniab Delta Walk**, a 6 km ramble that leads from the pump station in the Uniab Delta, past a waterfall, to the coast and back. No permit is required for this walk. For those keen to explore the desert on foot, the **Ugab Wilderness Trail** provides a unique experience. These guided hikes are conducted every second and fourth week from April to October. Starting on Tuesdays and ending on Thursdays, the trails offer a fascinating insight into various aspects of the Skeleton Coast. Namibia Wildlife Resorts, Private Bag 13267, Windhoek, tel (061) 23-6975 or 23-3845, fax 22-4900.

The camp site at **Torra Bay**, 51 km south of Terrace Bay, is open only during the December-January Namibian school holidays, when basic commodities and fuel are available. Reservations should be made well in advance.

At **Terrace Bay** visitors are accommodated on a full board basis in two-bed cottages. Amenities include a restaurant, shop, filling station and freezing facilities for anglers.

The stretch of the coast between the Hoarusib River and Cape Frio has been set aside as the **Skeleton Coast Park Concession Area**. Access to this area can only be gained by joining an exclusive fly-in safari conducted by the concessionnaire, Olympia Reisen.

Although game occur in small numbers, the emphasis of the safaris is on the wilderness atmosphere and the singular beauty and solitude of this remote area. Highlights of a visit include the **Clay Castles of the Hoarusib Canyon**, the **Roaring Dunes**, south of the Hoarusib Canyon, and the **Cape Frio seal colony**. There is also a possibility of seeing the rare **desert-**

dwelling elephants inhabiting this inhospitable area. Visitors are accommodated on a full board basis in a small camp in the Khumib River.

Swakopmund

Swakopmund, 35 km north of Walvis Bay, is Namibia's premier holiday resort and is especially popular during the summer months, when Namibians flock to the coast to escape the heat of the interior. The town has a distinctly German atmosphere, with stately German colonial buildings lining the streets, and German is widely spoken.

For tourist information on the Erongo Region, visit the **Namib I** office on the corner of Kaiser Wilhelm and Roon streets. It is one of the best tourism information offices in the country and has a wealth of information on the Erongo Region. Tel and fax (064) 40-4827. Open Monday to Friday 08:00 to 13:00 and 14:00 to 17:00; Saturdays 09:00 to 12:00.

The **Ministry of Environment and Tourism** office in Rittersburg, corner of Kaiser Wilhelm and Bismarck streets, has a reservation office and provides information on the coast and state-owned resorts. Tel (064) 40-2172. Open Monday to Friday 08:00 to 13:00 and 14:00 to 17:00.

The town's Khoekhoen name, Tsaokhaub, originates from the words *tsao* and *xoub*, which are translated as "posterior" and "excrement". The name apparently refers to the brown colour of the sea when the Swakop River is in flood.

Swakopmund owes its existence to a decision by the German Reich to establish a port along the coast to provide access to the interior of the German protectorate of Deutsch-Südwestafrika, proclaimed in 1884. As the Walvis Bay enclave had already been proclaimed a British possession and other possible sites were unsuitable, the choice fell on Swakopmund.

The first building – barracks for troops – was erected in September 1892, a month after the crew of the *Hyena* stepped ashore. On 23 August 1893, 120 *Schutztruppe* and 40 settlers disembarked from the *Marie Woermann* and by 1897 Swakopmund had 113 inhabitants.

What to do in Swakopmund

Swakopmund is a blend of stately German buildings, dating from the early 1900s, and modern buildings, and your visit

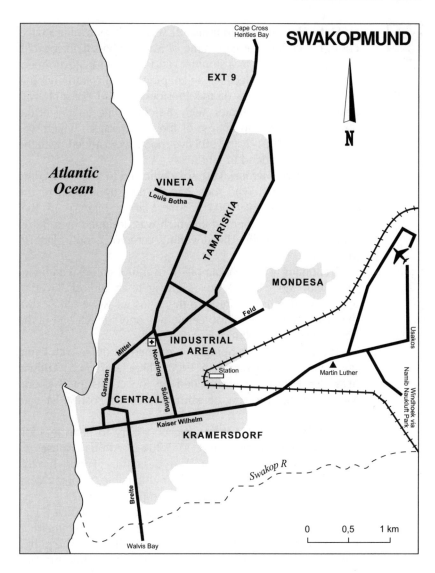

will not be complete without a **walking tour** through its streets. The following suggested walk should take about two and a half hours. Numbers marked on the Swakopmund town map on page 203 correspond to those in the text.

The **lighthouse** (1), a conspicuous Swakopmund landmark, originally consisted of an 11 m high stone tower, completed in July 1902. Eight years later its height was increased to 28 m.

State House Swakopmund (2) was built as a magistrate's court, hence the German name of *Kaiserliches Bizirksgericht*, and has also served as a summer residence for top government officials for several decades. In keeping with this tradition, it is the official residence of the President at the coast. It was designed by Carl Schmidt, with the chief state builder at the time, F W Ortloff, in charge of the construction, which was completed in 1901-2. In 1905 five rooms were added, with the wooden tower added in 1945.

The **Marine Memorial** (3) was dedicated to the First Marine Expedition Corps, who took part in the suppression of the Herero Uprising of 1904-5. The Marine Infantry in Kiel commissioned the memorial, which was designed by a Berlin sculptor, A M Wolff. The unveiling ceremony took place in July 1908.

Trendhaus (4) is an example of beautiful colonial architecture, with the window boxes giving it an almost Bavarian appeal. Carl Schmidt drew up the plans for Robert Stolz, but they were not followed too carefully – only the left half of the house appeared on the plans.

The Woermann Shipping Line opened an office with living quarters in Swakopmund in 1900. Three years later, **Ludwig Schröder House** (5) was added on the corner of Post and Molkte streets. The row of palm trees lining Post Street date back to 1911.

Not long after this it became necessary to provide additional accommodation and in 1904-5 **Altona House** (6) was built in Molkte Street. The design by Friedrich Höft incorporated a signal tower and an attic gable, to break what might have been a monotonous facade.

Swakopmund's telephone exchange and **post office** (7), as well as staff, were housed in this beautifully symmetrical building, which opened its doors on 1 April 1907. The public entrance was through the door in the centre, while the side doors gave access to the staff quarters on the first floor. Redecker drew up the plans, and the Bause brothers were responsible for the construction. The building served as a post office for 60 years, until a new building was taken into use just around the corner in 1967. Since then it has been used as municipal offices.

The foundation stone of the **Antonius Gebaude** (8), designed by Otto Erle, was laid in March 1907 and a hospital,

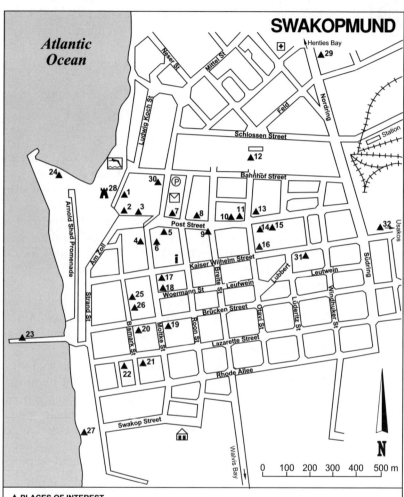

SWAKOPMUND

Atlantic Ocean

Henties Bay

▲ PLACES OF INTEREST

1	Lighthouse	17	Hotel Kaiserhof
2	State House Swakopmund	18	Deutsche-Afrika Bank
3	Marine Memorial	19	Hohenzollern
4	Trendhaus	20	MC Human Flats
5	Ludwig Schröder House	21	Kaserne
6	Altona House	22	Princess Rupprecht Home
7	Old Post Office	23	Jetty
8	Antonius Gebaude	24	Mole
9	Litfass-Saulen	25	Woermann House
10	Old Residence	26	Swakopmund Arts Association
11	Dr Schwietering House	27	National Marine Aquarium
12	Old railway Station	28	Swakopmund Museum
13	German School	29	Old Prison
14	Deutsche Evangelical Lutheran Church	30	Altes Ampsgericht
15	Parsonage	31	Otavi Bahnhof & OMEG Haus
16	Villa Wille	32	Martin Luther

staffed by sisters of the Franciscan order, was opened in March the following year. It served as a Catholic hospital until 1987.

In about 1905, **Litfass-Saulen** (9), or advertising pillars, became part of the town scene. These pillars were named after E Litfass, a printer who introduced the concept in Berlin in 1855. Businesses, including shops and hotels, displayed notices on the pillars, on which official announcements were also posted. The one here is the only original pillar remaining in the town.

Although you will pass a number of old German-style houses on your tour, it is worth stopping at the **old residence** (10) and the adjacent **Dr Schwietering House** (11) on the corner of Post and Otavi streets, which were used for many years as consulting rooms. Both houses date back to 1910.

Early in the 1900s Swakopmund was linked to the interior by two railway lines – the Otavi Line to Tsumeb and the State Line to Karibib and later Windhoek. Built in a style locally termed Wilhelminischer, the **old railway station** (12) was the terminus of the state railway line.

The ornate building, designed by C Schmidt and built in 1901, is one of the finest station buildings in southern Africa. It now serves as the reception hall of the Swakopmund Hotel and Entertainment Centre.

In June 1912 a design competition was announced for a building to house the **German government and the municipal secondary schools** (13). Separate entrances and classrooms were to be provided, while facilities such as the library would be shared. The winning design was submitted by Emil Krause, an employee of Metje and Ziegler. The building was completed in October 1913 and harmonises beautifully with the baroque style of the Lutheran Church and adjacent parsonage across the road.

In 1906 Dr Heinrich Vedder established a Lutheran congregation in Swakopmund and on 18 December 1910 the foundation stone of the **Deutsche Evangelical Lutheran Church** (14) was laid. The architect, Otto Ertl, was undoubtedly influenced by the reawakening of interest in baroque during the Wilhelminische era (1884-94). F H Schmidt was the builder and the church was consecrated on 7 January 1912. The bells in the tower were imported from Apolda, Germany, where they were cast by Franz Schilling. **The parsonage** (15), adjacent to the church, was completed in July 1911.

Karl Hermann Wille, a notable builder in the town, built the elegant **Villa Wille** (16) for himself. A single-storey dwelling was originally planned, but a double-storey house was built and its style is in keeping with the nearby church complex. The house was completed in 1911 and is one of the most beautiful in Swakopmund. The decorative tower is particularly eye-catching.

Situated on the corner of Kaiser and Molkte streets, the **Hotel Kaiserhof** (17) was opened in May 1905. Sixteen rooms on the first floor could accommodate 26 guests, with additional accommodation available on the ground floor. Fire destroyed the hotel in 1914, but it was later rebuilt as a single-storey building and housed the Standard Bank for some time.

On 4 October 1909 the Swakopmund branch of the **Deutsche-Afrika Bank** (18) opened for business. Constructed by the firm of F H Schmidt, its design incorporated several neo-classical features. Since 1922 it has been occupied by the National Bank, later Barclays, and then First National Bank, and over the years the exterior has not changed.

The **Hohenzollern building** (19), with its almost exotic decorations, is undoubtedly one of the finest examples of Victorian baroque in Swakopmund. It was built in 1905-6 as a hotel for Hermann Dietz and at one stage it was reputedly also used as a brothel. It later housed the municipal offices and in 1987 was renovated and converted into sectional title flats. A 1,8 m high cement cast of Atlas originally adorned the building. As it was feared that Atlas would collapse, the cast was replaced with a fibreglass replica during the renovations.

The building now known as **M C Human Flats** (20) was erected by the Bause brothers, who built several smaller houses in Swakopmund from 1902 onward. Their buildings are characterised by interesting facades, which were decorated with a wide variety of embellishments. As you continue down Bismarck Street, three old houses dating back to the early 1900s create a quaint street scene.

The Second Railway Company landed in Swakopmund in October 1904 to construct a wooden jetty and in 1906 completed the **Kaserne** (21), which served as barracks. Built in an L-shape, the Kaserne is similar in design to the Alte Feste in Windhoek and Fort Namutoni in Etosha. Although the massive building has every appearance of a fort, its purpose is evidenced by the large windows. Of interest are the crests of the then German Federal States and a plaque commemorating those killed in action, which can be seen on the wall of the entrance hall. The building serves as a youth hostel of the Ministry of Youth and Sport. Access to the Kaserne is from Lazarette Street.

Now a private hotel housing a maternity home in one wing, the original building of the **Princess Rupprecht Home** (22) dates back to 1901, when it was erected by the German authorities as a military hospital. It was located at the coast as the sea air was considered healthy for convalescents.

Construction of the solid iron **jetty** (23) started in 1911. Although it was originally planned to be 640 m long, only 262 m had been built when work was brought to a halt with the outbreak of World War I. As the necessary harbour facilities were available at Walvis Bay, the South African authorities did not complete the jetty. Two drill bits used in the construction of the old pier can be seen at the start of the jetty.

Over decades the pounding sea took its toll and by the mid-1980s the structure had become unsafe. A Save the Jetty Fund was established to raise funds and 17 iron pillars were encased in concrete. The jetty was reopened on 13 December 1986, but in March 1998 it was closed to the public, as the remaining iron pillars had become unsafe. An estimated N$800 000 will be needed to rehabilitate this well-known Swakopmund landmark.

The Mole (24) was an attempt by the early colonists to construct an artificial harbour which was planned by the government architect, F W Ortloff. Construction began in September 1899 and five months later the 375 m pier was completed. Unfortunately, the currents along the coast had not been considered and by July 1904 a sandbank had formed at the entrance, restricting shipping movements to high tide. By 1906 the harbour had silted up, creating a sheltered beach. Today, pleasure boats are launched from the Mole.

The following buildings have not been included in the walking tour as you would probably only appreciate them fully after a long rest. However, do make an effort to visit them during your Swakopmund visit.

Woermann House (25), with its elegant, panelled walls and stucco ceilings, is the pride of Swakopmund. Designed by Friedrich Höft as headquarters for the Damara and Namaqua Trading Company, the building was completed in 1905. The

"Damara Tower" was incorporated as a look-out post for ships, and for ox-wagons approaching from the interior.

In 1909 the building was bought by the trading firm of Woermann & Brock and became known as Woermann House. After World War I, it was used as a school hostel for 40 years, and gradually fell into an almost derelict state. It was restored in the mid-1970s and now houses the public library.

The view of Swakopmund from the top of the **Damara Tower** makes the climb up the steep staircase worthwhile. The key is obtainable from the library, which is open from 10:00 to 12:00 and 15:00 to 18:00 (Monday to Friday) and from 10:00 to 12:00 (Saturday). On Saturday and Sunday afternoons the key is obtainable from the Swakopmund Arts Association Gallery. Tel (064) 40-2473.

The **Swakopmund Arts Association Gallery** (26) is located on the first floor of Woermann House. The gallery has an interesting permanent collection of work by Namibian artists and is open Monday to Saturday from 10:00 to 12:00 and 15:00 to 17:00.

The focal point of the **National Marine Aquarium** (27) is an underwater glass tunnel through the oval-shaped 12 m by 8 m main tank. The tank, the first of its kind in Africa, contains a wide variety of marine species, including sharks, turtles, stingrays and typical West Coast fish species such as galjoen, kabeljou and steenbras. A visit is especially worthwhile when the fish are fed by divers at 15:00 on Tuesdays, Saturdays and Sundays. Various other forms of marine life, including anemones, starfish, rock lobster, deep-sea red crab and nudibranches, are displayed in several smaller tanks. Open Tuesday to Saturday 10:00 to 16:00; Sunday and public holidays 11:00 to 17:00; closed Monday and Christmas Day. Tel (064) 40-5744.

A visit to the **Swakopmund Museum** (28), built on the site of the original German customs house, should not be missed. Exhibits include the flora and fauna of the Namib Desert, several marine dioramas, a historical section with items from the German period and an excellent ethnological collection. An 80 page book, *Swakopmund – A Chronicle of the Town's People, Places and Progress*, is on sale at the museum and provides an invaluable insight into the development of the town. Tel (064) 40-2046. Open daily from 10:00 to 13:00 and 14:00 to 17:00.

The **old prison** (29) is easily bypassed without realising that it is in fact a jail. This is perhaps because it was designed by Otto Erle to provide staff accommodation in the main building, while the flanks served as the jail. Heinrich Bause was responsible for the construction, which was completed in 1909 at a cost of 121 500 German marks. As it is still used as a prison, photographs are forbidden.

The **Altes Amptsgericht** (30), or old magistrates' court, with its gables and turrets, is very similar to the jail (29). As it was also designed by Otto Erle and built during the same period (1907-8), the similarities are hardly surprising. The building was originally intended as a school, but lack of funds resulted in the state completing it for use as a magistrates' court. It was later used as a school hostel and in 1972 the municipality took over the building and restored it to provide office space.

The OMEG Line, built by the Otavi Minen- und Eisenbahn-Gesellschaft to export copper from Tsumeb, had its terminal building in Swakopmund at the **Otavi Bahnhof (Railway Station)** (31) in Kaiser Wilhelm Street. In 1910 the state took over the OMEG Line, as the State Line, which ran parallel to it for 145 km, had proved uneconomical and was closed. However, as the Otavi station was inadequate, the railway line was diverted to the State Line terminus. The building now serves as a museum depicting the development of transport and also houses a craft shop. The adjacent **OMEG Haus** served as a goods shed.

Just outside Swakopmund, alongside the B2, is one of Swakopmund's landmarks, **Martin Luther** (32), a steam tractor imported by Lieutenant Edmund Troost from Germany in 1896 to haul supplies from the port through the desert to the interior. After a few trips it was abandoned outside Swakopmund as a result of high maintenance costs and logistical problems in finding water for the boiler. It was subsequently dubbed Martin Luther, after a resident quipped that the engine can also say: "Here I stand; I cannot do otherwise." – a reference to the famous statement made by Luther in front of the German parliament in Worms in 1521.

The Namib Centre of the Wildlife Society of Namibia has established an interesting **2,5 km circular walking trail** on the outskirts of the town. Starting at the Angora Rabbit Farm, the route incorporates the Swakop River mouth and lagoon. A trail pamphlet with information about the birds, flora, history and geology of the trail is obtainable at the start of the walk. P O Box 483, Swakopmund, tel (064) 40-5442, ask for Gabby Tirronen-Heinrichsen.

Casual visits to **Rössing Uranium Mine** (see p 84) are not permitted. However, tours are conducted from Swakopmund on Fridays, departing at 08:00 and returning at 12:30. Reservations must be made in advance at the Museum (tel 064 40-2046) by 12:00 Thursdays.

About 12 km east of Swakopmund, on the D1901, is the well-known **Camel Farm** run by Elke Erb. Here you have the opportunity to ride a camel, a mode of transport which was fairly common for police patrols in the early 1900s. To add to the experience you can don a headdress similar to those worn by Arabs. Rides are conducted daily between 15:00 and 17:00 and bookings are essential, tel (064) 40-0363.

Organised tours and trips

Various day and half-day tours of Swakopmund, the Namib Desert and nearby attractions are conducted.

Charly's Desert Tours, P O Box 1400, Swakopmund, tel (064) 40-4341, fax 40-4821. Day trips to the Namib Desert, Sandwich, Kuiseb Delta, Spitzkoppe and half-day tours to Cape Cross and the Namib Desert. Overnight tours are also conducted.

Desert Adventure Safaris (DAS), P O Box 1428, Swakopmund, tel (064) 40-4459, fax 40-4664. Day and shorter trips to the Namib Desert, Cape Cross, Spitzkoppe and a gem tour to Rössing Mountain. Longer safaris to Kaokoveld.

Namib Adventure Centre, Commercial Bank Arcade, tel (064) 40-5216, fax 40-5165. One-stop booking office for coastal and desert tours, adventure activities, budget tours and budget accommodation.

Rhino Tours, P O Box 4369, Swakopmund, tel (064) 40-5751, fax 40-5757. Offers a wide range of day and overnight tours in and around Swakopmund, including full-moon trips to the Moon Landscape, pleasure-boat cruises and overnight safaris in luxury tents.

Abenteur Afrika Safari, P O Box 1490, Swakopmund, tel (064) 40-4030, fax 46-4038. Tours to the Namib Desert, Walvis Bay lagoon and dunes, sundowner trip and Cape Cross.

Air Flips

Atlantic Aviation, P O Box 465, Swakopmund, tel (064) 40-4749, fax 40-5832. Flights lasting from one hour to overnight trips.

Pleasure Flights & Safaris, P O Box 537, Swakopmund, tel and fax (064) 40-4500. Flights from one-and-a-half hours to full day trips.

Angling

Angling Tours Namibia, P O Box 3767, Swakopmund, tel (064) 40-2275, fax 46-4038. Specialises in shark fishing, as well as rock and surf angling.

Blue Marlin Adventures, Swakopmund, tel (064) 40-4134. Fishing, shark fishing, deep sea fishing and sightseeing tours.

Horse trails

Okakambe Trails, Swakopmund, tel (064) 40-2799, 40-4747 or 40-5258. Guided horse trails ranging from one-hour out-rides and day tours to trails of two to three days.

Shopping

Swakopmund offers visitors a varied shopping experience, with products ranging from art to gemstones and kudu hide shoes. Curios and handicrafts are sold at the **street markets** at Palmenstrand (below Café Anton) and opposite the Old Prison in Südring Street.

The town is home to several well-known Namibian artists and art galleries offer visitors an opportunity to invest in Namibian art. **Die Muschel,** 32 Breite Street, tel (064) 40-2874, has a good selection of art and books. There is also **Gallerie Rapmund**, Bismarck Street, tel (064) 40-2035 and the **Hobby Horse**, Brau-Haus Mall, between Roon and Molkte streets, tel and fax (064) 40-2875.

A wide selection of books on Namibia is available from **Swakopmunder Buchhandlung**, Kaiser Wilhelm Street, tel (064) 40-2613. It has been trading as a bookstore since 1896.

At **Karakulia**, Knobloch Street, tel (064) 46-1415, visitors can view the spinning and weaving of karakul carpets, rugs and wall-hangings from raw wool to finished product.

Swakop River Angoras, on the southern outskirts of the town alongside the Swakop River, tel (064) 40-5442, offers visitors an opportunity to watch angora rabbit wool being harvested and spun. Open Monday to Saturday 10:00 to 17:00.

Antique hunters should not miss a visit to **Peter's Antiques**, corner of Molkte and Brücken streets, tel (064) 40-5624, which offers a wide variety of crafts, books and memorabilia. The famous **Swakopmunder Veldskoen** is well known beyond Namibia's borders. In addition to genuine kudu leather shoes, a variety of leather goods, cured game skins and curios are available. 7 Leutwein Street, tel (064) 40-2633.

Where to eat

Swakopmund has a wide variety of restaurants, offering fare ranging from German home cooking to international cuisine. Seafood dishes are popular and are the speciality of several restaurants. Here are a few restaurants to try in Swakopmund.

Alt Swakop, 50 Breite Street, tel (064) 40-2333. German-style pub and restaurant.

Bayern Stübchen, 13 Garnison Street, tel (064) 40-4793. German home cooking.

Café Anton, 1 Bismarck Street, tel (064) 40-0331. No visit to Swakopmund is complete without a visit to Café Anton. Traditional German confectionery, light lunches.

Café Treff and Putensen Bäckerei, Kaiser Wilhelm Street, tel (064) 40-2034. Lively venue for coffee, cakes and light meals.

De Kelder Restaurant, Klimas Building, 11 Molkte Street, tel (064) 40-2433. Informal family restaurant. Steaks, spareribs, seafood and salads.

Erich's Restaurant, 21 Post Street, tel (064) 40-5141. Renowned for its fish and meat dishes. Open Monday to Saturday, evenings only.

Europa Hof Hotel Restaurant, Bismarck Street, tel (064) 40-5898. À la carte, seafood specialities.

Frontiers Restaurant, corner of Moltke and Woermann streets, tel (064) 40-4171. Traditional African dishes, game and fish.

Hansa Hotel Restaurant, 3 Roon Street, tel (064) 40-0311. À la carte international cuisine, fish, game.

Kuki's Pub and Seafood Restaurant, 22 Molkte Street, tel (064) 40-2407. A landmark in Swakopmund. Lively atmosphere and good food – seafood and steaks.

Napolitania Pizzeria, 33 Breite Street, tel (064) 40-2773. Pizzas and Italian dishes.

Papas, Shoprite Centre, Kaiser Wilhelm Street, tel (064) 40-4747. Pizzas and light meals.

Platform 1 Restaurant, Swakopmund Hotel and Entertainment Centre, tel (064) 40-0800. À la carte restaurant with excellent hot and cold buffet. Restaurant echoes railway theme of the reception hall.

Strand Café, Strand Hotel, tel (064) 40-0315. Light meals, daily specials, draught beer, coffee and cake.

The Tug, Arnold Shad Promenade, tel (064) 40-2356. Magnificent view over the ocean. À la carte menu with seafood and meat dishes.

Werner's Restaurant, Strand Hotel, tel (064) 40-0315. À la carte restaurant on beachfront overlooking the bay at the Mole. Seafood specialities.

Western Saloon, Molkte Street, tel (064) 40-5395. Small restaurant with excellent steak and seafood dishes.

Where to stay

Hotels

Reminiscent of a castle, **Burg Hotel Nonidas** was built around the ruins of a police station and a customs post dating back to 1892. The characterful bar forms part of the old building and photographs of the ruins before restoration are on display. Numerous museum pieces add to its authentic atmosphere to take you back to the turn of the century. Situated 12 km east of Swakopmund just off the B2.

The **Hansa Hotel** in Roon Street offers stylish accommodation in rooms with *en suite* facilities. Amenities include a restaurant, lounge, bar and a tranquil courtyard.

Hotel Europa Hof, Bismarck Street, with its *fachbauwerk* style offers accommodation in spacious rooms and German hospitality. Amenities include a restaurant (offering seafood specialities) and a lively bar.

Hotel Schweizerhaus, 1 Bismarck Street, is situated conveniently close to the beach, town centre.

Situated on the beachfront, the **Strand Hotel** has comfortable rooms, three restaurants and a bar.

The four-star **Swakopmund Hotel and Entertainment Centre** in Bahnhof Street is the most luxurious hotel in Swakopmund, offering luxury, stylish accommodation. Amenities include a heated outdoor pool and a restaurant. The Entertainment Centre comprises the Mermaid Casino (with slot machines and poker, blackjack and roulette tables), two cinemas, an action bar and speciality shops.

Pensions
Privat Hotel Deutsches Haus, 13 Lüderitz Street, offers accommodation in comfortable rooms. Facilities include an indoor swimming pool, sauna and private bar.

Owned and managed by the Rapmund family since 1968, **Hotel Pension Rapmund**, 6 Bismarck Street, offers good, clean accommodation at very reasonable prices. Located close to the beach and town centre.

Self-catering and budget
The **Kaserne** on the corner of Lazarette and Bismarck streets now serves as a youth hostel. Basic accommodation, with a self-catering kitchenettte, dining hall, lounge and braai area, is provided.

Fully equipped, tastefully furnished chalets are available at **Alte Brücke Resort and Conference Centre**.

Accommodation at **Brigadoon Guest Cottages**, 16 Ludwig Koch Street, consists of three tastefully furnished Victorian-style cottages. Fully equipped, self-catering and serviced daily.

Haus Garnison, 4 Garnison Street, has fully equipped holiday apartments serviced daily.

Accommodation at the **Swakopmund rest camp**, Cordes Street, ranges from two-bedroomed cottages to luxury four-bedroomed bungalows, or A-frame chalets.

Walvis Bay

The **Walvis Bay wetland** is the most important coastal wetland for birds in southern Africa and the second most important in Africa. It comprises the lagoon, other intertidal areas and the saltworks; each of which supports at least a third of the birds at some stage in the tidal or annual cycle. The number of birds fluctuates from year to year, ranging from 37 000 to 118 000.

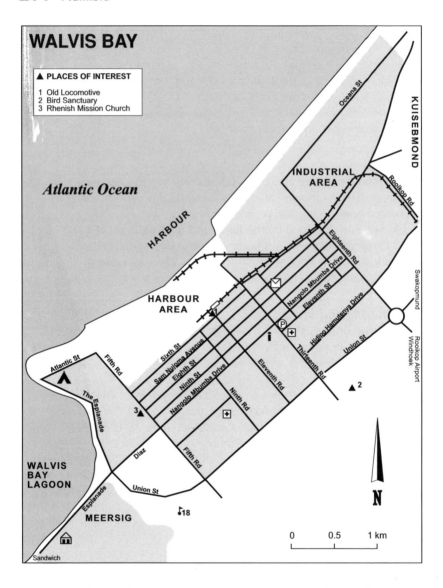

The wetlands offer excellent opportunities for birding, especially during the summer months when the numbers of resident species are swelled by over 20 migrant species.

The wetland is also of international significance, as it supports 50 per cent of the world population of chestnut-banded plover, as well as significant numbers of the world populations of greater flamingo (3 per cent), lesser flamingo (2 per cent) and curlew sandpiper (1 per cent). It is also home to 18 per cent of the southern African race of the black-necked grebe.

On a regional level, the wetland supports over 40 per cent of the southern African population of greater flamingo and 60 per cent of the subcontinent's lesser flamingos. Resident species include white pelican, kelp, grey-headed and Hartlaub's gulls, as well as Caspian and swift terns.

Keen birders will find a visit to the **Bird Paradise** at the municipal disposal works well worth a visit. When entering the town from Swakopmund, turn left into Thirteenth Road and continue 500 m to the signposted turnoff.

Walvis Bay is Namibia's only **deep-water harbour** and is expected to become a gateway for the expanding markets of southern Africa following the completion of the Trans-Kalahari and Trans-Caprivi highways. The harbour has eight berths with a combined length of 1 430 m, and a maximum depth of 10,6 m.

The town is the centre of Namibia's pelagic fishing industry, which is the mainstay of the town's economy. There are several factories; anchovy and maasbanker are processed into fishmeal and oil, while pilchards are canned.

Salt production is another important economic activity. The 3 500 ha saltworks south of Walvis Bay produces about 400 000 tonnes of salt annually; 95 per cent of the salt required by South Africa's chemical industry. *The saltworks is not open to the public.*

Walvis Bay is situated on the edge of a large bay, named Golfo de Santa Maria de Conceicão by Bartholomeu Dias on 8 December 1487. It was later renamed Golfo da Baleia, translated as "bay of the whales". As there was no fresh water along the coast, nearly three centuries passed before foreign powers began showing an interest in Walvis Bay. From 1784 American whalers began anchoring in the bay and when rumours of mineral deposits and large herds of livestock in the interior reached the Cape, the vessel *Meermin*, under the command of Captain F Duminy, was sent to annex the bay. On 23 January 1793 the Dutch flag was raised, but Dutch rule was short-lived. Two years later the Cape was occupied by the British and Captain Alexander was dispatched to Walvis Bay to establish Britain's claim over the enclave.

Settlers from the Cape arrived in 1844 and in the following year Heinrich Scheppmann of the Rhenish Mission Society established a mission station for the Topnaar Khoikhoi at Rooibank along the Kuiseb River, 40 km east of Walvis Bay.

The British viewed the increasing involvement of the Germans in Greater Namaqualand and Damaraland after 1840 as a threat to their interests and on 12 March 1878 the enclave was formally annexed by Commodore Richard Dyer. In 1884 the administration of the enclave was transferred to the Cape Colony and in 1910 Walvis Bay became part of the Union of South Africa. From 1922 to 1977 the enclave was administered as if it were part of its mandate over South West Africa.

The decision to transfer the administration of the enclave to the Cape Province in 1977 was strongly condemned by the United Nations General Assembly and in July 1978 the UN Security Council called for the reintegration of Walvis Bay.

Following Namibia's independence on 21 March 1990, international pressure for the return of Walvis Bay to Namibia increased. A joint administrative authority with South African and Namibian chief executive officers was established on 1 November 1992 and on 1 March 1994 the enclave and the offshore islands were reintegrated into Namibia.

Dating back to 1880, the **Rhenish Mission Church** in 5th Road was one of the first buildings in Walvis Bay. It was pre-fabricated from timber in Hamburg in 1879 and erected in the harbour area the following year. As a result of increased harbour activity, it was later moved to its present site. The outside walls were plastered to prevent wood rot from setting in.

The first service was held in 1881 and the church served its original purpose until 1966. It was subsequently saved from being demolished through the interest taken by the Walvis Bay Lions Club.

The lagoon is not only popular with birders (see p 213), but also with windsurfing and yachting enthusiasts. There is a slipway for pleasure craft near the angling clubhouse and visiting yachtsmen are welcome to call at the yacht club at the Esplanade. It is reached by following Nangolo Mbumba and then turning into the Esplanade.

A relaxing way of exploring the lagoon is to book a **sea kayak trip**, conducted by Jeanne Meintjies of Eco Marine Kayak Tours, tel (064) 20-3144. Two tours are offered: a two-hour lagoon birdwatching trip for the inexperienced and a five- to six hour tour off Pelican Point for the more experienced.

The Walvis Bay area offers good opportunities for **angling** with cob, galjoen, steenbras and blacktail especially sought after. Although angling is possible throughout the year, the summer months are generally the most rewarding.

Paaltjies, a popular angling spot about 12 km south of Walvis Bay, is reached by following a well-signposted road through the saltworks. It is renowned for steenbras and cob, especially between December and April. Also popular is the stretch of coast between Paaltjies and the northern boundary of Sandwich, Langstrand and Vierkantklip, just south of Swakopmund. The open season for rock lobster stretches from 1 November to 30 June.

Organised tours and trips from Walvis Bay

Inshore Safaris, P O Box 2444, Walvis Bay, tel (064) 20-2609, fax 20-2198. Angling trips, camping safaris, tours in and around Walvis Bay in specially designed off-road vehicles.

Mola Mola Safaris, P O Box 980, Walvis Bay, tel (064) 20-5511, fax 20-7593. Boat or shore angling, dolphin and seal cruises, pelagic bird trips, Sandwich.

Angling

Afri-Fishing & Safaris, P O Box 2156, Walvis Bay, tel (064) 20-9449, fax 20-9440. Shore angling tours along the Namib coast, freshwater angling in dams and tigerfishing in the Caprivi.

Levo Fishing and Pleasure Tours, P O Box 1860, Walvis Bay, tel and fax (064) 20-7555. Seal and dolphin cruises, bottom fishing, beach and shark angling, deep-sea trips by ski boat.

Kayaking

Eco-Marine Kayak Tours, Walvis Bay, tel and fax (064) 20-3144. Sea-kayak trips of Walvis Bay lagoon and offshore coastal areas.

Where to eat

Walvis Bay offers visitors a variety of restaurants and among the eateries you might want to try are:

Chi-Lin, Seagull Mall, 8th Street, tel (064) 20-9046. Chinese food and takeaways.

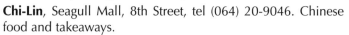

Hickory Creek Spur, 140 9th Street, tel (064) 20-7991. Steaks, burgers, spareribs, salads.

LaLainyas, Sam Nujoma Avenue, tel (064) 20-2574. Specialises in seafood.

O' Heilies Steakhouse and Pizzeria, 9th Street, tel (064) 20-5384. Steaks, pizzas, fish and home-style cooking.

The Raft, The Esplanade, tel (064) 20-4877. Magnificent view over the lagoon. À la carte, seafood, steaks.

Willi Probst Bäckerei, 9th Street, tel (064) 20-2744. Renowned for its breakfasts, bread, cakes and pies.

Where to stay

Visitors planning to spend one or more nights in Walvis Bay have a wide choice of accommodation options, ranging from hotels to caravan and camp sites.

Hotels and pensions

At the **Langholm Hotel Garni**, 24 2nd Street West, guests are accommodated in a homely atmosphere. Rooms are tastefully decorated and there is a lounge and private bar. Breakfast is included in the tariff.

The **Courtyard Hotel Garni**, 16 3rd Road, offers comfortable rooms, indoor heated pool and breakfast.

Opened in April 1997, the **Walvis Bay Protea Lodge** on the corner of Sam Nujoma Avenue and 10th Road offers comfortable accommodation, breakfast and refreshments from a service bar for guests. A variety of excursions can be arranged.

Self-catering and camping

Dolphin Park, 13 km north of Walvis Bay, offers accommodation in fully equipped and serviced four-bed bungalows. Camping and caravan facilities are also available.

Situated virtually on Walvis Bay lagoon, accommodation at **Esplanade Park** range from five- and seven-bed, fully equipped luxury bungalows to camp sites.

Lagoon Chalets in Meersig is 500 m from the lagoon. Accommodation is in self-contained bungalows. Amenities include a restaurant and ladies' bar.

ROUTE 16

SWAKOPMUND AND THE WELWITSCHIA DRIVE

DISTANCE: 150 km **TIME**: 4 to 5 hours **ROAD CONDITIONS**: gravel, good to fair, but can be corrugated
FUEL: Swakopmund **LINKING ROUTES**: Route 2

The **Welwitschia Drive** is one of the best ways to learn more about the desert. The excursion takes about three hours, but it is advisable to set half a day aside. This will allow you to visit **Goanikontes**, an old farm in the Swakop River, and to enjoy a picnic lunch at the shady picnic sites on the banks of the river. Permits and a trail pamphlet are available from the MET office in Swakopmund (during office hours) and from service stations (after hours).

From Swakopmund (see p 200), take the B2 toward Usakos for about 2 km and turn right onto the C28 (signposted Namib Park-Khomas Hochland), continuing for about 15 km to the Namib-Naukluft Park boundary. About 400 m after entering the park, turn left onto the D1991.

Several interesting features along the route are marked with stone beacons, whose numbers correspond with those in the trail pamphlet. Among them are lichens, desert-adapted plants, historical sites and spectacular views of the **Moon Landscape** of the Swakop River Valley.

About 16,6 km after turning onto the Welwitschia Drive, the D1991 turns off to the left to Goanikontes, 3,6 km further on. Backtrack for 3,6 km and then continue along the Welwitschia Drive. About 17 km beyond the Goanikontes turnoff, turn left and after passing a spectacular dolerite dyke you cross the Swakop River. As you drive out of the eroded Swakop River valley, numerous welwitschias can be seen sprawled across the desert plains. About 10 km beyond the Swakop River you will reach the **Giant Welwitschia of the Husab**. It is estimated to be about 1 500 years old.

From the Giant Welwitschia, backtrack for 18 km (the Swakop River picnic site is a good lunch stop) and then continue for 9 km to join the C28 from Windhoek to Swakopmund. Turn right and continue for 42 km to Swakopmund.

ROUTE 17

SWAKOPMUND TO TERRACE BAY

DISTANCE: 350 km **TIME**: 5 hours **ROAD CONDITIONS**: Salt and gravel; usually good **FUEL**: Swakopmund, Henties Bay, Terrace Bay **LINKING ROUTES**: Route 11

Heading north from Swakopmund (see p 200), the C34 hugs the coastline of the huge **National West Coast Tourist Recreation Area** which stretches northward for some 200 km to the Ugab River and about 50 km inland. The road is a mixture of brine and gravel (locally called a salt road) and in wet or misty weather you are advised to drive cautiously, as the surface can become very slippery.

Each year thousands of hopeful anglers are attracted to this stretch of coastline, which is renowned for its excellent catches of galjoen, cob, steenbras and blacktail. Anglers unfamiliar with the coast will find the angling column in the Friday edition of the *Namib Times* extremely useful. Details of angling regulations can be obtained from the Ministry of Fisheries and Marine Resources in Swakopmund, tel (064) 40-5744.

A peculiarity of the coast is that many of the places were named after their imperial distance north of Swakopmund, while others such as Bennie se Rooi Lorrie, Sarah se Gat, and Doep se Gat recall the favourite fishing spots of anglers.

Mile Four Caravan Park, just north of Swakopmund, offers accommodation ranging from fully equipped bungalows and fully furnished flats to rooms and camp sites with communal facilities. Other amenities include power points, freezing facilities and a laundromat.

The **Swakopmund saltworks area**, 7 km north of Swakopmund, is an important wetland with large populations of flamingos. Also of interest are great crested and black-necked grebes, as well as a variety of resident and migrant waders. Birding tours are conducted by Ms I Korl, tel (064) 40-4015 (pm only), and can be extended to the saltworks.

Production of the concentrated brine at a saltpan, known as Panther Beacon, began in 1933, but by 1952 the salt was depleted. Seawater has since been pumped into open evaporation and concentration ponds and the crystallised salt is then removed with mechanical scrapers. Impurities are removed in the washing and screening plant and the salt is graded in different grain sizes. It is used mainly in the plastic, chemical and paper industries.

Situated on part of the saltworks is the Richwater Oyster Company, which started cultivating oysters in 1985. The oysters are initially cultivated in a shallow seawater pond which offers protection and warmer water temperatures. They are then kept in a nursery pond until they are about 25 mm long and are then transferred to open shelves in cement channels. *The saltworks and oyster farm are not open to the public.*

Continuing along the C34, you pass the turnoff to the **Mile 14 camp site** to reach **Wlotzkasbaken** 32 km north of Swakopmund, named after a local fisherman of that name and a survey beacon along the coast. The quaint village began developing in 1936 and the houses and fishing shacks are all privately owned. There are no facilities here.

The Namib coast is renowned for its diversity of **lichens** and one of the best examples of these interesting plants can be seen on the plains east of the C34, about 4 km north of Wlotzkasbaken. To date well over 100 different lichen species have been identified along the Namib coast.

About 30 km north of Wlotzkasbaken, you pass the turnoff to the **Jakkalsputz camp site** and reach **Henties Bay**, a popular summer resort, 10 km further on. It was named after a Kalkfeld businessman, Hentie van der Merwe, who first visited the freshwater spring on the beach in 1929. The good fishing, fresh water and abundance of game birds and game brought him back year after year. As the popularity of the bay grew, it became known as Henties Bay.

The first permanent residents were mainly retired people, who started settling here in the early 1950s and for many years the settlement only saw activity during the summer holidays. Today, Henties Bay boasts several shopping centres, shops, restaurants, garages, a hotel and a post office. During the December-January school holidays the resident population of 2 000 swells to over 15 000. Sports facilities include tennis courts, a squash court and a 14-hole golf course in an old river course of the Omaruru Delta.

In addition to a restaurant in the **Die Duine Hotel**, there is a variety of other restaurants in Henties Bay; among them the **Eagle Steak Ranch**, Eagle Shopping Centre, which serves breakfasts, à la carte lunches and Sunday buffets. Tel (064) 50-0574. There is also the **Spitskoppe Pub & Restaurant,** which has an à la carte menu with seafood specialities. Tel (064) 50-0394.

Self-catering accommodation is available in fully equipped bungalows at **Die Oord. Eagle Holiday Flats** in Henties Bay are fully furnished and equipped holiday flats. The **Hotel De Duine** is an ideal base for anglers and holiday-makers to the west coast. It offers comfortable *en suite* rooms, restaurant, lounge bar, squash court and small swimming pool.

The coastal strip on the seaward side of the Swakopmund-Terrace Bay road is the breeding ground of a significant percentage of the world population of Damara tern. The numbers of this species in the National West Coast Recreation Area and the Skeleton Coast Park further north are estimated at 14 000.

They migrate from as far north as the Gulf of Guinea to breed along the Namib coast, arriving in September and migrating northward again in April.

Unfortunately, their breeding season overlaps with the peak tourist season and their habitat is being threatened by irresponsible off-road driving in the National West Coast Tourist Recreation area. Another concern is the destruction of the delicate lichen fields along the coast.

From Henties Bay the D2301 continues parallel to the coast, passing the turnoff to the **Mile 72 camp site** about 36 km beyond Henties Bay; the turnoff to **Cape Cross** (see p 183) is signposted 18 km on.

The northernmost camp site in the National West Coast Tourist Recreation Area, **Mile 108**, is reached 40 km on. Fuel and a mobile kiosk-cum-shop are available here and at Mile 72 during the Namibian December-January school holidays only. Water has to be trucked in to both camp sites and must, consequently, be bought.

After another 34 km you reach the Ugab River, the southern boundary of the Skeleton Coast Park. Permits to travel through the park via the Springbokwasser gate can be obtained at the gate until 15:00. Day visitors are, however, not allowed to visit Terrace Bay. Overnight visitors must be in possession of a reservation advice issued by the reservations office in Windhoek.

Continuing further north, there are several points of interest worth stopping at. About 16 km north of the Ugab Gate a signpost points the way to the site where a fishing vessel, the *Atlantic Pride*, ran aground. Still further north, about 10 km before reaching Toscanini, the rusty remains of an old oil rig bear testimony to the dreams of an optimistic entrepreneur.

About 104 km beyond Ugab Gate you reach the C39 to Khorixas via the Springbokwasser gate. Travelling further north, the road passes the **Torra Bay camp site** (open only during Namibian December-January school holidays) and then reaches the Uniab Delta (see p 199). Terrace Bay, a former diamond mining camp, is reached 49 km north of the C39 junction.

From Terrace Bay you can either backtrack to Swakopmund, or retrace your tracks for 49 km to the C39, following it in an easterly direction to its junction with the D2620 and route 11. From here you can either continue to Sesriem with route 11, or follow it in reverse, visiting Twyfelfontein, the Organ Pipes, Burnt Mountain and Petrified Forest *en route* to Khorixas.

ROUTE 18
SWAKOPMUND TO SANDWICH, SESRIEM AND SOSSUSVLEI

DISTANCE: 420 km **TIME**: 7 hours **ROAD CONDITIONS**: 45 km tar; remainder gravel, usually good but can be corrugated; Sandwich 4x4 only **FUEL**: Swakopmund, Walvis Bay, Solitaire, Sesriem **LINKING ROUTES**: Routes 3, 4

From Swakopmund (see p 200) the B2 heads south, hugging the narrow coastal strip hemmed in by the ocean and light-coloured dunes lying parallel to the coast.

Langstrand Holiday Resort is reached about 17 km south of Swakopmund. Located on the beach, the resort caters for campers and caravanners, as well as day visitors. Facilities include a tidal pool, shaded picnic places with braai facilities and a playground.

The **Langstrand Restaurant**, tel (064) 20-3820, has an à la carte menu with steak and seafood specialities. Another option is the **Waterfront Express**, tel (064) 20-7009, a restaurant in three train carriages overlooking the beach.

The coastal dunes around Langstrand are popular for a variety of dune sports such as sandboarding and paragliding, with lessons in sandskiing available during December and January. Contact Downhill Adventures, tel and fax (064) 20-4400.

About 2,6 km further south is the **Dolphin Recreation Park**, with its swimming pool, hydroslide, braai facilities and kiosk. Fully furnished chalets are available.

About 4 km on you will pass the guano platform on Bird Rock, about 400 m offshore. Work on the platform started in 1930 and over the years it was extended several times to its current size of 17 000 m². The platform is used mainly by Cape cormorants as a roosting place, but smaller numbers of white pelicans also converge on the platform.

The harbour town of **Walvis Bay** (see p 213) is reached 35 km south of Swakopmund. It is a haven for those seeking the outdoors and offers opportunities ranging from angling to a variety of water sports and birdwatching.

To find out more about the latest tourism developments in the area, visit **Walvis Bay Tourism**, in the Municipal Building in Nangolo Mbumba Avenue, tel (064) 201-3233, fax 20-4528. Open Monday to Friday 08:00 to 13:00 and 14:00 to 17:00 (16:30 on Friday).

A birdwatchers delight, **Sandwich Lagoon** (see p 192) lies about 40 km south of Walvis Bay, and is accessible only by four-wheel drive vehicle. Driving along the coast can be risky and the trip should not be attempted by inexperienced drivers. The journey to Sandwich should be undertaken when the tide is receding, and the return journey must be completed well before high tide. Advice on driving conditions can be obtained from the Ministry of Environment and Tourism's office in Swakopmund. From the northern boundary access is only permitted on foot.

From Walvis Bay, the C14 heads in a southeasterly direction and after about 5 km you will pass an embankment where the weathered remains of an old **narrow gauge railway line** can be seen. The line was built during the late 1800s and early 1900s to transport goods to and from the harbour and the terminus at Plum.

The terminus at Plum, east of the dunes, comprised a galvanised iron store, two-roomed cottage and stable. Goods were drawn on the line by mules, until a locomotive was landed in Walvis Bay in 1899. After it had been used at the harbour for some time, attempts were made to use it on the line between the harbour and Plum. Shifting sand, however, posed a constant threat and the line was eventually abandoned. In March 1905, the acting magistrate of Walvis Bay reported: "Some abandoned sections of the line are for more than half a mile buried under mountains of sand 30 feet high." The **narrow gauge locomotive**, Hope, can be seen in front of the Walvis Bay railway station in 6th Street.

About 3 km further, a road sign indicates the turnoff to the well-known **Dune Seven**, the highest easily accessible dune in the area. It is a small dune by Sossusvlei standards and its popularity and fame are largely because many soldiers stationed in Walvis Bay, when the enclave was still administered by South Africa, had to run up the dune with full kit as part of their training.

About 16 km east of Walvis Bay you cross into the Namib Section of the Namib-Naukluft Park (see p 186), passing Vogelfederberg, a large granite *inselberg*, or island mountain, 35 km on. Some 17 km on the D1982 to Windhoek via the Us Pass splits off to the left. Continue along the C14 for 46 km to a signpost indicating a turnoff to the right, which leads to Carp Cliff. The 6 km detour ends at a viewpoint overlooking the Kuiseb Canyon.

Rising in the Khomas Hochland near Windhoek, the Kuiseb River plays an important role in preventing the northward encroachment of the Namib sand sea. Its geological past is best seen from the **Carp Cliff viewpoint**, signposted 20 km west of the Kuiseb Canyon. Standing on the canyon rim, some 180 m above the present river, it is difficult to believe that you are in an ancient bed of an earlier Kuiseb. The well-rounded boulders and cobbles on the canyon rim were laid down on an enormous alluvial fan that stretched from near the Gamsberg area to south of Sandwich some 15-18 million years ago. At that time there was no deeply incised Kuiseb Canyon and the alluvial fan gravels were laid down in braided streams over an earlier Kuiseb drainage system.

This earlier system, dating back 20-40 million years, is represented by the greyish-brown to whitish sandstone underlying the gravels at Carp Cliff. During those earlier times, the Kuiseb River did not reach the Atlantic Ocean, but was blocked by dunes of an ancient sand sea, as the Tsauchab River is today at Sossusvlei.

The deeply incised course of the Kuiseb River is geologically a youthful feature. The incision is attributed to uplift of the southern African subcontinent some two to four million years ago. About one to one and a half million years ago, the Kuiseb bed was choked to some 30-40 m by its own sediments. These deposits were subsequently cemented by lime-charged underground waters, and can be seen today as terrace deposits lining the course of the Kuiseb.

Significantly, wedges of linear-type dunes are also incorporated into these conglomeratic terrace deposits, providing the first evidence of an association between the Kuiseb River, as we know it today, and the main Namib sand sea. This association also testifies to the antiquity of the barrier that the Kuiseb River has formed to the northward encroachment of the sand sea.

The **Carp Cliff viewpoint** is named after a nearby overhanging cliff, where two German geologists who feared internment during World War II, Henno Martin and Hermann Korn, lived for more than two years.

The name of their refuge might seem somewhat out of place, but during their stay here they found carp in the pools in the Kuiseb River; a discovery that caused much rejoicing. Their classic story, *The Sheltering Desert*, relates how they and their dog, Otto, survived against all odds in this inhospitable area.

Further along, the C14 makes its way down the Kuiseb Pass through spectacular scenery created by myriads of small streams, which cut steep valleys through the schist formations during a much wetter period. After crossing the Kuiseb River the road ascends steeply and about 8 km after leaving the park it is joined by the C26 from Windhoek via the Gamsberg Pass (see route 3).

Continuing south across the Namib plains, the road reaches the start of the Gaub Pass 17 km beyond the C26 junction, crossing the Gaub River, a tributary of the Kuiseb River, about 3 km on. After crossing the sparsely vegetated Namib plains the C14 is joined by the D1275 from Windhoek via the Spreetshoogte Pass (see route 4). Continue for 9 km and take the turnoff onto Main Road 36 to Sesriem and Solitaire. Despite its prominent position on the map, **Solitaire** is nothing more than a farm with a filling station, trading store and bottle-store. It is, however, a welcome stop for a cup of tea, to

stock up on some cold drinks and to buy some of the bread
Solitaire is famous for.

About 16 km south of Solitaire the turnoff to **Namib-
Naukluft Lodge**, an upmarket 14-room lodge with wide-ranging views over the Namib Plains, is signposted. Facilities
include a restaurant, open-air dining area, lounge, bar and
swimming pool. Daily excursions are conducted to Sossusvlei.

Still further on the **petrified dunes** on the farm Dieprivier
come into view. Visitors interested in geology will find the
Namib rest camp on the farm a fascinating stopover. Here the
Dieprivier has eroded the landscape to reveal fossilised sand
dunes, dating back some 20 to 40 million years, underlying the
present Namib sand sea.

Accommodation ranges from self-catering bungalows to
rooms and camp sites. The turnoff to the rest camp is signposted 29 km south of Solitaire.

Shortly after crossing the Dieprivier, a turnoff indicates the
way to **Weltevrede rest camp**, which offers true Namibian hospitality, good food and tranquillity at reasonable prices.
Bounded on three sides by the Namib-Naukluft Park, the rest
camp offers accommodation in bungalows or double rooms
on a self-catering basis, or inclusive of meals. There is also a
camp site. Amenities include a covered braai area and swimming pool. Among the activities offered are a 4x4 trail on the
farm and scenic walks.

A short way beyond the turnoff to Weltevrede, the road
enters the Namib-Naukluft Park corridor. The 20 km wide belt
was created in the early 1970s to enable gemsbok to migrate
from the Naukluft section of the park to the dune area, formerly known as Diamond Area II.

About 71 km south of Solitaire, turn right onto the D826,
which goes to the Sesriem (see p 193) entrance gate 12 km on.
Sossusvlei (see p 194) is reached 65 km west of Sesriem.

Alternatively, if you are seeking peace and tranquillity away
from the hustle and bustle of Sesriem, continue along Main
Road 36 for another 27 km to the signposted turnoff to
Sossusvlei Wilderness Camp, an upmarket camp offering
guests a unique desert experience.

Situated on the farm Witwater, the camp nestles among
granite outcrops overlooked by a large island mountain,
Sandkop, with expansive views over the gravel plains extending westward.

From the covered parking area visitors are transferred 6 km to the camp by four-wheel drive vehicle.

Each of the nine chalets has been designed individually to fit in with its setting. Boulders were incorporated into the walls and a combination of brick, timber and thatch gives the chalets an earthy feel. To enable guests to enjoy unimpeded views from their chalets, the bedrooms and lounge have large fold-away sliding doors. Each chalet also has a deck with a private plunge pool. A walkway of timber and rock leads from the chalets to the central lodge area, comprising a large deck, dining room, lounge, bar and curio shop.

Activities include guided trips to Sossusvlei, inclusive of a guided walk and a three-course breakfast. At the lodge guests can go on walks to explore the granite outcrops, while guided drives and sundowner drives are also offered. After sunset, guests can view the night sky through a telescope from the stargazing circle. One of the main attractions, however, is a hot-air balloon flight, which offers guests a bird's-eye view of the desert. Of geological interest on the farm is the **Hebron Fault**, which occurred a few million years ago when calcified gravel deposits were displaced by earth movements.

ROUTE 19
SESRIEM TO LÜDERITZ

DISTANCE: 480 km **TIME**: 7 hours **ROAD CONDITIONS**: 353 km gravel, fair to poor; 127 km tar **FUEL**: Sesriem, Wêreldsend (farm), Aus, Lüderitz **LINKING ROUTES**: Route 25

This scenic route meanders along the edge of the Namib Desert, providing stunning views of the dune sea, gravel plains and mountains. The road surface is generally very corrugated and it is advisable to obtain information on the condition of the road if you are travelling in a sedan car.

From Sesriem, take the D826 south to reach the turnoff to **Kulala Desert Lodge** after 18 km. Adjoining the Namib-Naukluft Park, the lodge is situated on a 32 000 ha farm with scenery ranging from pebble-strewn plains and rugged mountains to red and yellow sand dunes. Herds of gemsbok and springbok, as well as large flocks of ostrich, are conspicuous, but there is also a host of smaller animals, such as the bat-eared fox, ground squirrel and suricate.

Built from locally manufactured clay bricks, the lodge is an interesting combination of building styles from Cameroon, Niger and North Africa. The unusually shaped thatch roof of the main complex echoes the dunes which the lodge overlooks. It comprises the reception area, a spacious lounge and dining room. The decor is decidedly ethnic, with authentic Zaïrean masks, drums from Ghana and Zimbabwe and other *objets d'art*. Excellent French-style meals are served in the restaurant. Its tables are made from railway sleepers.

Kulala is a Swahili word for "sleeping place" and guests are accommodated in comfortable *kulalas* – tents on raised platforms with private verandas and sheltered by thatched roofs. *En suite* facilities are provided in an adobe-style hut with a rooftop sleeping terrace for those wishing to sleep under the starlit night sky.

A small plunge pool provides welcome relief on hot summer days. Activities include a nature drive with six viewpoints, each more spectacular than the preceding one. Guided trips are also offered to Sossusvlei.

For many visitors, however, the highlight of a visit to Kulala is a **hot-air balloon flight**. Flights are undertaken either from Kulala or from the Mövenpick Sossusvlei Lodge. Lasting about an hour, the flights provide a bird's-eye view of the island mountains, plains and dunes of the Namib. On landing a champagne breakfast is served.

About 15 km further you reach the northern boundary of the NamibRand Nature Reserve (see p 197). Remain on the D826 until you reach the junction with the D407, where you turn right, continuing for 24 km to the junction with the D707, and then turn right once more. The road now heads in a southwesterly direction, before turning south and skirting the eastern boundary of the Namib-Naukluft Park. It then swings in a southeasterly direction, skirting the ruggedly beautiful Tiras mountains, to join the C13 between Helmeringhausen and Aus 132 km beyond the previous turnoff.

On joining the C13, turn right and soon you'll be traversing the **Neisip Plain**, one of the most spectacular plains in Namibia. The road cuts across the plain for some 30 km before making a gentle 20 km ascent toward Aus. This drive is especially worthwhile during the early mornings and late afternoons, when the landscape is painted in pastel hues.

On reaching the B4, you can either continue to Lüderitz, 125 km to the west (see route 24), or travel to Keetmanshoop.

12

SOUTHERN NAMIBIA

The south of Namibia is a vast arid region, caught between the Kalahari Desert in the east and the Namib Desert in the west. Its scenic landscapes are characterised by low mountains, plains with scattered hills and isolated mountains and seemingly endless flat open spaces. Farming centres around small stock, mainly karakul sheep, sheep and goats, while diamond mining takes place in the southeast of the region at Oranjemund. Among the many attractions of this region are the Fish River Canyon, Lüderitz with its distinctly German atmosphere, and the ghost towns at Kolmanskop and Elisabeth Bay.

Duwisib Castle

The imposing Duwisib Castle, southwest of Maltahöhe, is a complete surprise to the unsuspecting traveller. The castle was built in 1908-9 by Captain Hans-Heinrich von Wolf and his wife, Jayta. Von Wolf, a member of the Saxon nobility, was born in Dresden in 1873. After completing school he entered military service and became an artillery captain in the Royal Saxon Army at Königsbruck, Dresden. In 1904 he was sent to serve with the *Schutztruppe* in German South West Africa and in a battle against the Nama he lost several field guns as a result of a tactical error.

Following the end of hostilities in 1907, Von Wolf returned to Germany and married Jayta Humphries, the stepdaughter of the American consul in Dresden. The couple decided to settle in South West Africa and by the end of 1907 they owned eight farms with a total area of 140 000 ha in the Maltahöhe district.

Von Wolf envisaged a home similar to the castles built by the *Schutztruppe* at Gibeon, Namutoni and Windhoek. In 1908 the renowned architect, Willi Sander, was commissioned to design a building that could serve as a home and a fortress. Stone for the castle came from a quarry some 3 km away, but all other material was imported from Germany via Lüderitzbucht. One can only appreciate the ambitiousness of the project when considering the logistics of transporting the material overland by ox-wagon. Twenty ox-wagons were used on the 640 km journey, half of which was across the Namib Desert. Skilled craftsmen also came from abroad: stonemasons and builders from Italy and carpenters from Sweden, Denmark and Ireland. The combined skills of these craftsmen resulted in a building which surpassed any comparable project in taste, craftsmanship and expense.

Duwisib consists of 22 rooms arranged in a U-shape, enclosed by a high wall at the open end. Central to the design was the requirement that the castle had to withstand any attack and most of the rooms have embrasures, not windows.

From the entrance you pass through an arch into the *Rittersaal*, or main hall. A narrow wooden staircase leads up to the *Herrenzimmer*, a room reserved for men, and a minstrels' gallery. Back downstairs, the main hall is flanked by sitting rooms with beautifully embellished fireplaces. In a country as hot as Namibia you will be surprised to find fireplaces in most rooms here. However, the thick stone walls, small windows and the southwesterly aspect necessitated fireplaces, especially during the cold winter months. During summer the castle remains pleasantly cool.

The castle was lavishly furnished with family heirlooms and fine furnishings and fittings bought during a visit to Germany in 1908. The walls of the castle were decorated with paintings, etchings and family portraits, as well as swords and rifles. Several of the paintings and etchings reflected Von Wolf's passion for horses.

The couple left for England to buy horses for their stud in August 1914, but the ship was diverted to South America on the outbreak of World War I. In Rio de Janeiro, Jayta obtained a berth on a vessel bound for Scandinavia, and Von Wolf and a companion were smuggled on board as stowaways. From Scandinavia they travelled to Germany, where Von Wolf joined the army. He was killed in the battle of the Somme in France in 1916 and his wife never returned to Duwisib.

The property was later sold to a Swedish family and in 1937 it was bought by a company. The castle, its contents and 50 ha of surrounding land were acquired by the state in the late 1970s and restored to former glory in 1991.

The castle is open daily from 08:00 to 17:00 throughout the year. Facilities for day visitors are limited to picnic sites.

Camping sites with braai places and hot water ablutions are available for overnight visitors to Duwisib Castle. The adjoining **Farm Duwisib rest camp** has fully equipped, self-catering bungalows. Activities include nature walks (to the quarry where the stone for Duwisib was quarried), farm tours and horse riding (pony rides for children).

Fish River Canyon & Ai-Ais

The Fish River Canyon is one of the great natural wonders of Africa and the second largest of its kind in the world. The canyon forms part of the Fish River Conservation Area, the nucleus of which was proclaimed a reserve in 1969. The 161 km long canyon is several kilometres wide in places and up to 549 m deep.

In addition to the main viewpoint, there are a number of others along the western rim, from where visitors can enjoy bird's-eye views of the canyon. Looking down into the canyon, its various geological formations can be clearly seen. The dark, steep slopes leading up from the riverbed were originally sandstone, shale and lavas deposited about 1 800 million years ago. During deep burial, about 1 300 to 1 000 million years ago, these deposits were intensely compressed and folded. At the same time they were heated to over 600 °C and metamorphosed. In this process they recrystalised and changed appearance. Together with intrusive granites of the area these rocks form the Namaqualand Metamorphic Complex. The dark lines that cut these rocks are dolerite dykes (lava that did not reach the surface) formed 900 million years ago.

The first major period of erosion began soon after this, exposing all the various rock types and levelling them into a vast peneplain which, some 650 million years ago, became the floor of a shallow sea that covered much of southern Namibia. Sediments of the Nama Group were deposited into this sea. The almost horizontal contact line between the Namaqualand Metamorphic Complex and the overlying, flat layers of the Nama Group can clearly be seen. In geological terms this is known as an unconformity, a term used to refer to a break in the geological record, during which time the deformed strata were exposed and eroded.

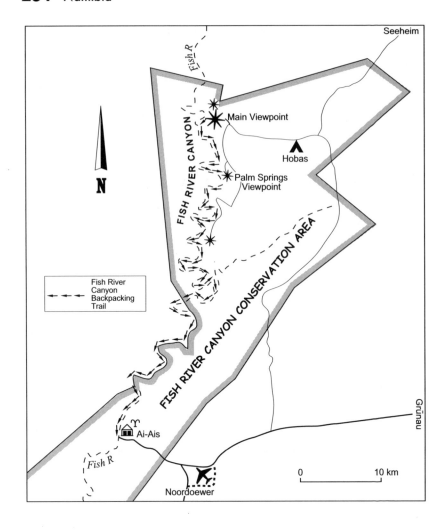

The base of the Nama Group is only a few metres thick and consists of a small-pebble conglomerate. Above this are 150-200 m of black limestones, grits and sandstones, followed by a 10 m capping of shale and sandstones.

Fracturing of the crust about 500 million years ago caused a north-south valley to form in the region of the Fish River. Slow erosion gradually removed the uppermost parts of the Nama Group and about 300 million years ago southward-moving glaciers deepened the valley.

The plains east of the canyon are the habitat of springbok,

while the canyon and the more rocky areas are home to Hartmann's mountain zebra, klipspringer, chacma baboon and rock dassie.

Birds on the plains include ostrich, Karoo korhaan, Burchell's and double-banded coursers, tractrac and Karoo chats. Purple gallinule and moorhen are attracted to reedbeds fringing the pools at Ai-Ais and in the riverine bush you could tick red-eyed bulbul, Karoo robin, black-chested prinia and dusky sunbird.

The 85 km long **Fish River Canyon Backpacking Trail** is one of southern Africa's most popular trails. From the northernmost viewpoint hikers descend to the canyon floor and then follow the meandering course of the river to Ai-Ais, a journey that usually takes four to five days. No facilities are provided along the route, necessitating self-sufficiency. Owing to excessive summer temperatures and the danger of flash floods, the trail is only open from 15 April to 15 September. It is advisable to make reservations well in advance.

Hobas camp site, 69 km north of Ai-Ais, is a mere 12 km from Main Viewpoint overlooking the canyon. Facilities consist of shady camp sites with braai places and tapped water, a field kitchen, communal ablutions and a kiosk. There is also a swimming pool. Day visitors have access to the viewpoints between sunrise and 22:00, but overnight visitors can view the canyon at any time.

Built in the lower reaches of the Fish River, the **Ai-Ais Resort** is situated in an almost lunar landscape. It is a popular stopover with travellers to and from South Africa. The focal point of the resort is the hot springs after which the resort has been named. The Khoekhoen name *Ai-Ais* is translated as "firewater", a reference to the scalding hot temperature of the water where it surfaces.

The spring was visited by white farmers in the late 1800s and during the Nama War of 1903-7 it was used as a base camp by the German forces. When the South African forces under General Louis Botha invaded South West Africa in 1915 German soldiers apparently sought refuge here to recover from their wounds. After World War I the spring was leased to a Karasburg entrepreneur, who provided basic facilities. In 1962 the canyon was proclaimed a national monument and seven years later a conservation area. The modern rest camp complex was officially opened on 16 March 1971, but just under a year later the Fish River came down in flood, causing extensive damage to the complex. Since then the rest camp has been flooded on a number of occasions.

In 1987 the Fish River Canyon Conservation Area was enlarged when state land west of the canyon, including the rugged Hunsberge, was incorporated into it. It borders on South Africa's Richtersveld National Park, south of the Orange River, and there is a possibility that the two parks could be managed as a single transnational park in future.

Accommodation at **Ai-Ais** includes luxury flats, four-bed flats and four-bed huts. Camping sites with braai places, field kitchens and communal ablutions are also available. Other amenities include a well-stocked shop, licensed restaurant, communal spa complex, outdoor swimming pool, tennis courts and filling station.

Kolmanskop Diamond Mining Ghost Town

Kolmanskop is the best known of several diamond mining ghost towns in the south of Namibia. It was here that one of August Stauch's labourers, Zacharias Lewala, discovered a diamond in April 1908. Stauch established his headquarters at Kolmanskop, which soon developed into the centre of the diamond industry. Prefabricated buildings clad with corrugated iron were initially imported from Germany, but they were later replaced by some fine, solid structures. Especially imposing are the mine manager's double-storey house and that of the mining engineer.

The social centre of Kolmanskop was the casino and skittle alley; the lemonade and sodawater factory must have been popular too, not only for its refreshing drinks, but also for the blocks of ice that were supplied to households free of charge.

Fresh water was every bit as much a problem as it had been for the settlers at Lüderitz. Although a pump station at Garub, about 100 km away, supplied some water, barrels of water were also shipped from Cape Town to Lüderitz, from where it was hauled through the sand by mules. Condensers were used to desalinate seawater and a 28 km long pipeline from Elisabethbucht supplied seawater to the mine's washing and treating plants.

CDM had its headquarters here until 1943, when the company moved to Oranjemund, and in 1950 all mining operations ceased at Kolmanskop. The last person left the town six years later, and the buildings were abandoned to the elements and pilferers. Nature soon claimed back what belonged to it. Sand streamed through open windows and doors and roofs were ripped off, turning the once booming mining town into a ghost of its former self.

Kolmanskop can only be visited by joining a guided tour lasting about an hour. Monday to Saturday 09:30 and 10:45; Sunday 10:00. Permits must be obtained from Lüderitz Safaris and Tours in Bismarck Street.

On completion of the tour you can visit the Kolmanskop Museum, which is open until 12:00. There is also a restaurant (closed on Sundays).

Lüderitz

Situated 337 km west of Keetmanshoop along the Diamond Coast, Lüderitz is a charming coastal town with many beautifully preserved German colonial buildings. Although it is not on any through route, a detour to this picturesque town is rewarding. It is advisable to arrive at Lüderitz by midday, because sandstorms on the last stretch of the trip are fairly common in the late afternoon and can "sandblast" your vehicle. Plan to spend at least two nights in Lüderitz to enable you to enjoy and see what the town has to offer.

The **Lüderitz Tourist Information Office** in the museum, Dias Street, provides up-to-date tourist information about Lüderitz and surroundings. Open Monday to Friday, 08:30 to 11:00 and 16:30 to 18:00 (summer) or 15:30 to 17:00 (winter), Saturday 09:00 to 11:00. Tel (063) 20-2532.

Tourist information is also available at the **Ministry of Environment and Tourism Office** in the Old Post Office, Schinz Street. Reservations can be made here for resorts managed by Namibia Wildlife Resorts. Open Monday to Friday 07:30 to 13:00 and 14:00 to 16:00. Tel (063) 20-2752, fax 20-3213.

Originally named Angra Pequena by the 15th century Portuguese navigators, Lüderitz was established by Heinrich Vogelsang, an agent of the Bremen merchant Adolf Lüderitz. Vogelsang arrived at Angra Pequena on 9 April 1883 to establish a trading station and after negotiating with the Bethanien

Khoikhoi chief, Joseph Fredericks, he obtained the land in an 8 km radius of Angra Pequena. The territory was proclaimed a German protectorate on 24 April 1884.

Lüderitz arrived at Angra Pequena in October 1883, but disappeared at sea three years later, when he sailed in a small vessel from the Orange River mouth to Angra Pequena.

What to do in Lüderitz

The beautiful Art Nouveau and German imperial-style buildings of Lüderitz will undoubtedly impress you. The town's German colonial atmosphere of yesteryear can only be truly experienced by exploring its streets on foot. The numbers of the buildings described on this **walking tour** correspond to the numbers on the map, starting in the centre of town.

An attractive feature of the **Deutsche-Afrika Bank** (1), built in 1907 by the Bause brothers, is the stonework of the lower storey and one corner of the upper storey. The building style is more decorative than that of Woermann House (9) and a bell-tower and Renaissance-style gable were incorporated into the design. Although not situated on a corner plot, the building was set back to allow the corner to be built in Wilhelminische style. The bank was established in 1905 as a private bank, with its headquarters in Hamburg.

Still the focal point of the town, the **station building** (2) is particularly interesting, as it is a combination of various building styles. Following the discovery of diamonds in 1908, goods and passenger traffic increased dramatically, and the original station building became inadequate. Lohse, the government architect, designed the building, which was constructed by the building division of Metje and Ziegler. It was completed in 1914, seven years after the railway line between Lüderitz and Aus was built.

The offices of the Ministry of Environment and Tourism are housed in the **Old Post Office** (3). Oswald Reinhardt, the railway commissioner of the southern line, drew up the original plans, but his successor, Rukwied, changed the design to include an upper storey with a tower. A public clock was placed on the tower and rang for the first time on New Year's eve 1908. However, in 1912 the clock was transferred to the church tower.

You are now in the *Altstadt* – the older part of the town. The semi-detached **Troost House** (4), with its jerkin head gable,

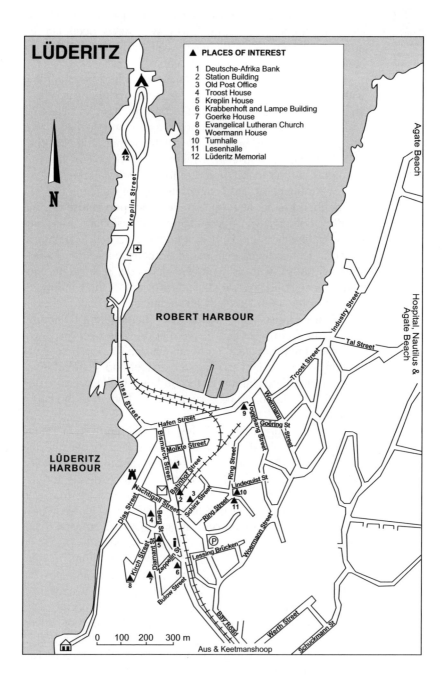

LÜDERITZ

▲ PLACES OF INTEREST

1 Deutsche-Afrika Bank
2 Station Building
3 Old Post Office
4 Troost House
5 Kreplin House
6 Krabbenhoft and Lampe Building
7 Goerke House
8 Evangelical Lutheran Church
9 Woermann House
10 Turnhalle
11 Lesenhalle
12 Lüderitz Memorial

N

ROBERT HARBOUR

LÜDERITZ
HARBOUR

Agate Beach

Hospital, Nautilus & Agate Beach

Industry Street

Troost Street

Tal Street

Woermann Street

Goering St

Vogelsang Street

Hafen Street

Bismarck Street

Molkte Street

Insel Street

Ring Street

Bahnhof Street

Lindequist St

Schinz Street

Ring Street

Nachtigall Street

Berg St

Dias Street

Krich Street

Diamant St

Zeppelin St

Lessing Brücken

Woermann Street

Bülow Street

Bay Road

Werth Street

Schuckmann St

Kreplin Street

0 100 200 300 m

Aus & Keetmanshoop

dates back to 1909. It was built in typical colonial style by Hermann Metje for Edmund Troost, who never occupied the house. Architecturàlly it blends in well with the adjoining residence with its symmetrical front gable.

Kreplin House (5), an impressive double-storey building with an asymmetrical facade, dates back to 1909. It was built for Emil Kreplin, a manager of the railway branch at Lüderitz and later a director of a diamond company and the first mayor of the town. It was built by Friedrich Kramer, and, together with Woermann House in Swakopmund, is one of the few examples of the second period of the Wilhelminische style.

The **Krabbenhoft and Lampe building** (6) was built in 1910 by Friedrich Kramer after he completed **Kreplin House** (5). The building, comprising a shop and adjoining residence, was owned by Krabbenhoft and Lampe, a trading firm with branches in Gibeon, Helmeringhausen and Keetmanshoop. The double-storeyed house, with its symmetrical facade, reflects the neo-Renaissance building style. Note, however, that the windows of the first storey are not directly above the ground floor arches.

Goerke House (7) is situated on Diamantberg (Diamond Mountain), from where you have a good view over the town, including the Evangelical **Lutheran Church** (8). The house was built in 1909 for Hans Goerke, a manager and shareholder of three companies. Unique to the building is the eye-catching sundial, a Wilhelminische decoration not known in the country at the time.

Goerke occupied the building until his return to Germany in 1912. Consolidated Diamond Mines (CDM) became the owner in 1920 and in 1944 the South West Africa Administration bought the property as a residence for the town's magistrate. CDM once again purchased the house in 1983 and restored the building to its former glory. It now serves as a guesthouse for officials and guests of NAMDEB, but is open to the public Monday to Friday, 14:00 to 15:00.

Also known as the *Felsenkirche*, or "The Church on the Rocks", the **Evangelical Lutheran Church** (8) dominates the skyline on Diamantberg. The first request to establish a Lutheran congregation was made in 1906, but because the population of Lüderitz was so small, the first minister arrived from Germany only three years later. Heinrich Bause built a parsonage the following year, while his brother, Albert, was responsible for the design and construction of the church. The foundation stone was laid on 19 November 1911 and the church was consecrated on 4 August 1912. Donations from Germany covered most of the building costs (46 300 German marks). The stained glass altar window was donated by Kaiser Wilhelm II, and his wife donated the altar Bible.

The architecture of the church is not in keeping with the German neo-Gothic building style of the time, but is more closely related to Victorian Gothic. This has been attributed to the fact that the Bause brothers had been influenced by the Cape Victorian building style. The church is open daily for about half an hour at 18:00 in summer and 17:00 in winter.

After the Woermann Line was entrusted with transporting German troops to Lüderitz, the company found it necessary to establish offices in the town. The plans for **Woermann House** (9) were drawn up by Friedrich Höft, but before construction could commence a hill on the site had to be levelled. The excavated rock was used in the foundations and the ground floor. The building is simple in design, but of interest was the inclusion of a water condenser, a technical innovation at the time.

The **Turnhalle** (10) was built in 1913 by Albert Bause and was initially a gymnasium. The four F logo above the entrance was the symbol of German gymnasiums and stood for "Frisch, Fromm, Frohlich and Frei, is die Deutsche Turnerei." The adjacent **Lesenhalle** (11), with its quaint tower, dates back to 1912, when it was taken into use as a library.

Not to be missed is a visit to the **Lüderitz Museum** in Dias Street, tel (063) 20-2532. The displays focus on the town's early days, minerals and diamond mining and the natural history of the Namib Desert. Of interest are 10 000-year-old giraffe bones recovered close to Elisabeth Bay, a diorama of seabirds occurring along the coast and a specimen of a toothed pygmy killer whale washed ashore at Griffiths Bay in 1968, the first record of this species south of the equator. The museum is open Monday to Friday, 08:30–11:00 and 16:30–18:00 (summer) or 15:30–17:00 (winter), Saturday 09:00–11:00. Mrs Looser, tel (063) 20-2582, can be contacted to make special arrangements outside these hours.

Exploring the Lüderitz peninsula

There are several delightful bays to be explored along the Lüderitz peninsula and an outing can be combined with a

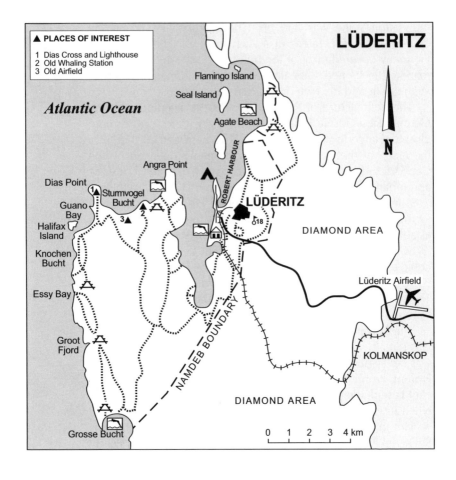

LÜDERITZ

▲ PLACES OF INTEREST

1 Dias Cross and Lighthouse
2 Old Whaling Station
3 Old Airfield

Flamingo Island

Seal Island

Atlantic Ocean

Agate Beach

ROBERT HARBOUR

N

Angra Point

Dias Point

Sturmvogel Bucht

LÜDERITZ

Guano Bay

618

DIAMOND AREA

Halifax Island

Knochen Bucht

Lüderitz Airfield

Essy Bay

NAMDEB BOUNDARY

KOLMANSKOP

Groot Fjord

DIAMOND AREA

0 1 2 3 4 km

Grosse Bucht

beach walk and a picnic, so set aside a few hours. The turnoff to the peninsula is at the southern end of the town.

The first bay, **Radford's Bay**, is named after the first white settler, David Radford, who lived here in a house constructed from jetsam. Radford sold dried fish and shark liver oil to Cape-bound ships and exchanged ostrich feathers for fresh water with northbound ships, as no water was available at Lüderitz.

Continue to **Second Lagoon**, which can be rewarding for birdwatchers. The lagoon attracts a variety of waders, including flocks of greater flamingo. Oysters are cultivated on rafts in the nutrient-rich water of the lagoon.

A few kilometres beyond Second Lagoon a turnoff to the left leads to **Grosse Bucht** (Large Bay). Along with Agate Beach, this 2 km long stretch is one of the few sandy bays along the peninsula and is, therefore, popular with sunbathers, anglers and strollers. Picnic facilities are available.

The road leading northward from Grosse Bucht gives access to a number of bays, and from the cliffs to the south of Guano Bay you have a good view over **Halifax Island**, which is home to a jackass penguin population. Continuing to Dias Point, you pass a **grave** with a wooden cross which reads "George Pond of London, died here of hunger and thirst 1906."

A short distance further you pass the **lighthouse** at Dias Point. The 28,8 m high lighthouse was built in 1910 to replace the one erected by the German authorities in about 1903. Dias Point is reached by way of a **wooden bridge**, built in 1911 to provide access to a steam-operated foghorn on the point.

During his journey southward, Bartholomeu Dias became the first white man to shelter in the protected bay at Lüderitz. He entered the bay with three ships on Christmas Day 1487 and named it Angra das Voltas, before continuing south to become the first navigator to round the Cape. On his return journey in July the following year, Dias renamed the bay Golfo de São Cristovão and erected a stone cross on Dias Point on 25 July 1488. Fragments of the cross were taken to Cape Town in 1856. A cross bearing no resemblance to the original padrão was erected in 1929. It was replaced by an exact **replica of the original padrão** during the Dias 88 Festival.

From Dias Point the road takes you past a **landing strip** built by the Germans in 1913, but long since abandoned. A short detour leads to **Sturmvogelbucht** (Sturmvogel is the German name for petrel, a seabird which visits the coast in summer). Here the remains of a Norwegian whaling station dating back to 1914 can be seen.

The adjacent **Griffiths Bay** was named after an American naval officer who was buried here by David Radford. During the American Civil War, Griffiths sought refuge at Angra Pequena, but was shot as a traitor when another ship arrived. The bay affords a magnificent view of the town across the lagoon.

Returning to town, you join the main access road which takes you past Second Lagoon and Radford Bay once again. Back in town, follow Bismarck Street into Hafen Street, where you turn left then right into Insel Street. A short way on a causeway takes you across to **Shark** or *Haifisch* **Island**. Among the historical buildings are the **Signal Station**, dating back to 1914, and the hospital, built in 1912. The site for the hospital was selected because of the scenic views, the lack of dust and its isolation. A **plaque** (12) along the rocky western shores of the island serves as a reminder of the founder of Namibia's oldest harbour town, Adolf Lüderitz.

Also to be seen are the tombstones of several *Schutztruppe* and a plaque recalling the exploits of a Brazilian, Captain Amyr Khan Klink, who rowed across the Atlantic for a research project on survival. Klink left Lüderitz on 10 June 1984 and arrived 100 days later at São Salvador in Brazil.

Finally, **Agate Beach** is also worth a visit, but do not count on finding agates here – they have long since been collected by beachcombers. This long, sandy beach, about 8 km out of town, is well-signposted from the turnoff at the junction of Hafen and Tal streets. Picnic facilities are provided, but take care to remain on hard-surface roads.

Angling

There are several rewarding angling spots along the peninsula where galjoen, steenbras and cob can be caught. Enquire with the Directorate of Fisheries and Marine Resources if you are not familiar with local regulations.

Desert roses

Lüderitz is well known for its desert roses – crystals of gypsum and calcium sulphate salts which occur in the desert sand and develop under damp, moist conditions. An exciting experience is to dig for your own desert roses. However, a permit must be obtained from the MET office in Schinz Street. Collectors are limited to three sand roses, or a total weight of 1,5 kg. Spades and other sharp objects may not be used, as they damage concealed sand roses. Collectors are allowed two hours and are accompanied by an MET official to ensure that all conditions are complied with.

Organised tours and trips

Bookings can be made at:
Kolmanskop Tour Company, P O Box 357, tel (063) 20-2445,

fax 20-2526. Tours to Elisabeth Bay and the Bogenfels, as well as yacht trips.

Lüderitzbucht Safaris & Tours, P O Box 76, tel (063) 20-2622, fax 20-2863. Day trips of the Lüderitz Peninsula and surroundings, yacht trips.

Weather permitting, **yacht trips** are offered daily on the 42 m steel sloop **"Sedina"** by the husband-and-wife team of Manfred and Gaby Wedell. These trips afford you beautiful views of Lüderitz and its numerous bays. Dusky dolphins are frequently seen playing near the bow of the yacht and a variety of seabirds can be seen. The trips depart early in the morning from Robert Harbour and the return journey to Dias Point takes two and a half to three hours. In calm seas the vessel sails to just off Halifax Island, where you can get close-up views of the jackass penguin colony.

Elisabeth Bay and the Bogenfels are situated within the restricted Diamond Area and can only be visited by joining an organised tour. Tours are conducted by Kolmanskop Tours.

The **Elisabeth Bay tour** is a 90 km round trip to the diamond mining ghost village of Elisabeth Bay, at one time the second largest diamond mining town in the Sperrgebiet. Mining began in about 1913, but was disrupted by World War I. Between 1926 and 1931 about 1,25 million carats were recovered. Production ceased in 1931 as a result of the Depression, but limited mining resumed in 1945. In 1948 the mine was finally abandoned and the buildings were stripped of all useful material. Over the years salt-laden winds eroded the bricks of the unplastered walls, leaving spectacular honeycomb patterns. Among the ruins to be seen are those of the recreation club, processing plant, CDM offices, station building, manager's house and the living quarters.

In March 1989 CDM decided to re-establish a mining operation at Elisabeth Bay and invested R135 million in a new plant and facilities. Production started on 1 June 1991 and the mine is expected to produce about 2,5 million carats during its estimated life span of 10 years.

The tour operates on weekdays only, departing at 08:30 and returning at 12:30.

Also on offer is a full-day safari to the **Bogenfels**, some 90 km south of Lüderitz. Extending into the sea, the 55 m high rock arch is the highest coastal rock arch in southern Africa.

The trip takes in the diamond fields of Idatal and the Märchental to Pomona, a deserted mining village which was abandoned to the elements in the mid-1930s.

The tour is conducted on weekdays only, departing at 08:00 and returning at 17:30.

As the Elisabeth Bay and Bogenfels tours are conducted inside the restricted Diamond Area, tours must be booked at least four working days in advance. The following information is required: full name, nationality, passport or identity number. Children under 14 are not permitted on the Elisabeth Bay Tour.

Shopping

At **Lüderitz Carpets** in the Krabbenhoft and Lampe Building, 25 Bismarck Street, tel (063) 20-2272, visitors can see how the karakul wool is first handspun and then handwoven into carpets, rugs and wall-hangings. Monday to Friday 08:00 to 12:30 and 14:30 to 17:30, Saturday 09:00 to 13:00.

Also in the same building is Herman Dierks' **Lüderitz Stained Glass**. Open Monday to Friday, 09:00 to 18:00, and Saturday, 09:00 to 13:00. Tel (063) 20-4322.

Where to eat

In addition to the restaurants at the **Sea View Zum Sperrgebiet** and **Nest** hotels, there are several other options:

Badger's Bistro, Dias Street, tel (063) 20-2818. A lively bistro. À la carte menu with steak and seafood specialities.

On the Rocks, Bay Road, tel (063) 20-3110. À la carte with seafood specialities.

S & S Coffee Shop, Bismarck Street, tel (063) 20-3478. Serves light meals.

Where to stay

With its panoramic views over Lüderitz Bay, the harbour and the town, the **Hotel Sea View Zum Sperrgebiet** offers high quality accommodation. Facilities include a restaurant, bar, heated swimming pool and sauna.

The **Nest Hotel** is situated on the beach front. The tastefully decorated rooms all have a sea view.

The **Hotel Zum Sperrgebiet** offers a choice of rooms or serviced self-contained holiday flats. Restaurant and bar.

The granite outcrops on Shark Island provide ideal camp sites, but conditions are often very windy. Amenities at the **Shark Island camp site** include field kitchens and communal ablutions.

Quiver Tree Forests

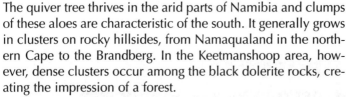

The quiver tree thrives in the arid parts of Namibia and clumps of these aloes are characteristic of the south. It generally grows in clusters on rocky hillsides, from Namaqualand in the northern Cape to the Brandberg. In the Keetmanshoop area, however, dense clusters occur among the black dolerite rocks, creating the impression of a forest.

The quiver tree belongs to the genus *Aloe* and is grouped with the tree aloes. The average size is 3-5 m, but occasionally examples reach a height of up to 8 m. Attractive bright yellow flowers are produced between May and July, attracting a variety of birds to the nectar.

The branches of these distinctive trees were hollowed out by the early San and used as quivers for their arrows, hence the name.

The little-known, but scenically very attractive, **Garas Park** is situated 20 km north of Keetmanshoop. Covering over 300 ha of black dolerite outcrops dotted with a profusion of quiver trees and other aloes, as well as succulents, Garas is a Nama name which appropriately means quiver tree. A visit is especially rewarding any time from May to July, when the bright yellow flowers of the quiver trees provide a blaze of colour. Paths meander around and over the outcrops, providing stunning views of the interesting landscape.

Also of interest are the fascinating rock shapes, some of which resemble a Land Rover, a cannon, pelican and a Herero woman with a headdress. At sunset the silhouettes of the rocks etched against the red sky create a very special atmosphere.

Facilities have purposely been kept rustic and comprise clearings among the rock outcrops. Amenities include reed-covered carports, mobile braai places, open-air cold showers, toilets, tapped water. Natural material such as rock serve as chairs, and wooden logs have been used for tables. There are also two typical Nama huts and a large tent.

The well-known **Quiver Tree Forest** is situated on the farm Gariganus, 14 km northeast of Keetmanshoop. Here, about 200 quiver trees are clustered among the dolerite outcrops.

Both quiver tree forests are best viewed in the early morning or late afternoon.

The **Quiver Tree Forest rest camp** offers accommodation ranging from rooms (with bed and breakfast or dinner, bed and breakfast) and fully equipped self-catering bungalows to camp sites. There is also a swimming pool and guests can undertake farm trips and visit the nearby Giant's Playground (see p 258).

ROUTE 20
REHOBOTH TO NOORDOEWER

DISTANCE: 705 km **TIME:** 7 hours **ROAD CONDITIONS:** Tar, except detours onto secondary (C) and district (D) roads **FUEL:** Rehoboth, Kalkrand, Mariental, Asab, Keetmanshoop, Grünau, Noordoewer **LINKING ROUTES:** Routes 21, 22, 24, 25

From Windhoek (see p 53) the B1 meanders along a scenic valley between the Auas mountains and the Gross Herzog-Friedrich Mountain before striking south to Rehoboth, where this route begins.

Rehoboth, 90 km south of Windhoek, is usually by-passed, as many tourists are unaware of the spa complex at the thermal spring in the town. Like many towns in Namibia, Rehoboth developed around a mission station, established in 1844 by a Rhenish missionary, Heinrich Kleinschmidt. The mission station was abandoned in 1864, but was rebuilt when the Basters under Hermanus van Wyk settled here in 1870. The Basters, a group of mixed European-Khoikhoi blood, originated in the Cape in South Africa, from where they gradually migrated northward, settling along the Gariep (Orange) River toward the end of the 18th century. Following legislation in 1865, which required all settlers to prove their right over property, a large number of Basters migrated northward and eventually settled at Rehoboth.

The Basters are extremely proud of their heritage and although the name (meaning half-caste) is generally considered derogatory, they insist on being called Basters. Afrikaans is still the home language of many Basters.

The town's main attraction is the **Reho Spa**, at a thermal spring which was originally known as *Aris*. The Khoekhoen name means "smoke" and is a reference to the steam rising off the spring on cold winter mornings. A recreation resort, comprising an outdoor pool with a temperature of up to 30 °C and an indoor thermal bath with a temperature of 39 °C, has been developed close to the spring.

The resort is open throughout the year. Overnight visitors with reserved accommodation may enter at any time, but may not leave between 23:00 and 07:00. Day visitors must leave the resort before 18:00.

The **Reho Spa Recreation Resort** offers accommodation in one-roomed bungalows with four, five and six beds. Units are equipped with a fridge, stove and kettle. Bedding is provided, but no crockery, cutlery or cooking utensils. There is also a camp site with communal ablutions.

Also of interest is the **Rehoboth Museum**, part of which is housed in the residence of the town's first postmaster, which dates back to 1903. Displays include the history of the Baster people, the Drierivier archaeological excavation and the vegetation and animals of the Rehoboth area. Also of interest are the traditional huts of the Damara, Nama, San, Himba and Owambo peoples. Visits to archaeological sites in the area can be undertaken, provided prior arrangements have been made. Tel (062) 52-2954. The museum is open Monday to Friday 08:00 to 13:00 and 14:00 to 17:00; Saturday 09:00 to 11:00.

The **Oanob Dam** on the western outskirts of the town is reached by turning off the B1 onto the D1237, about 5 km north of Rehoboth. Completed in 1990 to supply water to Rehoboth, the dam has a capacity of 35 million m³ and covers an area of 2,65 km² when full. The 55 m high dam wall stretches for 275 m across the Oanob River. A lookout point near the dam wall affords good views across the dam and the surrounding rolling countryside.

The dam offers opportunities for a variety of water sports – water-skiing, paddle-boating, aqua-biking and canoeing – and is especially popular over weekends. Amenities at the **Lake Oanob Resort** on the shores of the dam include a restaurant, marina, floating dock, launching ramp and picnic sites for day visitors. Open throughout the year, 24 hours a day.

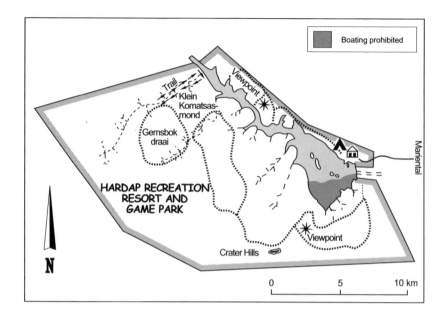

Accommodation at the resort is available in fully equipped, self-catering chalets and caravans with bedding. Camp sites with ablutions are also available.

From Rehoboth the B1 continues south to the signposted turnoff to the Hardap Recreation Resort, 15 km north of Mariental. Turn right and continue for 6 km to the entrance gate; the resort office is 2,5 km further.

Hardap Recreation Resort is a sought-after water sports destination and is also a popular overnight stop. The focal point of the resort and game park is **Hardap Dam**, Namibia's largest. The suitability of the area for a dam to harness the water of the Fish River was pointed out as early as 1897 by a German geologist, Dr Theodor Rehbock. Construction of a dam, however, only commenced in 1960 and was completed three years later. Behind the 39 m high dam wall, which stretches between two koppies over a distance of 865 m, lies a vast man-made lake with a capacity of 323 million m^3 and a surface area of up to 25 km^2. Up to 5 500 m^3 of water can be discharged per second via the four radial gates in the spillway.

Between the mid-1980s and 1996 the dam received little inflow and its level dropped to below 10 per cent. Early in 1997 heavy rains fell in the catchment area of the Fish River, filling the dam to capacity and resulting in the opening of the sluice gates for the first time in a decade.

The dam is popular for boating, windsurfing, sailing and angling. Seven fish species and a mudfish hybrid occur in the dam. Among the species to be caught are smallmouth yellowfish, carp, barbel, mud mullet, mudfish and blue kurper. Angling from the shore is restricted to designated angling and day camping sites on the dam's northeastern bank. Boat angling is also permitted, but there are restricted areas. Permits are obtainable from the tourist office.

A variety of freshwater fish species can be viewed in the aquarium, the only one of its kind in the country, adjacent to the resort office. There are also displays on the biology of fish and a distribution map of Namibia's freshwater fish. The Fresh Water Fish Institute (below the dam wall), where research is carried out into fish production and breeding, is closed to the public.

The **Hardap Game Park** is divided by the dam into two sections, covering 1 848 ha along the northern shore and 23 329 ha to the south and west of the dam. Wide plains interspersed with rondavel-type koppies and stony ridges characterise the landscape with its dwarf shrub savanna vegetation. Scattered trees such as camel thorn, wild green-hair and buffalo-thorn occur mainly in the river courses, while trumpet thorn (*Catophractes alexandri*) forms dense stands in some localities.

The section of the game park to the south of the dam is crisscrossed by an 82 km network of roads leading to viewpoints overlooking the dam and the appropriately named Crater Hills. It is reached by taking the road along the top of the dam wall.

Among the game to be seen are gemsbok, kudu, red hartebeest, springbok, Hartmann's mountain zebra, eland and ostrich. Black rhino were translocated to the park in 1990 in an effort to reintroduce this species more widely within its former range. This is the southernmost population of black rhino in Namibia.

Some 300 bird species have been identified to date in the diverse habitat types. The dam is one of only two breeding sites of the white pelican in Namibia and attracts up to 1 000 birds at times. White-breasted and reed cormorants, darter, squacco heron, Egyptian goose, South African shelduck, spur-winged goose and red-knobbed coot also occur and you might be fortunate to hear the challenging cry of the African fish eagle. Keep an eye out for osprey, which are present from October to April.

On a game drive you might tick kori and Ludwig's bustards, double-banded courser, a variety of larks and short-toed rock thrush. Birding is, however, most rewarding in the reedbeds along the Fish River and the dense stands of camel and sweet thorn below the dam wall.

Unless the dam is full, a visit to the Voëlparadys (Bird Paradise) is unlikely to be worthwhile. The alluring name was given to a stand of camel thorn trees that died after the dam filled to capacity in 1963. The dead trees provided ideal perches and attracted large numbers of white-breasted cormorants, but the birds abandoned their roosting sites when the water level dropped.

For those interested in getting a closer look at their surroundings a **circular walk** of 9 km or 15 km has been laid out in the vicinity of the Great Komatsas River. Before setting off, obtain a copy of the trail booklet from the resort office. In addition to information on various points marked along the trail, there is also a bird checklist. Be warned though, the area is favoured by black rhino and their huge spoor and dung serve as reminders of them along the trail. As these are dangerous animals you should remain alert at all times.

Overnight visitors may enter the resort at any time and provided accommodation and entry fees have been paid in full, visitors may leave the resort at any time. Day visitors are admitted from sunrise to 18:00.

Accommodation at **Hardap Recreation Resort** ranges from two- and five-bedded bungalows to camping sites, built on the cliffs overlooking the dam. The restaurant on the edge of the dam affords magnificent views over the large expanse of water. Adjoining the restaurant is a shop which stocks groceries, souvenirs and liquor. Other facilities include a swimming pool, tennis courts, children's playground and a filling station.

Continuing further south along the B1, the turnoff to Stampriet, Gochas and Mata Mata (see route 21) is reached 5 km on and after another 10 km you reach **Mariental**, the administrative capital of the Hardap Region.

Also known as the "Gateway to the South", the town is an important agricultural centre. It has the largest number of karakul sheep in the country and the ostrich farm just north of the town was the first commercial operation of its type in the country. Maize, lucerne, sultana grapes, sweet melon, watermelon and cotton are produced by farms of the Hardap Irrigation Scheme.

Before the arrival of white settlers, the Khoikhoi referred to the area as *Zaragaebis*, a word meaning "dusty" or "dirty face". It has been suggested that the name has its origin in the heavy dust storms which often occur here in summer.

The first German farmers to settle in the area, Hermann Brandt and Bernhard Mahler, bought a farm in 1895 from Nama chief Hendrik Witbooi, naming it Enkelkameeldoring (solitary camel thorn). Three years later Brandt married Anna-Maria Mahler and renamed the farm Mariental, in honour of her. The name is translated as "Mary's dale".

In 1895 a police station was established on Mariental and 10 years later the farm Koichas was sold to police sergeant E Stumpfe at 5 cents a hectare. Stumpfe gave 70 ha of his farm to the German railway authorities in April 1912 and in June the station was built and named Mariental. Two years later, Stumpfe requested the German administration to establish a village, but the following year the country was placed under military control, following the surrender of the German forces. In 1919 Stumpfe donated land to the Dutch Reformed Church and repeated his request to the military magistrate at Gibeon. The cornerstone of the first Dutch Reformed Church in the country was laid on 11 September 1920 and the town was proclaimed two months later.

Continuing south along the B1, you reach the C19 turnoff to Maltahöhe about 4 km south of Mariental (see route 22). Dominating the landscape to the east of the B1 is the Weissrand Plateau. **Gibeon railway station**, 63 km south of Mariental, is usually passed unnoticed. However, of interest here is a small **cemetery** – a reminder of one of the bloodiest battles of the 1914-15 German South West Africa campaign. The cemetery is reached by taking the turnoff to the station, but leave your vehicle near the station building. The cemetery is across the railway line, opposite the station building.

During the battle here on 27 April 1915 between a 1 500-strong force under Brigadier-General Sir Duncan Mackenzie and a German force of 800, commanded by General Von Kleist, 29 South Africans were killed or died of wounds and 66 wounded. The German losses were 12 dead and 30 wounded, while 188 were taken prisoner of war. Two field guns, four machine guns, a train, wagons with supplies and ammunition were also captured by the Union Forces. The battle resulted in a proclamation the following day that German territory south of Gibeon was under the control of the Union of South Africa Defence Force.

The small settlement of **Gibeon** is reached by taking the signposted turnoff opposite the station and travelling for another 9 km. The spring around which the settlement grew was originally known as *Gorego-re-Abes*, or "the drinking place of the zebras". As with several other settlements in the south of the country, Gibeon was founded by the Rhenish Mission. A mission station was established by missionary J Kana in 1863 and named after the biblical Gibeon (Joshua 10:2). The first church was built in 1876, but a few years later the mission station was destroyed. However, it was rebuilt later.

In 1894 Gibeon was declared a district, with the settlement as district town. In the same year a military post was established on the orders of Major Theodor Leutwein. While the fort was being built, non-commissioned officer Bahr and 14 troopers were temporarily accommodated in the mission church.

After the 1893-94 war against Hendrik Witbooi, Senior Lieutenant Von Burgsdorff was appointed *Bezirksampt* or district commander of the Gibeon district. On 4 October 1904 he was murdered at Mariental, after riding unarmed to Hendrik Witbooi's settlement in an unsuccessful final attempt to persuade him not to go to war.

In the late 1890s De Beers Consolidated Mines Ltd explored the Gibeon area, following the discovery of kimberlite pipes. Despite the absence of diamonds, hopeful explorers persisted and in 1902 the Gibeon Syndicate was formed. Two years later the syndicate changed its name to the Gibeon Schurf- und Handelsgesellschaft, but in 1910 abandoned its search.

The Gibeon area has attracted worldwide attention from astronomers, because one of the most extensive meteorite showers known of occurred here. The "**Gibeon Shower**" is estimated to have occurred over an area of 20 000 km^2, with the highest concentration in the Gibeon-Amalia area of approximately 2 500 km^2. It has been suggested that the meteors remained together after a violent explosion, an unusual occurrence, and struck the earth's atmosphere as a group after a relatively long journey through space.

In addition to the 37 meteorites collected for the *Landesmuseum* in Windhoek between 1911 and 1913 (see p 55), some 40 others have been recovered. They can be seen in museums throughout the world, including the British, Budapest and Prague museums, as well as the Washington and New York museums of natural history. The largest known Gibeon meteorite, one of 650 kg, was donated to the South African Museum in Cape Town.

On the weekend closest to 29 October – the day on which the renowned Witbooi Chief, Hendrik Witbooi, was killed in battle – Gibeon becomes a hive of activity when the **Witbooi Festival** is held at the town. During the festival Hendrik Witbooi's life story is related and battles and battle techniques are enacted, while traditional songs and dances are performed.

About 38 km south of Gibeon station you travel past Asab, from where travellers used to make a detour to **Mukurob**. This imposing rock formation was one of the most widely-known attractions in Namibia until its demise on the night of 7 December 1988. Only a small remnant of the neck has remained, but many tourists make the 25 km detour to the site.

The origin of Mukurob can best be understood when surveying the landscape east of the formation. As a result of the erosion of the softer shale and vertical seams, the sandstone escarpment of the Weissrand Plateau has been shaped into large blocks, most of which have collapsed. Mukurob originated when it became isolated from the escarpment and withstood the ravages of nature for some 50 000 years.

Research has shown that several factors, including the Armenian earthquake that registered strongly on the seismograph in Windhoek on the night that Mukurob collapsed, contributed to the demise of this well-known landmark. It has also been suggested that the heavy rain which fell in the area a few days before the collapse also played a role, weakening the mudstone neck of the precariously balanced pinnacle to such an extent that it could no longer support the head.

The formation towered 29 m above the landscape, with a sandstone head 12 m high and about 4,5 m at its widest. The head, with an estimated mass of 450 tonnes, was supported by a narrow neck, 3 m long and a mere 1,5 m wide.

Those not fortunate enough to have seen Mukurob before its demise can see a replica at the Southern Tourist Forum offices in Keetmanshoop.

Although the Khoekhoen name Mukurob is commonly associated with the English name, The Finger of God, the names bear no relation to each other. Mukurob is said to mean "look at the ankle", an apparent reference to the narrow neck between the pedestal and the head. It was also known by the Afrikaans names Vingerklip and, because of its resemblance to the profile of a Herero woman, Hererovrou.

As you head south from Asab, the landscape becomes increasingly dominated by the outline of **Brukkaros**, an extinct volcano measuring some 3,5 km from rim to rim. Because of its prominent position some 650 m above the surrounding plains, the mountain has served various purposes. In the early 1900s a heliograph station was established on the eastern rim by the Germans. The Smithsonian Institute conducted solar radiation observations from the western rim from 1926 to 1931. More recently a VHF radio mast was erected on the northern rim.

It is reached by turning off the B1 onto Main Road 98 (signposted Berseba), 52 km south of Asab. Some 36 km further on, about 1 km before the settlement of Berseba, you turn onto the D3904 (signposted Brukkaros). From here the road continues for 12 km, but travellers in sedan cars are advised to look for a suitable parking place after 10 km, where the road narrows to a steep track.

From the end of the road one has to continue on foot, following a well-defined path for about 30 minutes into the crater via the eroded southern rim. This path was constructed to provide access to the Smithsonian Institute's observatory. Once inside the crater, take some time to explore the floor with its quiver trees.

From the crater floor the path ascends steeply to the old observation station on the rim of the crater, gaining some 350 m in altitude in the approximately one hour walk. A short scramble brings you to the edge of the rim, from where there are wonderful views of the plains far below, dissected by numerous drainage lines radiating from the base of the crater.

The Nama name, *Geitsigubeb*, refers to the mountain's apparent resemblance to the large leather apron worn around the waist by Khoikhoi women. The German name, Brukkaros, is derived from the Khoikhoi name and is said to be a German adaptation of the Afrikaans names for trousers (*broek*) and leather apron *(karos)*.

Despite its volcanic origin, lava is surprisingly absent at Brukkaros. The evolution of the mountain began 80 million years ago with the intrusion of kimberlite-like magma (molten rock) into rocks about 1 km below the earth's surface. This magma must have encountered underground water, which would have turned into steam immediately. The extremely high pressure bulged the overlying rock into a dome 400 m high and 10 km across. More magma then intruded into the centre of the dome, where it also encountered underground water. Here the cover of overlying rock was thinner and a huge explosion of superheated steam blew out the dome's centre. As the underground water drained into the crater it encountered more intruding magma. This resulted in more explosions from successively deeper and deeper levels in the crater. In the end, rocks from as deep as 2 km within the earth's crust were being blasted out of the crater.

The highly shattered ejected rock fragments built up a rim of rubble and ash around the crater. Once explosive volcanism ceased, rain began to wash the fine material in the ash rim back into the crater, where it built up layers of sediment on the floor of the crater lake which had formed in the meantime. Numerous hot springs formed around the edge of the lake, and as they bubbled up through the sediments large quantities of fine-grained quartz were deposited. The sediments were gradually cemented into hard, weather-resistant rocks. Volcanism was very short-lived, lasting only a year or two, but sedimentation may have lasted hundreds of thousands of years.

Subsequent erosion gradually removed the surrounding rocks, leaving the cemented, weather-resistant crater lake sediments, once located down in the throat of the dead volcano, standing high above the centre of the dome that formed when the first magma intruded.

The settlement of **Berseba** is about 1 km beyond the turnoff to Brukkaros. Founded in 1850 by the Rhenish missionary Samuel Hahn, it takes its name from the biblical Berseba (Genesis 21:31), which means "well of the oath".

From the Berseba turnoff, continue south along the B1 to the turnoff to **Garas Park** (see p 247) 61 km on. Remaining on the B1, the turnoff to the **Quiver Tree Forest** (see p 247) is reached 18 km further. Turn left onto the C16 to Aroab and after about 800 m left onto the C17, then continue for 12 km to the Quiver Tree Forest.

The boulder-strewn landscape east of the Quiver Tree Forest has appropriately been named the **Giant's Playground** and is well worth a visit. It is 4,2 km beyond the Quiver Tree Forest along the C17.

The black rock, locally known as *ysterklip* (Afrikaans for iron rock), was formed when magma (molten lava) intruded into the overlying Karoo sediments some 180 million years ago. The magma subsequently cooled down to form dolerite and during this period a large number of fractures developed. Over millions of years the overlying Karoo sediments were eroded by the elements. Rain and ground water seeped deep into the dolerite, which became soft and could be washed away more easily by erosion. All that remains today is the more weather-resistant dolerite between the fractures.

The Giant's Playground is best viewed in the early mornings and late afternoons, especially at sunset, when the rock formations form striking silhouettes.

Keetmanshoop, the administrative capital of the Karas Region and an important agricultural centre, is reached 1,6 km south of the Quiver Tree Forest turnoff.

The **Southern Tourist Forum** in the Old Post Office, 5th Avenue, provides information on the south of the country. Tel (063) 22-3316. Open Monday to Friday 07:00 to 12:30 and 13:30 to 16:30 (Friday 16:00).

Originally a Nama settlement on the banks of the Swartmodder River, Keetmanshoop was known as *Nugoaes,* (translated as "black mud") – a reference to the river, which only flows after heavy rains.

In 1866 a Rhenish mission station was established and named after Johann Keetman, a prosperous industrialist and chairman of the Rhenish Missionary Society, who made funds available for the establishment of the mission. The first missionary, Johan Schröder, set about building a church, but in 1890 the building was swept away when the Swartmodder River burst its banks. A new church, built on higher ground, was completed in 1895 and was used until 1930. The building now serves as a museum which depicts the early history and development of the Keetmanshoop district. Open Monday to Friday, 07:00 to 12:30 and 13:30 to 16:30 (Friday 16:00).

Another building of interest is the **Old Post Office**, built in 1910 to plans drawn up by the government architect, Gottlieb Redecker. As a result of the decision to build the post office on a single erf, the plans had to be amended. In addition, as Kaiser Street ran at a slight angle to other streets, the northern wall of the post office was built at an angle too. The attractive facade incorporates a prominent pointed gable with a wide, rectangular tower, where a telegraph mast was attached. Part of the building now houses the Southern Tourist Forum.

Other interesting buildings include **Schutzenhaus** (1907) in Gibeon Street, the old hospital, also known as **Johanniter House** (1913), and the **German Evangelical Lutheran Church** (1935) on the corner of Kaiser Street and 3rd Avenue. Also of interest are the **Adelaars Monument** (Eagle Monument), dedicated to German soldiers killed during the 1904-7 war, and the site of the **spring** around which the town developed.

Accommodation in the **Canyon Hotel** in Keetmanshoop is in rooms with *en suite* bathrooms. Amenities include a restaurant, coffee shop, bar, beer garden, swimming pool and gymnasium facilities.

The **Keetmanshoop Municipal rest camp** is well maintained and offers shady camping or caravan sites with communal ablutions.

Travelling south from Keetmanshoop, the B1 traverses vast plains, punctuated by the Great Karas mountains, before heading south across more plains. About 12 km north of Grünau a signpost indicates the turnoff to the **White House rest camp**, where guests are accommodated, either on a self-catering or fully inclusive basis, in an old German farmhouse with lots of character.

Grünau, a small farming settlement, lies at the junction of the B1 to Noordoewer and Cape Town and the B3 to Ariamsvlei and Upington in South Africa. It also lies at the junction of the C12-D601 roads to **Hobas** and the viewpoints overlooking the **Fish River Canyon** (see p 233). From Grünau, take the C12 for 51 km to Holoog. Turn left onto the D601, continuing for 31 km to the turnoff signposted Fish River Canyon. Turn right here and after 3 km you will reach Hobas; the Main Viewpoint is a further 12 km on.

Continuing south from Grünau, the C10 to **Ai-Ais** (see p 235) is reached after 31 km. The resort is 74 km off the B1. The Namibian border post on the northern bank of the Gariep (Orange) River is 108 km beyond the C10 turnoff.

ROUTE 21
MARIENTAL TO GOCHAS AND THE SOUTHEAST

DISTANCE: 330 km **TIME**: 4 to 5 hours **ROAD CONDITIONS**: 63 km tar; 267 km gravel secondary road (C) **FUEL**: Mariental, Stampriet, Gochas **LINKING ROUTES**: Route 20

This route links Mariental with the Kalahari, but will only be a feasible option once the Mata Mata border post between Namibia and the Kalahari Gemsbok National Park in South Africa has been opened.

From Mariental, travel north along the B1 for 10 km to the turnoff onto the C20. After travelling for about 12 km the D1268 turnoff to the **Intu Africa Kalahari Game Reserve** is reached. If you plan to visit the lodge, turn left and continue for about 45 km to the signposted turnoff.

The reserve covers 15 000 ha of spectacular Kalahari landscape and among the game to be seen are gemsbok, springbok, blue wildebeest, Burchell's zebra, eland and giraffe. Activities include game drives, night drives, guided walks and two to three-day hikes guided by San trackers and guides. Accommodation ranges from luxury twin chalets and luxury twin rooms with *en suite* facilities to bungalows, a tented camp and a camp site.

Continuing along the C20, the farming settlement of **Stampriet** is reached after 40 km. With its artesian wells, this is an important fruit and vegetable farming area. Just outside Stampriet you turn onto the C15 (signposted Gochas) and after about 20 km you pass the farm **Gross Nabas**. Here a fairly inconspicuous monument to the left of the road is a reminder of one of the bloodiest battles of the Nama rebellion. Heavy losses were inflicted by the Witbooi Nama on a German force led by *Oberleutnant* von Burgsdorff during a battle here from 2 to 4 January 1905. About 24 km from this spot a granite monument to the left of the road marks the place where a German patrol of 14 men was killed when a surprise attack was launched on them on 4 March 1905.

The turnoff to Gochas is 24 km further on and at the far end of the four-way crossing, on the right-hand side of the road, the **grave** of the first missionary of Gochas, Heinrich Rust, can be seen under a large camel thorn tree. The village is reached by taking the signposted turnoff at the four-way intersection and then turning right again a few hundred metres on.

Gochas, on the banks of the Auob River, takes its name from a Khoekhoen name translated as "place of many !go-bushes" – a reference to the candle thorn. After Gibeon was declared a district in 1894, a non-commissioned officer and three soldiers were stationed at Gochas to maintain law and order. A fort was completed in 1897, but unfortunately the building has long since disappeared.

In the **cemetery**, a short distance beyond the post office in the village, the graves of a large number of soldiers, killed in the numerous battles along the Auob and in the vicinity with the Witbooi Nama and the tribe of Simon Koper, can be seen.

Two monuments, 10 km and 13,7 km southeast of Gochas, on the farm **Haruchas**, are further reminders of the battles fought here on 3 and 5 January 1905 by German forces, under *Hauptmann* Eugene Stuhlmann, against the Nama tribe of Simon Koper.

Situated on the banks of the Auob River, **Auob Lodge** is reached 68 km south of Stampriet. The lodge lies amid 8 000 ha of orange Kalahari dunes where gemsbok, red hartebeest, springbok, Burchell's zebra and giraffe roam freely. Guests are

accommodated in luxury rooms. Amenities include an à la carte restaurant, swimming pool and squash court. Game drives and horse riding are available.

After meandering alongside the Auob River for 111 km from Gochas, the road reaches the farm Tweerivier, where the Auob and the Olifants rivers meet. Mata Mata, the western gate to the Kalahari Gemsbok National Park in South Africa, is 67 km from there. Plans are afoot to reopen the Mata Mata gate and South African National Parks has already approved such a proposal. Visitors will be required to overnight in the park to prevent it from being used as a through route. No date has been set for the reopening of the gate; it is therefore advisable to enquire before taking this route.

ROUTE 22
MARIENTAL TO SESRIEM

DISTANCE: 290 km **TIME**: 4 hours **ROAD CONDITIONS**: 112 km tar; 178 gravel **FUEL**: Mariental, Maltahöhe, Sesriem **LINKING ROUTES**: Routes 5, 20, 23, 24

This is a convenient route to Sesriem for visitors entering Namibia from the south. The turnoff onto the C19 to Maltahöhe is signposted 4 km south of Mariental (see route 20). Travelling westward, the C19 traverses hilly country and plains before passing through plains with scattered hills approaching Maltahöhe.

Established in 1900, **Maltahöhe**, 111 km west of Mariental, was named after Malta von Burgsdorff, the wife of the commander of the garrison at Gibeon. More than 40 graves of German *Schutztruppe* who died in the numerous battles against Hendrik Witbooi and during the 1903-7 Nama rebellion can be seen in the graveyard to the east of the town. On the **farm Sandhof**, north of Maltahöhe, are two large pans which are often dry for years on end. After good rains, however, the pans become flooded and within a few days are covered in *Crinum paludosium* lilies. When these attractive white lilies reach a height of about 17 cm, the flowers are pollinated by beetles. This floral spectacle ends as abruptly as it started, as the flowers die soon after pollination. Visitors are likely to see this rare phenomenon only if they are fortunate enough to be in the area after good rains.

The **Maltahöhe Hotel**, with its cool verandah, dates back to 1907 and is renowned for its hospitality and characterful bar. It has a restaurant and a swimming pool.

From Maltahöhe, take the C14 toward Helmeringhausen (see route 23). The turnoff to **Daweb Guest Farm** is reached after 2 km. This well-known guest farm, where farm tours and walks can be enjoyed, offers visitors an opportunity to gain an insight into cattle farming. Accommodation is provided in double rooms.

Continuing further along the C14, the Schwartzrand (Black Ridge) is prominent to the south, with the flat-topped Zaris mountains dominating the landscape to the west. The turnoff to **Namseb Game Lodge** is signposted 16 km south of Maltahöhe. Situated on a plateau, the rest camp overlooks the hilly plains that merge with the Tsaris mountains. On a guided game-viewing trip visitors chance spotting giraffe, blue wildebeest, eland, red hartebeest, springbok and Hartmann's mountain zebra. Amenities include a restaurant, bar and swimming pool. Visitors are accommodated in bungalows or double rooms built from stone, either on a self-catering, half board or full board basis.

About 20 km south of Maltahöhe the road splits. The C14 continues to Helmeringhausen and Bethanie (see route 23), while Main Road 36 splits off to the right, continuing to Solitaire. Turn right onto Main Road 36, which goes in a westerly direction. After winding across the scenic **Zaris Pass**, the road meanders between the Nubib and Zaris mountains. It then traverses the Namib plains, passing the D854 (where route 5 links up) and the turnoff to **Sossusvlei Wilderness Camp** (see p 227), before reaching the D826 turnoff to Sesriem, 165 km beyond Maltahöhe. Sesriem (see p 193) is reached 12 km after turning onto the D826.

ROUTE 23

MALTAHÖHE TO BETHANIE AND B4

DISTANCE: 257 km **TIME:** 3,5 hours **ROAD CONDITIONS:** 30 km tar; 227 km gravel, usually good, but can be corrugated **FUEL:** Maltahöhe, Helmeringhausen, Bethanie **LINKING ROUTES:** Routes 22, 24

This route provides a convenient link between Maltahöhe and the B4 between Keetmanshoop and Lüderitz. From Maltahöhe follow route 22 for the first 20 km. Ignore the turnoff onto Main Road 36 after 20 km and head for Helmeringhausen along the C14. After about 18 km you reach the turnoff to the D824, which provides access to **Duwisib Castle** (see p 231). After

travelling for 12 km on the D824 you join the D831. Turn left here and after 16 km turn right onto the D826. The entrance gate to Duwisib is about 15 km further on. To rejoin the C14, backtrack to the D831; turn right and continue for 27 km to the junction with the C14.

Going south, the road makes its way through striking scenery dominated by the Schwartzrand (Black Ridge) to the east and the Rooirand (Red Ridge) to the west.

The turnoff to **Dabis Guest Farm** is signposted 10 km north

of Helmeringhausen. This well-known guest farm offers visitors an opportunity to join in the daily activities. In addition to participating in all aspects of farm life, guests can also take night drives. Accommodation is in five double rooms and typical Namibian food is provided. Amenities include a lounge and swimming pool.

Helmeringhausen is reached 142 km south of Maltahöhe. Despite its prominent position on maps it is nothing more than a farm with a hotel, general dealer and garage.

The interesting **open-air agricultural museum** adjacent to the Helmeringhausen Hotel is well worth a visit. A variety of

farming implements, an old fire engine used at Lüderitz and an ox-wagon used to transport building material and furniture from Lüderitz to Duwisib, are displayed. The key to the museum, established in 1984 by the Helmeringhausen Farmers Association, can be obtained from the hotel.

The quaint **Helmeringhausen Hotel** offers excellent value-for-money accommodation in a country setting. Amenities include a restaurant, bar and swimming pool. Trips can be arranged to view nearby rock paintings, the Konkiep Gorges, Duwisib Castle and attractions further afield.

Another option in the area is **Sinclair Guest Farm**, which lies northwest of Helmeringhausen. One of the oldest guest farms in the country, it is renowned for its hospitality and beautiful scenery. Guests can go for walks, undertake farm trips and explore an old copper mine. There is also a swimming pool. The turnoff is signposted 54 km northwest of Helmeringhausen on the D407.

From Helmeringhausen, travellers can take the C13, which traverses the spectacular **Neisip Plain** before reaching Aus. If you are headed for Bethanie and Keetmanshoop, however, continue along the C14.

About 19 km south of Helmeringhausen the turnoff to **Mooifontein Cemetery** is signposted along the C14. About 1 km beyond the turnoff is the farmhouse, but continue along a track to the left of the reservoir to the cemetery about 1 km further on.

Mooifontein was originally known as Chamis and during the German colonial period a military station was established here. In 1899 a wooden, prefabricated house was shipped from Germany to Lüderitz, whence it was transported by ox-wagon to Chamis. This prefabricated house, erected on the northern banks of the Konkiep River, served as barracks and mess for German troops for a number of years. It was later replaced by a permanent double-storey structure, which was converted to a single-storey house that serves to this day as a farmhouse.

Unlike most others in the country, this cemetery is not only of historic, but also of architectural, interest. It is surrounded by an attractive stone wall, which forms a half-circle on one side, with the tombstones of German troops and NCOs who died during the Nama wars recessed into the wall. In the centre of the cemetery is a memorial resembling a chapel. Also of interest are the heavy iron gates, forged from the rims of ox-wagon wheels.

Bethanie is reached 85 km south of Helmeringhausen along the C14. A mission station to serve the Nama was established here in 1814 by the German missionary Heinrich Schmelen of the London Missionary Society. Known as Uigantes to the !Aman Nama, who had settled in the area in about 1804, the station was first named Klipfontein, but was soon renamed Bethanien.

Intertribal conflicts forced Schmelen to abandon Bethanien in 1822 and his attempts in 1823, 1827 and 1828 to re-establish the mission station failed; not only because of the intertribal friction, but also because of drought and locust plagues. Schmelen left Bethanien after 14 years service and, following the transfer of the society's rights to the Rhenish Missionary Society in 1840, the Rev Hans Knudsen was sent here in 1842.

In Keetmanshoop Street you will see **Joseph Fredericks House**, erected in 1883 by Captain Joseph Fredericks as a dwelling and council chamber. The first "protection treaty" between the Germans and the Bethanien Nama was signed in the house by Captain Fredericks and the German Consul General, Dr Friedrich Nachtigal, in October 1884.

The turnoff to **Schmelen House** is signposted opposite Joseph Fredericks House. Shortly after turning into Quellen Street you will see the Rhenish Mission Church on your right. It was inaugurated on 30 May 1899 as a replacement for the original twin-tower mission church. From Quellen Street turn left into the grounds of the Evangelical Lutheran Church.

Schmelen House, built by Schmelen in 1814, was burnt down after he left the mission station, but was rebuilt by missionary Knudsen. All that remains from Schmelen's original house are the stone walls, the oldest colonial structure in Namibia. The historic building houses an interesting photographic display on the mission station's history and the surrounding area, as well as some archaeological artefacts. The key is kept at the front door of the house.

In the nearby **cemetery** the graves of several missionaries who served the Bethanien parish can be seen. Also to be seen is the limestone church built in 1859 by missionary Hermann Kreft. The church originally had twin towers, but they became dilapidated and had to be demolished. Following the inauguration of a new church, the building was used as a school, a purpose it served until about 1970, when a new school was taken into use.

From Bethanie the C14 is tarred and after 25 km you join the B4 between Keetmanshoop and Lüderitz (see route 24).

ROUTE 24
KEETMANSHOOP TO LÜDERITZ

DISTANCE: 334 km **TIME**: 4 hours **ROAD CONDITIONS**:
Tar **FUEL**: Aus, Lüderitz **LINKING ROUTES**: Routes 20, 23, 25

From Keetmanshoop the B4 winds through dolerite koppies,
dominated by the Kaiserkrone, a prominent dolerite-capped
outcrop. As you travel westward, however, the landscape alternates between hills and plains with scattered hills, to the low
mountains of the Great Escarpment, until it finally gives way to
the white dunes of the Namib Desert.

About 34 km west of Keetmanshoop the turnoff onto the
D545 and Naute Dam (see route 25) is signposted. The turnoff
to the railway siding at Seeheim, signposted Fish River Canyon,
Ai-Ais, Grünau (see route 25), is passed a few kilometres on.

Continuing along the B4, the bridge over the Fish River is
reached after about 1,5 km. Some 11 km further, on the farm
Naiams, a national monument signboard indicates the turnoff
to the **ruins of an old German fort**, which is accessible either
on foot or by four-wheel drive vehicle. After passing through
the gate opposite the Naiams farmhouse, turn left and follow
the track for about 1 km to the ruins.

Dating back to 1905-6, the fort was built to protect traffic
on the road between Keetmanshoop and Lüderitz against
attacks by bands of raiding Nama. As travellers were particularly vulnerable in the narrow valley and at the nearby waterhole, a small contingent of German *Schutztruppe* was stationed here. On the way up to the fort the original road and the
nearby graves of two *Schutztruppe* can be seen.

At Goageb the C14 from Maltahöhe, Helmeringhausen and
Bethanie (see route 23) joins the B4 and after 105 km the C13
from Helmeringhausen (see route 19) links up with the B4. The
small settlement of **Aus**, just off the B4, is passed 212 km west
of Keetmanshoop. The name is Khoekhoen in origin and is said
to mean "snake fountain" or "place of snakes".

During World War I, a **prisoner-of-war camp** for German
non-commissioned officers and other military personnel was
established just east of the village. The site is reached by turning left at the T-junction as you enter Aus. Travel for 3 km until
you reach the road signposted to Rosh Pinah. Ignore the turnoff

and continue straight for another 0,6 km before turning right. From there it is a short distance to a clearing where a national monument's plaque on a boulder marks the site.

Following the surrender of the German forces at Khorab, just north of Otavi, on 9 July 1915, Aus was selected as the site for a prisoner-of-war camp because of its strategic and logistical location. By August 1915, 1 552 prisoners of war, as well as 600 South African Veteran Regiment guards, had been settled in tents at Aus. The tents offered little protection against the elements and as no attempts were made to improve conditions the prisoners were left to improve their own lot. They did so by making bricks to build their own houses and by April 1916 tents were no longer in use. Bricks were also sold to the guards at 10 shillings per 1 000.

The houses were ingeniously constructed and tins were flattened and joined to make tiled roofs. The houses were generally one roomed, and some were semidetached, giving the impression of a small closed neighbourhood. In some buildings the floor was well below ground level, with the roof just above the ground.

Water was initially obtained by pipeline, and later from three boreholes sunk in the camp. An extensive tramway, stretching for almost 5 km around the camp, was completed in February 1917.

With the signing of the Treaty of Versailles at the end of the war, the first two groups left the camp on 19 and 20 April 1919. Others followed gradually and when the last group left on 13 May 1919, the camp was officially closed.

Unfortunately, the elements have reduced this historic site to a few walls and lumps of clay. A copy of the book *Aus 1915-1919* will enhance your visit to the site. The book is unfortunately only available in Afrikaans, but the map will help you to orientate yourself.

The farm **Klein Aus Vista**, signposted 2 km west of Aus, lies amid the granite outcrops of the Aus mountains and offers spectacular views over the plains of the Namib Desert.

Visitors can simply relax in the superb surroundings, or explore this historically interesting area on foot. The **Namib Feral Horse Hiking Trail** covers 34 km and can be hiked in three or four days. Along the route hikers are rewarded with spectacular views over the plains, where the wild horses of the Namib roam. Facilities include three overnight huts equipped

with beds, fireplaces, showers and toilets. The hut at the starting point also has a fully equipped kitchen with a gas stove
and fridge.

Other activities include **guided horseback trips**, a one-day
mountain biking trail (own cycles required), sightseeing and
historical trips, and excursions to see the wild horses of the
Namib.

Accommodation is provided in chalets set among the boulders. Camp sites with ablution facilities are also available.

About 11 km west of Aus you enter the area formerly
known as Diamond Area 1. It became known as the
Sperrgebiet (Prohibited Territory) in 1908 when the Deutsche
Diamanten Gesellschaft was granted exclusive prospecting
and mining rights over a large tract of the Namib Desert.
Covering 26 000 km², this area stretched from the Orange
River northward to 26 ° S latitude. Although diamond mining
was restricted to within a few kilometres of the coast, the area
stretched inland for 100 km to deter would-be intruders and
strict security measures were enforced.

In 1920 the assets and all mineral rights in the *Sperrgebiet*
were bought by Consolidated Diamond Mines (CDM), a subsidiary of De Beers. After holding virtually exclusive rights to
Namibia's diamonds for nearly 75 years, De Beers signed an
agreement with the Namibian government in November 1994,
giving Namibia a 50 per cent stake in CDM. At the same time
CDM was transformed into the Namdeb Diamond
Corporation, and relinquished about half of its concession area
to the state. The future use of this vast tract of land is still under
discussion and until such time as the land use has been
finalised access will remain restricted.

On entering the *Sperrgebiet*, the B4 becomes the southern
boundary of the Namib-Naukluft Park, which stretches northward to the Swakop River (see p 219). Road signs warning you
of the danger of horses must be heeded, especially if you are
travelling after dark, when the horses often stand in the road.

Continuing across the wide, open plains of this almost
untouched land, those to the north of the road are dominated
by an island mountain, known as **Dicke Wilhelm**. Rising
600 m above the plains, it served as a German heliograph station during the early 1900s.

About 20 km west of Aus you reach **Garub**, where water is
pumped into a trough for the **wild horses of the Namib**. There

is a **hide** with benches and toilet facilities about 1 km north of the tar road, and this is where you are likely to have the best views of these famed horses. Their numbers depend on the condition of the veld and although the average is between 150 and 160, they can number up to 276.

The horses have seemingly evolved physiological mechanisms to survive under desert conditions. They have been observed to drink only once in five days during dry periods and can reabsorb water at twice the rate of domestic horses when they are dehydrated.

There are several theories on the origin of these horses – one of possibly only five populations of feral horses in the world. The most popular theory is that they are descendants of horses owned by Captain Von Wolf of Duwisib (see pp 231-232). Another theory is that they are descendants of horses abandoned by German *Schutztruppe* when they retreated from Aus during the South West Africa campaign in 1915.

About 8 km before reaching Lüderitz the forlorn station building at **Grasplatz**, where August Stauch was posted as railway supervisor in 1907, looms up unexpectedly.

The diamond mining ghost town of **Kolmanskop** (see p 236), one of the most popular attractions in the south of the country, is reached about 10 km east of Lüderitz. Lüderitz (see p 237) is 337 km west of Keetmanshoop.

ROUTE 25
KEETMANSHOOP, NAUTE DAM, FISH RIVER CANYON AND AI-AIS

DISTANCE: 235 km **TIME:** 4 hours **ROAD CONDITIONS:** 32 km tar; 203 km gravel, usually good, but can be corrugated **FUEL:** Keetmanshoop, Ai-Ais Resort **LINKING ROUTES:** Route 24

This is a convenient route from Keetmanshoop to Hobas and the viewpoints overlooking the Fish River Canyon, and then on to Ai-Ais Resort in the lower reaches of the canyon.

From Keetmanshoop take the B4 toward Lüderitz for 32 km and turn left onto the D545. From the turnoff it is about 18 km to **Naute Dam** which is open for viewing from 08:00 to 18:00. Visitors must, however, obtain the key from the nearby purification works.

Situated in the Löwen River, a tributary of the Fish River, the dam was completed in 1971. Behind the 150 m long multiple arch dam wall up to 83,5 million m³ of water can be impounded. The dam is the main water supply of Keetmanshoop and also provides water for irrigation downstream of the dam.

Nestling among black dolerite outcrops, with the flat-topped Klein Karas mountains forming a spectacular backdrop, the dam is one of the most scenic in the country. It is popular with water sports enthusiasts and freshwater anglers. Although there are no facilities, informal camping is permitted along the southwestern shores of the dam.

Along the shores of the dam is a 23 000 ha game park, set aside in 1989, but still to be developed. An experimental date plantation has been established below the dam wall.

About 15 km beyond the dam you join the C12 to Grünau; turn left here and continue for 32 km to the signposted turnoff to the **Fish River Lodge**, which is 22 km beyond the farm turnoff. The lodge caters for budget travellers and offers a different perspective of the Fish River Canyon to those who have hiked Namibia's most popular official trail.

The farm area borders on the Fish River in the west for 32 km, with the spectacular Löwen River traversing the farm for 11 km. There is a choice of two overnight trails: one is 75 km long and the other a more demanding 85 km. Day hikes of 10 km or less are also available. Among the other attractions are fascinating rock formations such as the Three Pinnacles, rock engravings and far-reaching views over the Fish River Canyon. Four-wheel drive trips into the canyon are also conducted.

Amenities include a base camp for hikers at the lodge, and breakfast and dinner before and after the trail (not included in the trail fee). Groups are limited to a maximum of 20 hikers. P O Box 1840, Keetmanshoop, tel and fax (063) 22-3762.

Continuing further south along the C12, the railway siding at Holoog is passed. Here two lone graves under a camel thorn tree on the banks of the Gaub River serve as a reminder of the war fought in the south of the country between Namas and Germans early in the 1900s.

About 9 km further, turn right onto the D601, and continue for 31 km to the signposted turnoff to Hobas and the Fish River

Canyon viewpoints (see p 233). To reach Ai-Ais Resort, backtrack to the D601-D324 junction and turn right.

The turnoff to **Cañon Lodge** is signposted 7 km south of the junction. The lodge lies within the Gondwana Cañon Nature Park, a private nature park adjoining the Fish River Canyon Conservation Area. Nestling among granite boulders, the bungalows are a skilful blend of natural rock, wood walls and thatch roofs. A farmhouse, built in 1910, serves as a restaurant and there is also a swimming pool. The striking landscape, with its impressive rock formations and quiver trees, is ideal hiking country. It is a mere 20 km from the main viewpoint overlooking the canyon.

Travelling south to Ai-Ais, the road traverses mainly flat terrain, with scattered mountains and ridges, characterised by a dwarf shrub savanna. Typical trees and plants include clumps of milkbush (*Euphorbia gregaria*), quiver trees and shepherd's trees, with camel thorn and wild green-hair trees conspicuous along river washes.

After about 43 km, the D324 joins the C10, which is followed for 24 km to **Ai-Ais** (see p 233). Depending on your next destination, you can join the B1 either by taking the D316 (if you are headed for Noordoewer), or the C10 (if you are heading for Grünau).

WHERE TO STAY IN NAMIBIA

In recent years the number of accommodation establishments in Namibia has grown rapidly. Visitors to Namibia now have a choice of well over 400 accommodation establishments, ranging from luxurious lodges and top-class hotels to bed and breakfast facilities and backpackers' hostels.

All accommodation establishments must be registered with the Ministry of Environment and Tourism and are graded. The grading system currently in use (December 1998), however, dates back to the 1960s and is completely outdated. In addition, there is a huge backlog in processing applications for grading and regrading, while there are no clear guidelines on the definition of a lodge. Lodge establishments, therefore, range from hotels to guest farms and tented safari camps.

The **Hospitality Association of Namibia (HAN)** is a voluntary organisation representing the interests of registered accommodation establishments. Founded in 1987, it has played an important role in promoting tourism and improving standards in the accommodation industry. The association has over 200 members, all registered and graded by the Ministry of Environment and Tourism. HAN members are expected to comply with internationally accepted standards with regards to the quality of rooms and service.

In the past few years the demand for more personalised and affordable accommodation has increased steadily, resulting in a proliferation of **bed and breakfast, self-catering, backpackers'** and **home-based residential** establishments. Existing legislation does not make provision for the registration and grading of them. The Budget and Home Accommodation Association represents their interests and has a membership of over 80 countrywide. A membership list is available from the Budget and Home Accommodation Association, P O Box 90270, Windhoek, Namibia.

Hotel Gradings

★★★★★   There are currently no five-star hotels in Namibia.

★★★★   A superb hotel (751-900 points), currently the highest grading awarded in Namibia. Requirements include: all rooms with wall-to-wall carpeting, private bathrooms and showers, air-conditioning and heating, radio and 24-hour telephone service; air-conditioning and heating in dining rooms; valets from 07:00-20:00; à la carte meals available until 23:00; 24-hour floor service for light refreshments, floor service of 14 hours for light meals; 24-hour reception service; furniture and equipment of high quality; transport and secretarial services available for guests.

★★★ A really good hotel (651-750 points) with the following facilities: wall-to-wall carpets and private bathrooms or showers in at least 75 per cent of the rooms; three-channel radio and telephone in each room; heating in all rooms and public lounges; valets on the premises; a 1:6 ratio of communal bathrooms and toilets to beds in ordinary rooms; à la carte meals available daily, 18-hour floor service for light refreshments; 24-hour reception service; furniture and equipment of high quality; transport available for guests.

★★ A good hotel (551-650 points) with the following facilities: private bathrooms and showers for at least 50 per cent of the rooms; room heating on request; at least one bathroom and toilet for every seven beds in ordinary rooms; 16-hour floor service for light refreshments; reception service of 14 hours.

★ A standard hotel (400-550 points) which, in addition to 71 basic minimum requirements, must offer the following: private bathrooms or showers for at least 25 per cent of the rooms; one or more communal bathrooms and toilets for every eight other beds; 16-hour floor service for light refreshments.

Hotel pension garnis are small, congenial establishments with a minimum of 10 rooms. Unlike hotels, they are not required to have full restaurant facilities, but must serve breakfast.

Guest Farm and Rest Camp Gradings

The highest grading for these establishments is a three-star rating. The following ratings are applicable:

★★★ excellent
★★ very good
★ good

Accommodation

The following list of accommodation establishments is arranged according to the tourist regions used in this guide, and placed under the nearest town, and in some cases, tourist attraction.

Accommodation in state-owned conservation area and resorts is listed separately at the end of the chapter.

Windhoek

City Centre

Hotels

Continental Hotel (★★), P O Box 977, Windhoek, tel (061) 23-7293, fax 23-1539.

Fürstenhof (★★), P O Box 316, Windhoek, tel (061) 23-7380, fax 22-8751.

Kalahari Sands Hotel (★★★★), P O Box 2254, Windhoek, tel (061) 22-2300, fax 22-2620.

Safari (★★★), P O Box 3900, Windhoek, tel (061) 24-0240, fax 23-5652.

Safari Court Hotel (★★★★), P O Box 3900, Windhoek, tel (061) 24-0240, fax 23-5652.

Thüringer Hof (★★), P O Box 112, Windhoek, tel (061) 22-6031, fax 23-2981.

Windhoek Country Club Resort (★★★★), P O Box 30777, Windhoek, tel (061) 205-5911, fax 25-2797.

Hotel Pension Garni

Alexander, P O Box 1911, Windhoek, tel and fax (061) 24-0775.

Cela (★★), P O Box 1947, Windhoek, tel (061) 22-6294, fax 22-6246.

Christoph (★), P O Box 6116, Windhoek, tel (061) 24-0777, fax 24-8560.

Eros, P O Box 9607, Windhoek, tel (061) 22-7020, fax 24-2919.

Etambi, P O Box 30547, Windhoek, tel (061) 24-1763, fax 24-2916.

Handke (★), P O Box 20881, Windhoek, tel (061) 23-4904, fax 22-5660.

Heinitzburg, P O Box 458, Windhoek, tel (061) 24-9597, fax 24-9598.

Kleines Heim, P O Box 22605, Windhoek, tel (061) 24-8200, fax 24-8203.

Moni (★), P O Box 2805, Windhoek, tel (061) 22-8350, fax 22-7124.

Steiner, P O Box 20481, Windhoek, tel (061) 22-2898, fax 22-4234.

The Guest House, P O Box 11948, Windhoek, tel (061) 22-5500, fax 22-6768.

Uhland, P O Box 20738, Windhoek, tel (061) 22-9859, fax 22-0688.

Villa Verdi, P O Box 6784, Windhoek, tel (061) 22-1994, fax 22-2574.

Self-catering
Jan Jonker Holiday Apartments, P O Box 21511, Windhoek, tel (061) 22-1236, fax 23-8794.

Windhoek North

Guest Farms/Lodges
Düsternbrook (★★), P O Box 870, Windhoek, tel (061) 23-2572, fax 23-4758.
Elisenheim (★★), P O Box 3016, Windhoek, tel and fax (061) 26-4429.
Okapuka Ranch (★★★), P O Box 5955, Windhoek, tel 22-7845, fax 23-4690.

Rest Camps/Lodges
Sundown Lodge (★★★), P O Box 5378, Windhoek, tel (061) 23-2566, fax 23-2541.

Windhoek South

Guest Farms/Lodges
Auas Game Lodge, P O Box 80887, Windhoek, tel (061) 24-0043, fax 24-8633.

Guest Houses
Landhaus Aris, P O Box 5199, Windhoek, tel (061) 23-6006, fax 23-4507.

Rest Camps/Lodges
Arebbusch Travel Lodge, P O Box 80160, Olympia, Windhoek, tel (061) 25-2255, fax 25-1670.

Windhoek East

Guest Farms/Lodges
Finkenstein (★★), P O Box 167, Windhoek, tel (061) 23-4751, fax 23-8890.
Heja Safari Lodge, P O Box 588, Windhoek, tel (062) 25-7151, fax 25-7148.
Leopard Lodge (★★), P O Box 90049, Windhoek, tel and fax (062) 54-0409.
Mountain View Game Lodge (★★), P O Box 9061, Windhoek, tel (062) 56-0008, fax 56-0009.
Okambara Country Lodge, P O Box 11864, Windhoek, tel (062) 56-0217.
Ondekaremba, P O Box 5468, Windhoek, tel (062) 54-0424, fax 54-0133.
Silversand (★★), Private Bag 13161, Windhoek, tel (062) 56-0200, fax 23-5501.

Rest Camps/Lodges
Airport Lodge, P O Box 5913, Windhoek, tel (061) 24-3192, fax 23-6709.
Trans-Kalahari Caravan Park, P O Box 11084, Windhoek, tel (061) 22-2877, fax 22-0335.

Windhoek West
(Khomas Hochland, Gamsberg Region)

Guest Farms/Lodges
Corona (★★), P O Box 11958, Windhoek, tel (062) 57-2127, fax (061) 24-3179.
Eagle Rock Leisure Lodge, P O Box 6176, Windhoek, tel (061) 23-4542, fax 25-7122.
Niedersachsen (★★), P O Box 3636, Windhoek, tel (062) 57-2200.
Okatore Lodge, P O Box 2868, Windhoek, tel and fax (061) 23-2840.
Swartfontein (★★), P O Box 32042, Windhoek, tel (062) 57-2004.
Weissenfels (★★), Private Bag 13144, Windhoek, tel (062) 57-2112.

Rest Camps/Lodges
Namibgrens, P O Box 21587, Windhoek, tel (062) 57-2021, fax (061) 23-4345.

Central Namibia
Dordabis

Guest Farms/Lodges
Eningu Clayhouse Lodge, P O Box 9531, Windhoek, tel (062) 57-3580.
Hope (★★), P O Box 21768, Windhoek, tel (062) 57-3109.

Rest Camps/Lodges
Arnhem Cave, P O Box 11354, Windhoek, tel (062) 57-3585.
Scheidthof, P O Box 6292, Windhoek, tel (062) 57-3584.

Gobabis

Hotels
Central Hotel, P O Box 233, Gobabis, tel (062) 56-2094, fax 56-2092.
Gobabis Hotel, P O Box 942, Gobabis, tel (062) 56-2568, fax 56-2641.

Guest Farms/ Lodges
Ohlsenhagen (★★), P O Box 434, Gobabis, tel (062) 56-2330, fax 56-3536.
Zelda, P O Box 75, Gobabis, tel (062) 56-0427, fax 56-0431.

Rest Camps/Lodges
Harnas Lion, Leopard and Cheetah Farm, P O Box 548, Gobabis, tel (062) 56-8020 or 56-8788, fax 56-8738.

Welkom Rest Camp, P O Box 450, Gobabis, tel (062) 56-3762, fax 56-3584.

Karibib

Guest Farms/Lodges
Albrechtshöhe (★★), P O Box 124, Karibib, tel and fax (062) 50-3363.
Etusis Lodge, P O Box 5, Karibib, tel (064) 55-0826, fax 55-0961.
Kansimba Game Lodge, P O Box 23556, Windhoek, tel (062) 50-3966, fax 50-3967.

Okahandja

Guest Farms/Lodges
Haasenhof (★★), P O Box 72, Okahandja, tel (062) 50-3827, fax 50-3465.
Kahn River, P O Box 278, Okahandja, tel (062) 50-3883, fax 50-3884.
Matador (★★), P O Box 214, Okahandja, tel (062) 50-3428, fax 50-4142.
Midgard Lodge (★★★), P O Box 16, Windhoek, tel (062) 50-3888, fax 50-3818.
Moringa (★★), P O Box 65, Okahandja, tel and fax (062) 50-1106.
Mt Lieven Safari Ranch (★★), P O Box 66, Okahandja, tel (064) 55-0848, fax (061) 23-4470.
Okomitundu (★★), P O Box 285, Okahandja, tel (062) 50-3901, fax 50-3902.
Oropoko Lodge, P O Box 5017, Windhoek, tel (061) 26-2395, fax 21-7026.
Otjiruze (★★★), P O Box 297, Okahandja, tel and fax (062) 50-3719.
Otjisazu (★★★), P O Box 149, Okahandja, tel (062) 50-1259, fax 50-1323.
Ozombanda, P O Box 449, Okahandja, tel (062) 50-3870, fax 50-3996.
The Rock Lodge, P O Box 1297, Okahandja, tel (062) 50-3840, fax 50-3170.
Wilhelmstal-Nord Haase, P O Box 641, Okahandja, tel and fax (062) 50-3977.

Usakos

Rest Camps/Lodges
Ameib Ranch, P O Box 266, Usakos, tel (064) 53-0803, fax (061) 23-5742.

Witvlei

Hotels
Doll's House (★), P O Box 18, Witvlei, tel (062) 57-0038.
Rest Camps/Lodges
Ehoro Lodge, P O Box 10626, Windhoek, tel (062) 57-0081, fax 57-0059.

Northern Namibia
Etosha

Hotels
Mokuti Lodge (★★★★), P O Box 403, Tsumeb, tel (067) 22-9084, fax 22-9091.
Guest Farms/Lodges
Etosha Aoba Lodge, P O Box 469, Tsumeb, tel (067) 22-9100, fax 22-9101.
Ongava Lodge (★★★), P O Box 6850, Windhoek, tel (061) 22-5178, fax 23-9455.
Sachsenheim Game Ranch, P O Box 1713, tel (067) 23-0011, fax 23-0072.
Toshari Inn (★★), P O Box 164, Outjo, tel and fax (06548) 3702, fax (067) 31-3040.

Grootfontein

Hotels
Meteor Hotel (★), P O Box 346, Grootfontein, tel (067) 24-2078/9, fax 24-3072.
Guest Farms/Lodges
Dornhügel, P O Box 173, Grootfontein, tel (06738) 8-1611, fax (067) 24-3503.
Rest Camps/Lodges
Olea Rest Camp, P O Box 23, Grootfontein, tel (067) 24-3100, fax 24-2930.

Kalkfeld

Guest Farms/Lodges
Mount Etjo Safari Lodge, P O Box 81, Kalkfeld, tel (067) 29-0174, fax 29-0172.

Rest Camps
Dino's Camp Site, Otjihaenamaperero, tel (067) 29-1053.

Omaruru

Hotels
Central Hotel (★), P O Box 29, Omaruru, tel (064) 57-0030, fax 57-0481.
Hotel Staebe (★), P O Box 92, Omaruru, tel (064) 57-0035, fax 57-0450.
Guest Farms/Lodges
Boskloof (★★), P O Box 53, Omaruru, tel and fax (06532) 3231.
Epako Game Lodge, P O Box 108, Omaruru, tel (064) 57-0551, fax 57-0553.
Erindi Onganga, P O Box 20, Omaruru, tel (067) 29-0112, fax (061) 23-2624.
Immenhof (★★), P O Box 250, Omaruru, tel (067) 29-0177.
Okosongoro (★★), P O Box 324, Omaruru, tel and fax (067) 29-0170.
Omapyu, P O Box 425, Omaruru, tel (064) 57-0811.
Omaruru Game Lodge (★★★), P O Box 208, Omaruru, tel (064) 57-0044, fax 57-0134.
Omburo Health Resort, P O Box 138, Omaruru, tel 081-129-1140.
Onduruquea Lodge, P O Box 38, Omaruru, tel (064) 57-0832, fax (061) 22-5363.
Otjandaue, P O Box 44, Omaruru, tel (064) 57-0821, fax 57-0481.
Otjikoko, P O Box 404, Omaruru, tel (064) 57-0364, fax 57-0365.
Schönfeld, P O Box 382, Omaruru, tel (067) 29-0090, fax 29-0190.

Ondangwa

Hotels
Punyu International Hotel, P O Box 247, Ondangwa, tel (065) 24-0556, fax 24-0660.
Rest Camps/Lodges
Nakambale Museum Rest Camp (Olukonda), c/o ELCIN, Private Bag 2018, Ondangwa, tel (067568) 8-4622.

Oshakati

Hotels
Euro-Frique, P O Box 510, Oshakati, tel and fax (065) 23-0363.
Guest Houses
International Guest House, P O Box 958, Oshakati, tel (065) 22-0175, fax 22-1001.
Oshandira Lodge, P O Box 958, Oshakati, tel (065) 22-0443, fax 22-1189.

Santorini Inn, P O Box 5569, Oshakati, tel (065) 22-0457, fax 22-0506.

Otavi

Hotels
Otavi Gardens Hotel (★), P O Box 11, Otavi, tel (067) 23-4333, fax 23-4336.

Guest Farms/Lodges
Gauss Guest Farm, Private Bag 6, Kombat, tel (067) 23-1083, fax 23-1077.
Khorab Safari Lodge, P O Box 186, Otavi, tel and fax (067) 23-4352.

Rest Camps/Lodges
Zum Potjie (★), P O Box 202, Otavi, tel (067) 23-4300, fax 22-2010.

Otjiwarongo

Hotels
Hotel Hamburger Hof (★★), P O Box 8, Otjiwarongo, tel (067) 30-2520, fax 30-3607.
Otjibamba Lodge (★★), P O Box 510, Otjiwarongo, tel (067) 30-3133, fax 30-4561.

Guest Farms/Lodges
M'Butu Lodge (★★), P O Box 1389, Otjiwarongo, tel (067) 30-4062.
Mon Desir, P O Box 767, Otjiwarongo, tel (067) 30-3873, fax 30-3874.
Oase, P O Box 1661, Otjiwarongo, tel and fax (0658) 1-4222.
Okonjima (★★), P O Box 793, Otjiwarongo, tel (067) 30-4563, fax 30-4565.
Otjiwa Game Ranch (★★), P O Box 1231, Otjiwarongo, tel (067) 30-2665, fax 30-2668.
Wabi Game Lodge (★★★), P O Box 973, Otjiwarongo, tel and fax (0658) 15313.

Outjo

Hotels
Etosha Garten Hotel, P O Box 31, Outjo, tel (067) 31-3130, fax 31-3419.
Hotel Onduri, P O Box 14, Outjo, tel (067) 31-3405, fax 31-3408.

Guest Farms/Lodges
Bambatsi Holiday Ranch (★★), P O Box 120, Outjo, tel (067) 31-3897, fax 31-3331.
Bergplaas Paresis, P O Box 60, Outjo, tel (067) 31-3842, 31-3000.
Danube, P O Box 255, Outjo, tel (06548) Otjikondo 4840, fax (067) 30-2616.

Gasenairob, P O Box 299, Outjo, tel (067) 31-3898, fax 31-3331.
Gelukspoort, P O Box 158, Outjo, tel (067) 30-2025, fax 31-3000.
Namatubis (★★★), P O Box 467, Outjo, tel and fax (067) 31-3061.
Ombundja Wildlife Lodge, P O Box 318, Outjo, tel and fax (067) 31-2123.
Otjitambi (★★), P O Box 580, Outjo, tel (067) 31-2138.
Rest Camps/Lodges
Camp Setenghi, P O Box 533, Outjo, tel and fax (067) 31-3445.
Ombinda Country Lodge, P O Box 326, Outjo, tel (067) 31-3181, fax
31-3478.

Tsumeb

Hotels
Makalani Hotel (★★), P O Box 27, Tsumeb, tel (067) 22-1051, fax (067)
22-1575.
Minen Hotel (★★), P O Box 244, Tsumeb, tel (067) 22-1071, fax (067)
22-1750.
Guest Farms/Lodges
La Rochelle (★★), P O Box 194, Tsumeb, tel (067) 22-1326, fax 22-0760.
Rest Camps/Lodges
Punyu Tourist Park, P O Box 319, Tsumeb, tel and fax (067) 22-1996.
Tamboti Nature Park, P O Box 163, Tsumeb, tel (067) 22-0140, fax
22-1718.

Western Namibia

Damaraland

Rest Camps/Lodges
Aba-Huab Camp Site near Twyfelfontein (no reservations).
Etendeka Mountain Camp, P O Box 21783, Windhoek, tel (061) 22-6979,
fax 22-6999.
Fort Sesfontein Lodge, P O Box 22114, Windhoek, tel (061) 22-8257, fax
22-0103.
Khowarib Camp Site, 73 km north of Palmwag (no reservations).
Ongongo Camp Site, 90 km north of Palmwag (no reservations).
Palmwag Lodge (★★), P O Box 339, Swakopmund, tel (064) 40-4459 or
40-2434, fax 40-4664.
The Damaraland Camp, P O Box 6850, Windhoek, tel (061) 22-5178, fax
23-9455.

Kamanjab

Hotels
Oase Garni, P O Box 86, Kamanjab, tel (067) 33-0032.
Guest Farms/Lodges
Hobatere Lodge, P O Box 90538, Windhoek, tel and fax (061) 25-3992.
Kavita Lion Lodge, P O Box 118, Kamanjab, tel (067) 33-0224, fax (061) 22-6999.
Otjitotongwe Lodge, P O Box 60, Kamanjab, tel and fax (067) 33-0201.
Rustig, P O Box 25, Kamanjab, tel (067) 33-0250.

Kaokoland

Rest Camps/Lodges
Epupa Camp, P O Box 90466, Windhoek, tel (061) 24-6427, fax 24-6428.
Ngatutungwe Pamwe Camp Site, 100 km northwest of Sesfontein near Purros (no reservations).
Omarunga Camp (Epupa), Ermo Safaris, P O Box 27, Kamanjab, tel (067) 33-0220.

Khorixas

Guest Farms/Lodges
Huab Lodge, P O Box 180, Outjo, tel (061) 22-6979, fax (061) 22-6999.
Vingerklip Lodge (★★), P O Box 11550, Windhoek, tel (061) 23-3691, fax 24-8718.
Rest Camps/Lodges
Khorixas Rest Camp, P O Box 2, Khorixas, tel (067) 33-1196, fax 33-1388.

Opuwo

Rest Camps/Lodges
Ohakane Lodge, P O Box 8, Opuwo, tel (065) 27-3031, fax 27-3025.

Uis

Rest Camps/Lodges
Brandberg Rest Camp, P O Box 35, Uis, tel and fax (064) 50-4038.

Northeastern Namibia
Bushmanland

Rest Camps/Lodges
Omatako Valley Rest Camp, 133 km west of Tsumkwe (no reservations).
Tsumkwe Lodge, P O Box 1899, Tsumeb, tel (064) 20-3581 and book a
radio call to 531.

Caprivi

Hotels
Zambezi Lodge, P O Box 98, Katima Mulilo, tel (0677) 3203, fax 3631.
Rest Camps/Lodges
Caprivi Cabins, P O Box 2029, Katima Mulilo, tel (0677) 2288, fax 3158.
Hippo Lodge, P O Box 1120, Katima Mulilo, tel and fax (0677) 3684.
Impalila Island Lodge, P O Box 70378, Bryanston 2021, South Africa, tel
and fax (011) 706-7207.
Kubunyana Camp Site, 10 km south of Kongola (no reservations).
Lianshulu Lodge, P O Box 90392, Klein Windhoek, tel (061) 21-4744, fax
21-4746.
Kalizo Lodge, P O Box 1854, Ngweze, tel (0677) 2802, fax 2803.
Zambezi Queen & King's Den, P O Box 98, Katima Mulilo, tel (0677)
3203, fax 3631.

Grootfontein (District)

Rest Camps/Lodges
Roy's Camp, P O Box 755, Grootfontein, tel (067) 24-0302, fax (067)
24-2409.

Kavango
(Popa Falls, Mahango Game Park)

Rest Camps/Lodges
Ndhovu Safari Lodge, Box 559, Swakopmund, tel (064) 40-3141, fax
40-3142.
Suclabo Lodge, P O Box 894, Rundu, tel and fax (067) 25-5796.

Rundu

Hotels
Omashare River Lodge, P O Box 294, Rundu, tel (067) 25-5753, fax
25-6111.

Rest Camps/Lodges
Hakusembe Lodge, P O Box 1497, Tsumeb, tel (067) 25-7010, fax 25-7009.
Kaisosi River Lodge, P O Box 599, Rundu, tel (067) 25-5265, fax 25-6566.
Kavango River Lodge, P O Box 634, Rundu, tel (067) 25-5244, fax 25-5013.
Kayengona Rest Camp, fax (067) 25-5467.
Nkwasi Lodge & Camping Site, P O Box 1623, Rundu, cell 081-127-4010, fax (067) 25-5467.
Sarasunga River Lodge, P O Box 414, Rundu, tel (067) 25-5161, fax 25-6238.

Namib Desert
Henties Bay
Hotels/Pensions
Hotel De Duine (★★), P O Box 1, Henties Bay, tel (064) 50-0001, fax 50-0724.
Rest Camps/Lodges
Die Oord (★★), P O Box 82, Henties Bay, tel and fax (064) 50-0239.
Eagle Holiday Flats (★★), P O Box 20, Henties Bay, tel (064) 50-0032, fax 50-0299.

Sesriem/Naukluft Area
Guest Farms/Lodges
Ababis (★★), Private Bag 1004, Maltahöhe, tel (063) 29-3362, fax 29-3364.
Büllsport (★★), Private Bag 1003, Maltahöhe, tel (063) 29-3371, fax 29-3372.
Camp Mwisho, P O Box 5197, Windhoek, tel (063) 29-3233, fax 29-3241.
Haruchas (★★), P O Box 113, Maltahöhe, tel (063) 29-3399.
Kulala Desert Lodge, P O Box 40584, Windhoek, tel (063) 29-3234, fax 29-3235.
Mövenpick Sossusvlei Lodge, P O Box 6900, Windhoek, tel and fax (061) 24-8338.
Namib-Naukluft Lodge, P O Box 22028, Windhoek, tel (061) 26-3082, fax 21-5356.
Nomtsas, P O Box 12, Maltahöhe, tel and fax (0668) 1803.

Wolwedans Dune Camp and Wolwedans Dune Lodge, P O Box 5048, Windhoek, tel (061) 23-0616, fax 22-0102.
Zebra River Lodge, P O Box 11742, Windhoek, tel (063) 29-3265, fax 29-3266.

Rest Camps/Lodges
Hammerstein Lodge (★★), P O Box 250, Maltahöhe, tel (0668) 5111.
Namib Rest Camp (★★), P O Box 1075, Swakopmund, tel (063) 29-3376, fax 29-3377.
Weltevrede Rest Camp, Private Bag 1009, Maltahöhe, tel (063) 29-3374, fax 29-3375.

Skeleton Coast Park

Lodges
Olympia Reisen Concession, Olympia Reisen, P O Box 5017, Windhoek, tel (061) 26-2395, fax 21-7026.

Swakopmund

Hotels
Atlanta Hotel (★), P O Box 456, Swakopmund, tel (064) 40-2360, fax 40-5649.
Burg Nonidas (★), P O Box 1423, Swakopmund, tel and fax (064) 40-0384.
Europa Hof Hotel (★★), P O Box 1333, Swakopmund, tel (064) 40-5898, fax 40-2391.
Grüner Kranz Hotel (★★), P O Box 211, Swakopmund, tel (064) 40-2039, fax 40-5016.
Hansa Hotel (★★★), P O Box 44, Swakopmund, tel (064) 40-0311, fax 40-2732.
Jay Jay's Hotel (★), P O Box 835, Swakopmund, tel (064) 40-2909.
Schütze Hotel (★), P O Box 634, Swakopmund, tel and fax (064) 40-2718.
Schweizerhaus Hotel (★★), P O Box 445, Swakopmund, tel (064) 40-0331, fax 40-5850.
Strand Hotel (★★), P O Box 20, Swakopmund, tel (064) 40-0315, fax 40-4942.
Swakopmund Hotel & Entertainment Centre (★★★★), P O Box 616, Swakopmund, tel (064) 40-0800, fax 40-0801.

Hotel Garni/Pension
Adler (★★), P O Box 1497, Swakopmund, tel (064) 40-5045, fax 40-4206.
Deutsches Haus (★), P O Box 13, Swakopmund, tel (064) 40-4896, fax 40-4861.

Dig By See (★), P O Box 1530, Swakopmund, tel (064) 40-4130, fax 40-4170.

Prinzessin-Rupprecht Heim (★), P O Box 124, Swakopmund, tel (064) 40-2231, fax 40-2019.

Rapmund (★), P O Box 425, Swakopmund, tel (064) 40-2035, fax 40-4524.

Rest Camps/Lodges

Alte Brücke (★★★), P O Box 3360, Swakopmund, tel (064) 40-4918, fax 40-0153.

El Jada Rest Camp, P O Box 1155, Swakopmund, tel and fax (064) 40-0348.

Haus Garnison (Holiday Apartments) (★★), P O Box 2188, Swakopmund, tel and fax (064) 40-4456.

Mile 4 Caravan Park, P O Box 3452, Swakopmund, tel (064) 46-1781, fax 46-2901.

Swakopmund Rest Camp (★), Private Bag 5017, Swakopmund, tel (064) 40-2807, fax 40-2076.

Walvis Bay

Hotels/Pensions

Atlantic Hotel (★★), P O Box 46, Walvis Bay, tel (064) 20-2811, fax 20-5063.

Casa Mia Hotel (★★), P O Box 1786, Walvis Bay, tel (064) 20-5975, fax 20-6596.

The Courtyard, P O Box 2416, Walvis Bay, tel (064) 20-6252, fax 20-7271.

The Langholm Hotel, P O Box 2631, Walvis Bay, tel (064) 20-9230, fax 20-9430.

Walvis Bay Protea Lodge, P O Box 30, Walvis Bay, tel (064) 20-9560, fax 20-9565.

Rest Camps/Lodges

Dolphin Park, Private Bag 5017, Walvis Bay, tel (064) 20-4343.

Esplanade Park, Private Bag 5017, Walvis Bay, tel (064) 20-6145, fax 20-4528.

Langstrand Resort, Private Bag 5017, Walvis Bay, tel (064) 20-3134.

Levo Guest House & Chalets, P O Box 1860, Walvis Bay, tel and fax (064) 20-7555.

Southern Namibia

Aus

Guest Farms/Lodges
Namtib Desert Lodge, P O Box 19, Aus, tel (06362) ask for 6640.

Rest Camps/Lodges
Klein Aus Vista, P O Box 25, Aus, tel (063) 25-8102.

Bethanie

Hotels/Lodges
Bethanie Hotel (★), P O Box 13, Bethanie, tel and fax (063) 28-3013.

Fish River Canyon/Ai-Ais

Rest Camps/Lodges
Cañon Lodge, P O Box 80205, Windhoek, tel (061) 23-0066, fax 25-1863.

Gochas

Guest Farms/Lodges
Auob Lodge, P O Box 17, Gochas, tel (063) 25-0101, fax 25-0102.

Grünau

Hotels
Grünau Hotel (★), P O Box 2, Grünau, tel (063) 26-2001, fax 26-2009.

Rest Camps/Lodges
Vastrap Rest Camp, P O Box 26, Grünau, tel and fax (063) 26-2063.
White House Rest Camp, P O Box 9, Grünau, tel and fax (063) 26-2061.

Helmeringhausen

Hotels/Pensions
Helmeringhausen Hotel (★), P O Box 21, Helmeringhausen, tel (063) 28-3083, fax 28-3132.

Guest Farms/Lodges
Dabis (★★), P O Box 6213, Helmeringhausen, tel (06362) 6820, fax (061) 24-9937.
Sinclair (★★), P O Box 19, Helmeringhausen, tel (06362) 6503, fax (061) 22-6999.

Karasburg

Hotels/Pensions
Kalkfontein Hotel (★), P O Box 205, Karasburg, tel (063) 27-0172, fax 27-0457.

Guest Farms/Lodges
Mount Karas Game Lodge (★), P O Box 691, Keetmanshoop, tel (063) 22-5158.
Oas Holiday Farm, tel (06342) Stinkdoring 4321.

Keetmanshoop

Hotels/Pensions
Canyon Hotel (★★★), P O Box 950, Keetmanshoop, tel (063) 22-3361, fax 22-3714.
Pension Gessert, P O Box 690, Keetmanshoop, tel and fax (063) 22-3892.

Rest Camps/Lodges
Keetmanshoop Municipal Rest Camp, Private Bag 2125, Keetmanshoop, tel (063) 22-3316, fax 22-3818.
Lafenis Rest Camp, P O Box 827, Keetmanshoop, tel (063) 22-4316, fax 22-4309.
Quiver Tree Forest Rest Camp, P O Box 262, Keetmanshoop, tel and fax (063) 22-2835.

Koës

Rest Camps/Lodges
Kalahari Game Lodge, P O Box 22, Koës, tel (06662) 3112, fax 3103.

Lüderitz

Hotels/Pensions
Bay View Hotel (★★), P O Box 100, Lüderitz, tel (063) 20-2288, fax 20-2402.
Kapps Hotel (★), P O Box 218, Lüderitz, tel (063) 20-2345, fax 20-3555.
Nest Hotel, P O Box 690, Lüderitz, tel (063) 20-4000, fax 20-4001.
Sea View Hotel Zum Sperrgebiet, P O Box 373, Lüderitz, tel (063) 20-3411, fax 20-3414.
Zum Sperrgebiet Hotel Garni, P O Box 373, Lüderitz, tel (063) 20-2856, fax 20-2976.

Maltahöhe

Hotels
Maltahöhe Hotel (★), P O Box 20, Maltahöhe, tel (063) 29-3013, fax 29-3133.

Guest Farms/Lodges
Daweb (★★), P O Box 18, Maltahöhe, tel and fax (063) 29-3088.

Rest Camps/Lodges
Farm Duwisib Rest Camp (★), P O Box 21, Maltahöhe, tel (06638) ask for Namgorab 5304, fax (061) 22-3994.
Namseb (★★), P O Box 76, Maltahöhe, tel (063) 29-3166, fax 29-3157.

Mariental

Hotels/Pensions
Mariental Hotel (★★), P O Box 619, Mariental, tel (063) 24-2466, fax 24-2493.

Guest Farms/Lodges
Anib Lodge (★★), P O Box 800, Mariental, tel (063) 24-0529, fax 24-0516.
Intu Afrika Kalahari Game Lodge (★★), P O Box 40047, Windhoek, tel (061) 24-8741, fax 22-6535.

Rehoboth

Rest Camp
Lake Oanob Resort, P O Box 3381, Rehoboth, tel (062) 52-2369, fax 52-4112.

Uhlenhorst

Rest Camps/Lodges
Bitterwasser Lodge & Flying Centre (★), Private Bag 13003, Windhoek, tel (06672) 3830, fax (061) 25-0621.

Accommodation in State-owned Rest Camps and Resorts

Following is a list of accommodation in state-owned conservation areas and resorts, administered by **Namibia Wildlife Resorts**. All reservations must be made through Namibia Wildlife Resorts in the Oude Voorpost, cnr Molkte and John Meinert streets (north of the Kudu statue). The postal address is Private Bag 13267, Windhoek, Namibia, tel (061) 23-6975, 23-3845, 22-3903, 22-1132, fax 22-4900. Alternatively, reservations can also be made through the **Swakopmund office**, tel (064) 40-2172, fax 40-2796, or the **Namibia Tourism** offices in Cape Town, tel (021) 419-3190/1, fax (021) 421-5840 and Johannesburg (011) 784-8024/5, fax 784-8340.

Reservations and payments are accepted Mondays to Fridays from 08:00 to 15:00. Information is provided Mondays to Fridays 08:00 to 17:00. The office is closed on Saturdays and public holidays. Written reservations are accepted 18 months in advance but only confirmed 11 months prior to the date required.

Detailed information of accommodation and facilities in the following conservation areas and resorts is provided either in the descriptions of major attractions at the start of each region, or in the relevant route.

Fish River Canyon: Ai-Ais (see p 236) and Hobas (see p 235)
Daan Viljoen Game Park (see p 88)
Duwisib Castle (see p 233)
Etosha National Park (see p 105)
Gross Barmen (see p 74)
Hardap Recreation Resort (see p 252)
Khaudum Game Park (see p 163)
Lüderitz (camping only) (see p 247)
Namib-Naukluft Park: Naukluft (see p 192), Namib section (see p 188), Sesriem (see p 194)
National West Coast Recreation Area: Mile 14 (see p 221), Mile 72 (see p 222), Mile 108 (see p 222) and Jakkalsputz (see p 221)
Popa Falls (see p 165)
Skeleton Coast Park: Terrace Bay (see p 199), Torra Bay (see p 199)
Von Bach Recreation Resort (see p 77)
Waterberg Plateau Park (see p 110)

Note: For **Caprivi Game Park** (see p 169) as well as **Mamili and Mudumu national parks** (see pp 173-177) contact the Ministry of Environment and Tourism in Katima Mulilo, tel (0677) 3027, fax 3322.

USEFUL ADDRESSES

Namibian Diplomatic Missions Abroad
Africa

Angola (Embassy)
Rua Dos Coqueiros No 37
Luanda

P O Box 953
Luanda
Tel +244 2 39-5483, fax 33-3923

Botswana (High Commission)
2nd Floor
Debswana House
Gaborone

P O Box 987
Gaborone
Tel +267 30-2181, fax 30-2248

Ethiopia (Embassy)
Higher 17, Kebel 19
House No 002
Addis Ababa

P O Box 1443
Addis Ababa
Tel +251 1 61-1966, fax 62-1677

Nigeria (High Commission)
Plot 1395 Tiamiyu
Savage Street
Victoria Islands
Lagos

Tel +234 1 261-8606, fax 261-9323

South Africa (High Commission)
702 Church Street
Pretoria 0002

P O Box 29806
Sunnyside, Pretoria 0001
Tel + 27 12 344-5992, fax 343-7294

Zambia (High Commission)
6968 Kabanga Road, Addis Ababa Drive
Rhodes Park
Lusaka

P O Box 30577
Lusaka
Tel +260 1 25-2250, fax 25-2497

Zimbabwe (High Commission)
31A Lincoln Road
Avondale
Harare

Tel +263 4 30-4879, fax 30-4855

Europe

Austria (Embassy)
Strozzigasse 10-14
1080 Vienna   Tel +43 1 402-9374, fax 402-9370

Belgium (Embassy)
Avenue de Tavuren
B1150 Brussels   Tel +32 2 771-1410, fax 771-9689

France (Embassy)
80 Avenue Foch 17
Square de L'Avenue Foch
Paris   Tel +33 1 4417-3265, fax 4417-3273

Germany (Embassy)
Mainzer Strasse 47
53179 Bonn   Tel +49 228 34-6021, fax 34-6025

Russian Federation (Embassy)
2nd Kazachy Lane
House No 7
Moscow   Tel +7 095 230-0113, fax 230-2274

Sweden (Embassy)
Luntmakargatan 86-88   P O Box 26042
111 22 Stockholm   Tel +46 8 612-7788, fax 612-6655

United Kingdom (High Commission)
6 Chados Street
London WIM OLQ   Tel +44 171 636-6244, fax 637-5694

North America and the Caribbean

Cuba (Embassy)
Hotel Neptuno
P O Box 92, Miramar
Havana   Tel +53 7 24-1430, fax 24-1431

United States of America (Embassy)
1605 New Hampshire Avenue, N.W.
Washington, D.C. 20009   Tel +1 202 98-6054, fax 986-0443

Asia and Far East

China (Embassy)
House No 58
Beijing Riviera No 1 Xiang Jiang
Bei Road, Chaojong District
Beijing 100015   Tel +86 10 6435-1317, fax 532-4549

India (High Commission)
D-6/24 Vasant Vihar
New Delhi
India, 110 057   Tel +91 11 611-0389, fax 611-6120
Malaysia (High Commission)
Suite 08.03, 8th Floor
Menara Lion
165 Jalan Ampang
50450 Kuala Lumpur   Tel + 60 3 264-7015, fax 264-7017

Diplomatic Representatives Accredited to Namibia

Africa

Algeria (Embassy)
111A Gloudina Street   P O Box 3079
Ludwigsdorf   Windhoek
Windhoek   Tel (061) 22-1507, fax 23-6376

Angola (Embassy)
Angola House   Private Bag 12020
3 Ausspann Street   Windhoek
Ausspannplatz   Tel (061) 22-7535, fax 22-1498
Windhoek

Botswana (High Commission)
101 Nelson Mandela Avenue   P O Box 20359
Windhoek   Windhoek
     Tel (061) 22-1941, fax 23-6034

Congo (Embassy Republic of Congo)
1st Floor, Tal House
Tal Street
Windhoek   Tel (061) 25-7517, fax 24-0796

Egypt (Embassy)
10 Berg Street   P O Box 11853
Klein Windhoek   Windhoek
Windhoek   Tel (061) 22-1501, fax 22-8856

Ghana (High Commission)
5 Nelson Mandela Avenue   P O Box 24165
Klein Windhoek   Windhoek
Windhoek   Tel (061) 22-0536, fax 22-1343

Kenya (High Commission)
5th Floor, Kenya House   P O Box 2889
134 Robert Mugabe Avenue   Windhoek
Windhoek   Tel (061) 22-6836, fax 22-1409

Libya (Embassy)
69 Burg Street
Luxury Hill
Windhoek

P O Box 124
Windhoek
Tel (061) 23-4454, fax 23-4471

Malawi (High Commission)
56 Bismarck Street
Windhoek West
Windhoek

Private Bag 13254
Windhoek
Tel (061) 22-1391, fax 22-7056

Nigeria (High Commission)
4 Omuramba Road
Eros Park
Windhoek

P O Box 23547
Windhoek
Tel (061) 23-2103, fax 22-1639

South Africa (High Commission)
RSA House
Cnr Jan Jonker and
Nelson Mandela Avenue
Klein Windhoek, Windhoek

P O Box 23100
Windhoek
Tel (061) 22-9765, fax 22-4140

Zambia (High Commission)
Zambia House
Cnr Sam Nujoma Drive and Mandume
Ndemufayo Avenue
Windhoek

P O Box 22882
Windhoek
Tel (061) 23-7610, fax 22-8162

Zimbabwe (High Commission)
Cnr Independence Avenue and
Grimm Street
Windhoek

P O Box 23056
Windhoek
Tel (061) 22-8134, fax 22-6859

Europe

European Union (Delegation)
4th Floor, Sanlam Centre
154 Independence Avenue
Windhoek

P O Box 24443
Windhoek
Tel (061) 22-0099, fax 23-5135

Finland (Embassy)
5th Floor, Sanlam Centre
154 Independence Avenue
Windhoek

P O Box 3649
Windhoek
Tel (061) 22-1355, fax 22-1349

France (Embassy)
1 Goethe Street
Windhoek West
Windhoek

P O Box 20484
Windhoek
Tel (061) 22-9021, fax 23-1436

Germany (Embassy)
6th Floor, Sanlam Centre
154 Independence Avenue
Windhoek

P O Box 231
Windhoek
Tel (061) 22-9217, fax 22-2981

Netherlands (Embassy)
2 Crohn Street
Windhoek

Private Bag 564, Windhoek
Tel (061) 22-3733, fax 22-3732

Portugal (Embassy)
28 Garten Street
Windhoek

P O Box 443, Windhoek
Tel (061) 22-8736, fax 23-7929

Romania (Embassy)
3 Hamerkop Road
Hochland Park
Windhoek

P O Box 6827
Windhoek
Tel (061) 22-4630, fax 22-1564

Russian Federation (Embassy)
4 Christian Street
Klein Windhoek
Windhoek

P O Box 3826
Windhoek
Tel (061) 22-8671, fax 22-9061

Spain (Embassy)
58 Bismarck Street
Windhoek West
Windhoek

P O Box 21811
Windhoek
Tel (061) 22-3006, fax 22-3046

Sweden (Embassy)
9th Floor, Sanlam Centre
154 Independence Avenue
Windhoek

P O Box 23087
Windhoek
Tel (061) 22-2905, fax 22-2744

United Kingdom (High Commission)
116 Robert Mugabe Street
Windhoek

P O Box 22202
Windhoek
Tel (061) 22-3022, fax 22-8895

North America, South America and the Caribbean

Brazil (Embassy)
52 Bismarck Street
Windhoek West
Windhoek

P O Box 24166
Windhoek
Tel (061) 23-7368, fax 23-3389

Cuba (Embassy)
31 Omuramba Road
Eros
Windhoek

P O Box 23866
Windhoek
Tel (061) 22-7072, fax 23-1584

Mexico (Embassy)
3rd Floor, Southern Life Tower
39 Post Street Mall
Windhoek

Private Bag 13220
Windhoek
Tel (061) 22-9082, fax 22-9180

United States of America (Embassy)
14 Lossen Street
Ausspannplatz
Windhoek

P O Box 12029
Windhoek
Tel (061) 22-1601, fax 22-9792

Venezuela (Embassy)
3rd Floor, Southern Life Tower
39 Post Street Mall
Windhoek

Private Bag 13353
Windhoek
Tel (061) 22-7905, fax 22-7804

Asia and the Middle East

China, People's Republic (Embassy)
13 Wecke Street
Windhoek

P O Box 22777, Windhoek
Tel (061) 22-2089, fax 24-9122

India (High Commission)
97 Nelson Mandela Avenue
Klein Windhoek
Windhoek

P O Box 1209
Windhoek
Tel (061) 22-6037, fax 23-7320

Indonesia (Embassy)
103 Nelson Mandela Avenue
Klein Windhoek
Windhoek

P O Box 20691
Windhoek
Tel (061) 22-1914, fax 22-3811

Iran (Embassy)
13 Am Wasserberg Street
Klein Windhoek
Windhoek

P O Box 24790
Windhoek
Tel (061) 22-9974, fax 22-0016

Malaysia (High Commission)
10 Von Eckenbrecher Street
Klein Windhoek
Windhoek

P O Box 312
Windhoek
Tel (061) 25-9344, fax 25-9343

Emergency Numbers

Air Ambulance

Aeromed, Windhoek (061) 24-9777; Swakopmund (064) 40-0700 or 081 124 1709; Walvis Bay (064) 20-7207, or 081 129 4444.
Medrescue, Windhoek (061) 23-0505; Walvis Bay (064) 20-0200.

Ambulance

Windhoek: Contact Aeromed (061) 24-9777; Medrescue (061) 23-0505; Windhoek Municipality (061) 21-1111; Windhoek Central Hospital (061) 203-2270; Town Ambulance Services (061) 203-2270.

Gobabis (062) 56-2275
Grootfontein (067) 24-2141
Katima Mulilo (0677) 3012
Keetmanshoop (063) 22-3388
Khorixas (067) 33-1064/5
Lüderitz (063) 20-2446
Mariental (063) 24-2331, 24-2333
Okahandja (062) 50-3030
Oshakati (065) 22-0211
Otjiwarongo 081 129 6300 (Aeromed), (067) 30-3734/5
Rehoboth (062) 52-3646, (062) 52-3811, 52-2006 (after hours)
Rundu (067) 25-5025
Swakopmund (064) 40-5731
Tsumeb (067) 22-1911/2, 22-0796/7
Walvis Bay (064) 20-5443

Police/Flying Squad
Countrywide 10111

Hospitals
Windhoek:
Catholic Hospital (061) 23-7237
Medi Clinic (061) 22-2687
Rhino Park Private (Day) Hospital (061) 22-5434
Windhoek Central (State) Hospital (061) 203-9111
Otjiwarongo: Medi Clinic (067) 30-3734
Swakopmund: (064) 40-2341

Breakdown Services
For breakdowns in Windhoek, contact the **AA of Namibia**, tel (061) 22-4201, or
22-0823, 24-0733. In the major towns the following 24 hour tow-in service
garages are contracted to the AA of Namibia:
Gobabis: Visser Panelbeater (062) 56-2781, 56-3050 (a/h); Fanie Kuhn Panel-
beaters (062) 56-2438, 56-2213 (a/h)
Grootfontein: Blits Panelbeater (067) 24-2556
Katima Mulilo: Caprivi Toyota (0677) 3020, 3080 (a/h)
Keetmanshoop: Rassie's Breakdown Service (063) 22-2119, or (063) 124-7141;
Wimpie's Breakdown Service (063) 22-4186, 22-3613 (a/h)
Lüderitz: Diamond Motors, (063) 20-2497
Mariental: Hoofstraat Motors (063) 24-0391, 24-2265 (a/h); Mariental Toyota
(063) 24-0353, 24-2718 (a/h)
Okahandja: Poolman Motors (062) 50-1311, or 081 124-7476
Otjiwarongo: Hohenfels Garage (067) 30-3535, 30-2166 (a/h)
Swakopmund: Knoblochs Garage (064) 40-2286, 40-2860 (a/h); Steenbras Service
Station (064) 40-2131, 40-5544

Tsumeb: Auto Clinic (067) 22-0242, 22-1767
Usakos: Usakos Auto Repairs (064) 53-0181
Walvis Bay: Car Care (064) 20-5499, 20-2088

Useful Information Lines

AA of Namibia
(061) 22-4201

Airport information
Chief Hosea Kutako International Airport
Passenger services (062) 54-0229
Arrivals and departures (062) 54-0316
Airport bus (Intercape Mainliner) (061) 22-7847

Eros Airport
Airport manager (061) 23-9850

Weather forecasts
(061) 208-2170

Tourism Offices

Namibia Tourism offices abroad
Germany: Bad Homburg +49-6172-406650, fax 406690
South Africa: Cape Town*   +27-21-4193190/1, fax 21-5840; Johannesburg*
    +27-11-784-8024/5, fax 784-8340
Spain: Madrid +34-1-350-15.32, fax 350.18.10
United Kingdom: London +44-171-636-2924/8, fax 636-2969
United States of America: New York +1.212. 465-0619, fax 868-1654
* Reservations for accommodation in state-owned conservation areas and resorts
only can be made at these offices.

Namibia Tourism office in Namibia
Windhoek: (061) 284-2111, fax 284-2364

Ministry of Environment and Tourism/
Namibia Wildlife Resorts
Tourism Help Line: (061) 22-0640

Tourism offices:
Windhoek*: (061) 23-6975-8, 23-3845, 22-3903, 22-4097
Lüderitz: (063) 20-2752
Swakopmund*: (064) 40-2172

* Reservations for accommodation in state-owned conservation areas and resorts only can be made at these offices.

Regional/town tourist information centres
Lüderitz Tourist Info Office: (063) 20-2532
Namib I (Swakopmund): (064) 40-4827
Otjiwarongo Tourist Centre: (067) 30-3658
Southern Tourist Forum (Keetmanhoop): (063) 22-3316
Tsumeb Tourism Centre: (067) 22-0728
Walvis Bay: (064) 201-3233
Windhoek Information & Publicity: (061) 290-2092

INDEX

Entries marked with an asterix (*) are national monuments